**Marian Salzman** and **Ira Matathia** are the most respected and influential futurists at work today. Together they set up a unique unit within the TBWA Chiat/Day advertising agency called 'The Department of the Future', which revolutionized the science and art of trend analysis, plugging into vast and divergent sources of information from around the globe.

Marian Salzman pioneered youth and Generation X research at her consultancy BKG Youth for clients that included Levi's, Reebok, Nike and Kodak. On selling her share of BKG Marian joined Chiat/Day, becoming Worldwide Director of TBWA International's Department of the Future after TBWA's merger with Chiat/Day. In this position she led the agency's global study of new media, new consumers and everything and anything about the future.

She is now Director of Brand Futures Group at Young & Rubicam, the world's third largest advertising agency, which lists amongst its clients such international giants as Time-Warner, Colgate-Palmolive, Xerox and Dupont.

Ira Matathia joined Chiat/Day advertising agency in 1984, eventually becoming President of its New York operation. In mid-1996 he assumed responsibility for the Department of the Future, and by the end of 1996 he was its full-time CEO. In addition to providing a powerful weapon for agency new business, the DOF was instrumental in generating a significant press profile for the agency's new thinking style regarding trends, change and consumer behaviour.

Ira is now on special assignment with Omnicom, and studies and writes about change, branding for the future, and what's next for commerce and marketing.

**Ann S. O'Reilly** and **Christy Lane Plummer** are co-heads of research and published products for Young & Rubicam's Brand Futures Group, where they share responsibility for the management of the department's editorial and research staff.

# Next:
# A Vision of Our Lives
# in the Future

**Ira Matathia, Marian Salzman**

**Ann O'Reilly, Christy Lane Plummer**

HarperCollins*Publishers*

HarperCollins*Publishers*
77–85 Fulham Palace Road,
Hammersmith, London W6 8JB

Published by HarperCollins*Publishers* 1999
1 3 5 7 9 8 6 4 2

First published in the Netherlands by Anthos
under the title *Trends Voor De Toekomst* 1997

A catalogue record for this book is
available from the British Library

ISBN 0 00 257041 6

Set in Meridien by
Rowland Phototypesetting Ltd,
Bury St Edmunds, Suffolk

Printed and bound in Great Britain by
Caledonian International Book Manufacturing Ltd, Glasgow

# Contents

# Preface

People tend not to think about the future. In fact, I would wager that most of us have a pretty limited sense of what we're likely to be doing any time after next Wednesday. The authors, on the other hand, do very little other than think about the future – in fact, they virtually live there.

But, unlike so many 'futurists', this team of authors has a genuine capacity to generate knowledge about trends and social movements that business people can actually use. And, today, that's one of the most valuable skills around. After all, nowadays just keeping up with life is a defensive proposition.

Technology and information are moving at a breathtaking pace. We've created enough gadgets to keep us busy pretty much every waking hour. And that's getting to be all twenty-four, since we can go online all night long – to check a stock market halfway around the world or buy anything from a paperback to a three-bedroom apartment.

As consumers and corporations alike teeter on the brink of overload, who has time to think ahead? Or to try to understand the impact all this change will have on our world, our attitudes, everything? The present is overwhelming enough.

Of course, there's a huge opportunity in all this uncertainty. Marketers have always needed to understand consumers' current concerns and experiences with their brands. But if they are to thrive in the years ahead, they must also anticipate where technology, social trends and a myriad of other change agents are leading, so that their new products and services will have a place in the consumer future.

Ed Vick
Chief Operating Officer, Young & Rubicam Inc.

# Introduction: The Times are Changing

We're living in a fascinating age, for even those people who claim to be immune to millennium fever can't help but wonder what lies on the other side of the date we've long held to represent the future. In these last days of the twentieth century, we're focused not so much on the triumphs of the last hundred years as on the promise and uncertainty of the next hundred. If this century saw the global adoption of automobiles and electric lights, men walking on the moon and advances in medicine that have extended average life expectancies into one's seventies or eighties, what might the next century bring? How will those of us who will be alive in 2050 be living? What will our homes be like? How will we get from one place to another? How will we shop – and what will we be shopping for?

While literature abounds with long-term prognostications about life next, our view is more pragmatic. Here's why. International. Global. Worldwide. We're living in what we used to call 'the future'. In 1955 Canadian academic Marshall McLuhan on *Take Thirty* (CBC Television) explained, 'There are no remote places. Under instant circuitry, nothing is remote in time or in place. It's now.' McLuhan is credited with being the first person who genuinely understood that technology was changing and would change mass media, and that mass media and contemporary life are so interconnected that everything would change, fast and hard. Those of us who spent part of the seventies contemplating his work recognize that we are already living in his 'global village' and understand how essential it is to decode our present, rather than live life with an eye on the rearview mirror. In the nineties, the present is an enormously important tool for those in the trendtracking business, and especially for those in global marketing communications.

Why do advertising people care about trends? On a simplistic level, the success of an ad campaign is predicated on whether the marketing message is on trend. It's often said that advertising is a window on culture. We think that's true, and that's why anything that can be used to monitor change and change agents is a fundamental tool for effective marketing communications. So, in our work as advertisers, we appreciate the degree to which accurate trendtracking is critical to the marketing process. Accurately spotting and forecasting trends is of fundamental importance in determining whether an ad is a genuine asset to a brand (ideally by becoming a part of popular culture) or simply a negligible wave over which channel surfers pass.

Think of trends as human: they have a life cycle. That is, they are sown or fertilized, they gestate, they grow, mature, age and eventually die. Some trends are reincarnated a decade or more later, often in slightly different form.

How do we track trends? Like other major trendtrackers, our approach is interdisciplinary. We study and analyse traditional and non-traditional media, in both the specialized and popular categories. Because opportunity is missed by those who view the world only through the eyes of their chosen profession, we are confirmed generalists, tracking scores of themes daily. When we get onto something, we turn to the experts – and then consider critically their points of view. Notice how often the so-called experts disagree and restate the obvious to emphasize their particular take on a situation or scenario. Notice, too, that one's 'expertness' is empowering; sometimes predictions can become self-fulfilling as a result of media hype.

When all is said and done, trendtracking, like communication, is part art, part science. An effective trendtracker must have a talent for the rhetorical, as well as a pragmatic view of the message impact. What will trend X mean for me? For everyone else? As observed by futurist Wendell Bell, 'The primary goal of futurists is not to predict the future, but to uncover images of possible, probable, and preferable futures that enable people to make informed decisions about their lives.' Our trendtracking style is about identifying the probable for life and work next – and about proposing conceivable implications if what's probable happens . . .

We view the future through contemporary popular culture, a trait that puts us in good stead when trying to connect with readers outside the advertising community. Advertising is, after all, one of the world's common cultural touchpoints. From the Pillsbury Dough Boy to the dancing California raisins to the hyperactive Energizer bunny, advertising's icons are a part of popular culture around the globe. These 'figures of sale' and taglines tie us together with consumers in other countries, serving as a common reference for conversation in just about any language.

The publication of *Next* is in part the result of our two-year global odyssey. Our unique take on the world now and next is genuinely shaped by Ira and Marian having had the exposure that comes with being two of the privileged few who have jumped from continent to continent absorbing the cultures, media and lifestyles of trendsetters in many, many countries. We hope our zest for what's different, as well as our respect for culture, pervades all our observations and the implications we propose.

## What to Expect from *Next*

For the sake of making *Next: A Vision of Lives in the Future* an easier read, we have created a few devices to highlight the key themes.

- 'Big Nexts' are the megatrends that are so big they transcend place and point of view and touch almost everyone.
- 'Nexts' are the key trends that are influencing the influencers – and that will shape life and work next, as we countdown into the next century.
- 'What's Nexts?' are sprinkled throughout this book. It's a technique which allows thoughtful speculation on probable scenarios – the ultimate product of credible trend analysis.

## Experience Gathering

This book records the changes we've noted in Europe, North America, and elsewhere, and it cites the sources that helped us to identify key shifts and corroborate major patterns of life and work next. Our approach is intended to empower readers to begin the process of interpolating for yourselves the information you consume via traditional news channels and on and off the Internet. By harnessing the power of the information you receive each day, rather than being overwhelmed by it, you will become adequately equipped to manage future change.

# [1]

# Big Nexts

As we noted in the introduction this travelogue to the future is not some vision of the 'brave new world'. Rather, it is a practicum – filled with things that are just on the horizon, trends we are watching move from the periphery to Main Street. Also addressed are the potential commercial implications of those movements. We start with the 'Big Nexts': observations about human behaviour and interactions that, in our view, are the overarching factors defining our collective journey to whatever and wherever is next. You will note that many Big Nexts have been expressed as paradoxes. The apparent contradictions suggest that, as part of our future, making things work will require a more expansive world view.

## Big Next: The Ever-more-demanding Consumer

Imagine you're sitting at your desk, waiting for an important contract. You check your fax machine, your email, and even for FedEx and courier deliveries. And then you call the person who drew up the contract and he says, 'Don't worry, you'll get it. I dropped it in the mail slot yesterday.' Fifteen years ago, that response wouldn't have raised an eyebrow. But who has time today to wait for snail mail? We want everything yesterday, and we grow increasingly frustrated by people who waste our time with antiquated means of communication.

Well, that's actually how today's consumers feel. Having made new technologies a part of our lives, we want everything faster than ever before. Anything that's not immediate is s-l-o-w. Same-day delivery. Instant news. Nuked meals. DirecTV. PC banking. Increasingly, we have no patience for products and services we can't access right NOW. And, of great commercial significance, our satisfaction with brands is more and more defined by immediacy rather than quality of service. In North America, in particular, retailers are discovering that customers aren't willing to wait till the store reopens at 9 a.m. to buy milk. We want it now – and we'll get it, whether via a competitor that stays open late or at a twenty-four-hour convenience store. The result is a burgeoning number of twenty-four-hour retail establishments, from bookstores and copy shops to doughnut shops.

More than that, consumers around the world are rejecting the notion that 'one size fits all'. A popular T-shirt one sees today reads, 'I ask only that you treat me no differently than you would the Queen.' The T-shirt may be meant as a joke, but the attitude is pure reality. As new technologies have made it easier for companies to target individuals, consumers have grown accustomed to white-gloved treatment. *Time* magazine comes with a printout showing how the subscriber's local representatives voted on critical issues. Levi Strauss lets us order computerized-fit jeans. Parents can buy personalized storybooks, videos and dolls for their children. And customer service centres around the world are scrambling to put a touch of 1:1 marketing in their responses. GTE Telesystems in the US, for example, rates each call coming into its customer service centre with three graphic devices (calendar pages to indicate customer longevity, sticks of dynamite to indicate past service problems and money bags to indicate volume). The system allows personnel to respond more appropriately to each caller's problem.

As consumers, we're being led to expect products that meet our specific needs. (Why should I sit through world forecasts on the Weather Channel when I can have my particular city's weather report emailed to me each morning?) We want to access these products via distribution mechanisms that are convenient to us – whether through one-stop shopping, twenty-four-hour superstores, home delivery or some equally agreeable method. And we want an immediate and satisfactory customer service response when problems arise.

Our desire to remain in control in an uncertain world – combined with our insistence on having things when and how we want them – also translates into a demand for personalized marketing campaigns.

The reality is that mass marketing is obsolete in high-tech cultures. Complex technology-based products, increased competition and additional channels of communication have a net result of declining advertising effectiveness.

In the near term, one can expect to see many more examples of increased interactivity between advertisers and targets in the form of consumer-data collection and 1:1 marketing campaigns. In addressing the Public Relations Society of America at New York's Harvard Club, Larry Weber commented: 'The information economy and the new communications channels are going to require a new kind of marketing communications . . . Here's one small example of a new communications channel. Imagine that you're at your local supermarket, buying a six-pack of Coca-Cola. The scanner that recognized the six-pack of Coke also triggers a software program, which spits out a 50-cents-off coupon for a six-pack of Pepsi. Automatically. Let's say you ignore the coupon, or you take it home and lose it. The next time you buy Coke, the scanner recognizes the Coke and your debit card. The software looks up your record, knows you didn't respond to the last coupon, and spits out a one-dollar-off coupon for Pepsi. Next time, it's a dollar fifty. If you don't switch in three tries, the software gives up on you for now. That's an actual system now being tested. Retailing is not about merchandise anymore. It's a war of information and communication.'

The reality is that developments such as customized products and 1:1 marketing initiatives are creating in consumers an expectation that they will be catered to. In some parts of the world, mail-order goods take weeks to arrive at their destination. In the US today – because we have grown accustomed to top-flight service – many of us get impatient if we can't have a product delivered overnight or if we're unable to have our customer service problem solved at 3 a.m. on a Sunday. This isn't going to go away. As new technologies are developed and as production and distribution methods are improved, consumers will grow ever more demanding, not just in the US, but around the world. Any company that thinks the way it did business in 1970 is going to cut it with today's consumer is going to be blown away.

## Big Next: Seeking Security

Just twenty years ago, most of us worked in offices without PCs, fax machines and voicemail. Our homes were not equipped with VCRs; our phones were not equipped with Caller ID. Many of us would have scoffed at the notion that computer technology would fundamentally alter the way we live and work in just two decades' time. And now, with the new millennium upon us, we are taking a peek into the future, imagining how our world will change in the *next* twenty years.

One of the terms that has emerged in the past couple of years is 'premillennial tension'. In the Western world, the general population's anticipation of the year 2000 (or 2001, in the case of sticklers for detail) is tempered with concern, even fear. James Baldwin wrote, 'Most of us are about as eager to be changed as we were to be born, and go through our changes in a similar state of shock.' We know there will be changes in the coming years, but we don't know what exactly they'll be – or how dramatic their impact. The result: an intensified search for security.

### Trust No One

A key reason we've become so demanding as consumers is that we no longer trust businesses to look out for our best interests. This attitude has been honed by years of being lied to and misled – not just by 'big business', but by government leaders, celebrities and just about everyone else in the media spotlight. In our travels across Europe, we spoke with citizens who are no longer willing to tolerate corruption in any form. Whether the offence be tax evasion, money laundering, bribes, undue influence or any other such crime, Europeans are now demanding that justice be served. The result has been the toppling of such high-visibility people as NATO General Secretary Willy Claes, Norwegian Central Bank Governor Torstein Moland and Alcatel Alsthom CEO Pierre Suard. One of the forces contributing to this 'shakedown' is increased access to information. Whether from the Internet, cable or satellite television, or independent 'zines, today's consumers simply have more access to breaking news than in the past, as well as an increased ability to pursue stories of interest.

## Fear

One result of having weathered scandal after scandal is that we've grown more cynical. We're wiser to the ploys of politicos, preachers, priests, teachers and, yes, advertisers and marketers. We're bombarded with infinitely more messages than we were a dozen years ago. We're worried about our futures, our countries, our jobs, our cities and villages, our schools and violence down the street and overseas. And we're anxious about what the millennium holds.

Adding to the collective fears of new consumers in Europe is the uncertainty surrounding both the European Union and increased globalization. With regard to the EU, many citizens are disturbed by the realization that belonging to the EU will require their national governing bodies to relinquish a certain amount of control. Denmark, for instance, experienced such a situation first-hand when the EU required that the country adopt France's less-stringent rules regarding the use of preservatives in baby food. Understandably, many Danes were distraught to see bureaucrats in faraway Brussels dictate what can be put into food for their children. Other small countries are similarly concerned that they will lose their autonomy and simply be swallowed by the big European crowd.

With the future uncertain, we don't know where to turn to find answers to the big questions in our lives – like where we should bring up our kids – and to smaller questions – like which brand of soup we should choose. We're looking for things we can hold on to. Things we can trust. We're looking for relationships with brands, not just products to buy. To assuage these concerns, consumers are seeking long-term product/service 'partners' that will help them to survive and thrive both professionally and personally. Whether peddling instant breakfasts or computer software, the obvious challenge for marketers is to earn a place within the consumer's trusted brand set. What criteria do consumers use to evaluate prospective partners? Most look for three things: managerial vision (Does this company know where the world is heading? How their products/services need to be reinvented?); marketplace integrity (customer support, solid warranties); and an in-depth understanding of 'my' needs and desires.

One of the interesting dichotomies we see in the new consumers is their simultaneous embrace of novelty and fear of change that is too rapid. They want everything to be smaller, better, faster – but only if it fits comfortably within the world they're used to. They place an enormous value on physical and emotional safety, and covet 'classic' products they can trust.

Laurence Bernstein, a colleague of Marian's, described how he believes premillennial tension is affecting people in his part of the world: 'The most significant trend in Canada right now is a profound change in the Canadian world view, moving people from a society with a therapeutic perspective ("We can do it now because everything can be fixed") to a society driven by a prophylactic sense of caution ("Whatever we do now, we must be careful because we may not be able to fix it in the future.")' Bernstein contends that this shift 'is evident in almost every aspect of life and can be viewed as the force behind such social phenomena as environmental concern (people actually recycling), the anti-smoking campaign, etc.'

People in many parts of the world are undergoing a similar shift from a therapeutic to a prophylactic perspective. As we attempt to take advantage of the benefits of new technologies and other conveniences, we remain acutely aware of the potential pitfalls. And, in a world travelling at hyperspeed, it's a brave (or delusional) person who never once has questioned whether he or she is going to be able to keep up.

## Big Next: Global vs Hyperlocal

As the world gets smaller and smaller, we aren't just becoming more globally aware, we're also becoming increasingly focused on the hyperlocal places and communities in our lives. The authors of this book are decidedly global. In a typical few months Ira holidayed with his family in Italy and visited Berlin with Marian to speak to international business people and journalists. Marian also travelled to Copenhagen, Amsterdam and Kuala Lumpur (Malaysia) in the course of her job.

The two of us are also decidedly hyperlocal. In a representative week Ira raced from a session with a prospective publisher to a school board meeting in the Connecticut town where he lives, and where one of his children attends a public elementary school. He also belongs to a number of committees related to the advertising community that do good works. Meanwhile, Marian had a date with her university alumni club, because that's the community that has been the most important to her over the last decade. She also attended a Women in New Media breakfast – networking is an eighties buzzword that in the nineties translates into forging hyperlocal ties.

It seems to us that achieving a balance between global and hyperlocal will be of increasing importance both to people and brands in the years ahead. For people, hyperlocal ties help us to partition the world into manageable chunks. I may not know how to solve the problems that may arise from Europe's new single currency, but I can create a workable budget for my homeowners' association or chess club. I may feel a bit overwhelmed when surfing through Usenet newsgroups, but I feel very much at home when chatting with people in my online hobbyist group.

For brands, the push and pull of the global and hyperlocal continuum is somewhat different. Aided by their embrace of new technologies – which keep them plugged into world events and points of view – new consumers have developed the rudiments of a global outlook that infuses the way they think, the way they act – the way they buy. Transnational commerce is leading, in turn, towards media globalization. As the 'global consumer' becomes more of a reality, we're seeing a deepening awareness that marketing messages can – and should – be transmitted across borders. Disney, Coke, Nikon, Apple, IBM, Levi's and Nike are just some of the brands already globally consistent.

Today's drive towards globalization means companies need to make hard decisions on everything, from whether brand names need to be globally consistent to which brand messages translate across cultures, to what logo or icon can best represent their brand around the world. Not every company can have a symbol as globally recognized as the Nike swoosh – but all of them would like to! As brands consider the implications of going global, it's important that they recognize, too, the enormous draw of hyperlocal connections. Forging hyperlocal links with consumers is a must for tomorrow's brands – no matter how global. The trick lies in providing messages that balance universal appeal with sufficient 'localization' to attract and retain the interest of consumers in each market. In fact, we can safely assume that tomorrow's mass-appeal brands will share three commonalities: global relevance, hyperlocal desirability and strong ties to multiple niches.

How can a product have both global relevance and hyperlocal appeal? Some smart brands will take advantage of convergence opportunities. When done right, convergence is about brands bonding because their combined power is greater than the sum of their parts. Moving forward, we can expect to see global champions such as Frito-Lay co-brand with such local winners as the Netherlands' Smith's crisps, thereby ensuring that ubiquity and familiarity are in sync.

Smart marketers are also coming up with other ways to give mass-produced products local appeal. How many of us have been fooled by seemingly 'homegrown' microbrews and speciality snack products in our grocery stores, which are, in fact, manufactured by the very same conglomerates selling mass products a bit further down the aisle? Slap on a local-sounding name or the colours of a local sports team, and consumers are apt not to read the small print about the product's true origins.

In the fast-food world, the Jollibee chain is a good example of how to combine successfully a global product with local touches. Although the Filipino chain sells hamburgers, it tailors these 'all-American delights' to suit the local market's tastes (Jollibee's hamburgers in the Philippines, for instance, come with sweet-and-sour sauce flavouring.) The result: Jollibee has not only outmanoeuvred McDonald's in the Philippines, but has also opened multiple outlets in south-east Asia and the Middle East. Jollibee recently took on McDonald's on its home turf, opening outlets in San Francisco and Los Angeles, home to large Filipino populations.

On a city level, one can see how globality and hyperlocality can co-exist and actually enrich one another. Amsterdam, for instance, despite being a comfortable participant on the world stage, has managed to retain a sense of being a village of locals. When Adidas, one of the most on-trend brands in the world, relocated many of its creative, marketing, promotions and sales functions to Amsterdam, the Dutch press explained it thus: 'Amsterdam is chosen as second headquarters for its international cosmopolitan feel, in a village setting; a wonderful lifestyle.'

Contrast the June 1997 European Union summit (a.k.a. Eurotop) in Amsterdam with the Olympic Games at Nagano. The Amsterdam event felt as if the world had been invited to a New Age picnic (BYOB) and musical celebration of the future. In striking contrast, the rural, sleepy, isolated village of Nagano, in Japan, seemed to be resisting the exhortations of CBS to 'spend a moment with the world'. Amidst reports that local businesses were actually turning away 'foreigners', the prevailing view of the townsfolk was that this intrusion from the outside world was simply to be 'suffered' as they eagerly awaited a return to anonymity.

## Big Next: Nostalgia and Futurism: a Winning Yin and Yang

Throughout our global village, residents are being asked to accommodate change at an unprecedented pace. As the new world order demands that we adapt to a broad array of new cultural, political, economic and technological influences, we can't fail to recognize the truth in the adage, 'Change is life's only constant.'

In the West, anxiety about change is exacerbated by premillennial tension. As observed by John Naisbitt, the millennium is a metaphor for the future; wrapped up in it are our greatest hopes – and our greatest fears. We're uncertain how the changes to come will affect us personally. The result has been oscillation between optimism and anxiety. Indeed, the two of us have been struck by how much of society's 'future view' is caught up in such paradoxes. Today's trends include a push towards risk *and* safety, indulgence *and* cost-consciousness. But no paradox is as interesting, nor as marketable, as that of nostalgia and futurism. As put by marketing consultant James Rosenfield, 'People seem to be trying on both the past and the future for size.'[1]

These co-existing tendencies toward nostalgia and futurism are not unexpected – when confronted with accelerated change, people gravitate to that which is most familiar and most comfortable, whether it be a particular brand of food, an old TV show or a retro fashion. But because swearing off the future and change is simply not an option, we alleviate our anxieties by finding a balance between what has been, what is and what is to come. The exact 'comfort' equation is as unique to each individual as his or her fingerprints, but most involve creating a sturdy bridge that spans past, present, and future. Marketers and product developers must take this consumer duality into account in order to strike a balance that's appropriate for their target. Chanel's fall '98 ready-to-wear collection rose to the challenge by featuring both very, very long skirts (a nod to the attire of Coco's youth) and a new bag designed for the millennium called '2005'.

When we consider brands for the future (a.k.a. millennium brands), it's clear to us that, whether classic or newly minted, these brands will share a capacity to be reinvented, reinterpreted and reoriented at an extraordinary rate. Rather than be motivated by a chameleon-like hypocrisy, such change will be an extension of the brand's guiding force. Authenticity is also all-important. Worn down by an endless barrage of questionable product claims and an unrelenting need to 'read the fine print', consumers gravitate towards – and actively seek out – people and products that deliver honesty and integrity.

The fact that Citibank sponsored Elton John's 1998 world tour speaks worlds about that brand's commitment to being what its customers need it to be: honest, human, humane and spirited. What more could a brand ask for than a celebrity endorser who has aired all and been lauded for his integrity, for his passion for his art and for the causes he's supported and moved the world to support? When we consider Sir Elton John, we are really considering the quintessential millennium brand, an individual who has risen above his blemishes and warts, has been transported by his ambition, commitment and talent, and who remains firmly rooted in the real world while he lives a life far beyond anything a working-class kid from England could have ever imagined. Elton John is a millennial brand because he is trusted, because he is genuine – and because he is familiar. We *know* him, and we draw comfort from that.

Smart marketers have been quick to take advantage of consumers' nostalgic leanings. Microsoft launched Windows 95 with help from the Rolling Stones; Nissan reconnected to its history with the aid of Van Halen and G.I. Joe. Around the world, we're most definitely seeing a rise in 'stake claiming' to the past, as companies work to ensure that tomorrow is familiar because of its linkage to yesterday. Going forwards, we'll see that the most effective marketing strategies meld the essence of nostalgia (reliability, quality, beauty, familiarity) with the positive elements of futurism (functionality, convenience, versatility).

## Big Next: 'Perpetual Youth' and our Ageing World

It used to be that people over fifty were old, and people under thirty were young. Then Mick Jagger turned fifty and continued to strut his stuff on-stage, and our entire theory of ageing had to be revamped. Today, 'midlife crises' occur not on one's thirty-fifth birthday, but on one's forty-fifth, fifty-fifth or even later. Men and women in their seventies and eighties are remaining physically (even sexually) active, travelling the world, and are sometimes even involved in running companies – and countries.

Throughout much of Europe and North America, women are delaying childbirth until their thirties or even forties. Adults are running around in tennis shoes and short shorts, working out at the gym in an attempt to delay some of the normal ravages of ageing – and having plastic surgery to mask much of the rest. The fashion industry has been forced to redesign its 'youth' fashions to fit the bodies of the middle-aged men and women who continue to wear them rather than adopting more 'grown-up' fashions.

In the years ahead, expect the world's 'elders' (whether ageing boomers or their parents) to command unprecedented attention from marketers and the media, and to have an enormous impact on the rest of the population. The reality is that we're entering into an era in which the elderly will make up a larger proportion of the global population than ever before. Already, the most rapidly growing age group is made up of those aged eighty-five plus. In the US this group will double in size by 2025 and increase fivefold by 2050. Consider the implications: By the year 2030, approximately 20 per cent of the US population will be over age sixty-five. That's 69 million people. Around the world, half of all people aged sixty-five and over who have *ever* lived are alive today.

Our ageing population promises to influence everything from financial planning and home design to the way products are made and sold. Likely developments include everything from 'adult friendly' caps on medicine bottles to wider car doors and foods that compensate for changing tastes and dietary needs. We'll also see even greater shifts with regard to our attitudes regarding what it means to 'age'. As the number of elderly continues to increase, so will this group's power in terms of influencing public policy. Images of the elderly as victims will become historical; instead we will see seniors who grow more active in politics and who maintain and even increase their economic power as they move fully into their second half century of life. Socially, politically – and certainly economically – the implications of this 'Big Next' will be felt by us all.

We've chosen to place our final two Big Nexts – the United States of Europe and an Independent Asia – in a separate chapter. These Big

Nexts differ from our usual 'stock in trade' in that they focus on geopolitics and regional economics rather than on consumerism, popular culture and the like. Whether one lives in one of the regions in question or in the Americas, Africa or elsewhere, the implications of life next in Europe and Asia will be enormous.

# 2

# It's a Small World Next

## Big Next: United States of Europe

For many of Europe's 350 million-plus citizens, the next five to ten years will be the most exciting, promising, and/or disturbing era of their lives. Only those with vivid memories of the 1939–45 war or the radical sixties might find these millennial years less than seminal. The quarrelsome patchwork of nations, peoples, cultures, economies, climates and topographies loosely known as Europe is facing the next millennium more united – or at least more closely bound together – than anyone could have dreamed just fifty years ago.

### Brussels

The capital of Belgium has become shorthand for the ambitious project of European integration that started in the early 1950s. The changing names of the project over the decades reflect the broadening ambitions of the 'Eurocrats' and the visionary politicians who have driven it – the European Coal and Steel Community (1952), the European Economic Community (1957), the European Community (1967) and now, the European Union (1993). What started out as a forum for collaboration among six countries in a limited area of industry has evolved into nothing less than a drive to create, in effect, a United States of Europe, with its own single currency and supranational legislature currently covering fifteen countries, with more in the waiting room.

Not everybody in Europe is on board. The sort of people who used to be known as 'right wing' – typified by Britain's Conservative Party and its former leader Margaret Thatcher – resent the political dimension. They think the project should stick to fostering trade and commerce and keep its hands off social policy, let alone political integration. Some 'left-wing' Europeans see the whole thing as a vehicle for big business to have its wicked way with workers, playing off those in high-wage countries against those in lower-cost areas.

As the process grinds on through committees, white papers, debates and summits, it may seem like a typically European phenomenon – long-winded, ponderous, bureaucratic, short on star performers and sex appeal. But it's worth remembering that the western Europeans who have grown up watching this process are the first in many generations who haven't taken time out to knock the hell out of each other in battle. And as recent events in former Yugoslavia have shown, Europe's capacity for ethnic violence can never be completely discounted.

Slowly but surely, nations across Europe are in the process of uniting their destinies with former foes, of handing over strands of sovereignty previously held dearer than life itself. Long term, for many Europeans it will mean living under rules invented by other Europeans who don't even speak the same language. This sort of prospect used to lead to fighting in Europe, but so far it has only sparked a war of words between the 'Europhiles' and the 'Eurosceptics' within countries.

With a fair wind, the early years of the next millennium should see the laborious but peaceful emergence of a true European Union, put together by committees rather than by combatants, but nevertheless a heroic achievement. What the late General de Gaulle said of his native France is even more applicable to Europe as a whole: 'My friend, you can't expect to unify overnight a country which boasts 257 different types of cheese.'

## Déjà History

One of Europe's big problems (and points of pride) is that the past is always getting in the way of the present and the future. For example, engineers trying to excavate tunnels for the city metro in Rome routinely came across ancient Roman relics – cue to stop digging and call in the archaeologists again. In London developers in the financial district have faced similar problems with buried Roman relics.

Even the idea of unifying Europe goes back a long way. On the eve of the first millennium, the year zero, the Romans were on their way to ruling an empire that would cover much of the territory now in the European Union. A thousand years later, the German-speaking area of Europe was engaged in a long-running attempt to put together a second empire – the would-be Holy Roman Empire. And after Napoleon's short-lived conquest of Europe in the early 1800s, Hitler made his bid for the Third Reich (Third Empire), which crumbled in 1945.

On a less grand scale, many of the European social and workplace attitudes prevalent for much of this century are steeped in a sense of the past – the dynamics of left-wing/right-wing class politics and the efforts of workers to protect their interests. Workers' 'struggles' are remembered as heroic, and even today, large numbers of Europeans are loath to give up hard-won privileges for the uncertain prospect of global next.

In short, Europeans' history, their perception of history, and the legacies of history have all too often served to keep them apart and stuck in the past. But now, it seems that the grip of history is loosening across the whole Continent – although people in the Balkans might disagree on that point. New generations of Europeans have grown up amid peace and plenty, eating the same fast food, drinking the same soft drinks, driving the same cars and increasingly sharing the same tastes in music, movies and TV. These New Europeans display a mindset that breaks with the thinking of previous generations – much more focused on the here and now, on themselves and their own futures, much less interested in where they are from and more concerned with where they are going.

To paraphrase Francis Fukuyama, we may well be witnessing something akin to the end of history in Europe – or at least the beginning of the end of Europe's obsession with history.

## The Euro Nightmare

With the approach of the year 2000, computerized countries all over the world are facing the same Y2K 'millennium bug' problems. Computers in which dates were programmed as two digits rather than four will be completely thrown when 99 (of 1999) clicks over to 00 (of 2000).

But as Y2K fever heats up, Europe will add its own complication to the computer systems nightmare – a new currency, the euro, which is the flagship of an ambitious project of economic and monetary union. Banks and businesses in Europe currently have to deal with transactions between the fifteen currencies of the European Union, whose exchange rates constantly vary within fairly narrow bands. In order to simplify cross-border business in the future, Europe is going to phase in a single currency. The euro should make things much easier in the long term, but a lot more complicated in the short term. To quote from *Peter Pan*, the whole undertaking promises to be 'an awfully big adventure'.

Europeans will be able to start using the euro on 1 January 1999, and for a three-year transition period it will be used in parallel with existing national currencies – the French franc, the German mark, etc. After that, it will be goodbye to the franc, the mark and all the other currencies that will cease to be legal tender in the summer of 2002. During the transition period, the euro will be the cross-rate hub – exchange rates will be calculated on the basis of each currency's rate versus the euro, rather than directly between the currencies.

It's not clear whether the European authorities were fully aware of the Y2K problem when they decided on the single European currency schedule. What is sure is that the timing is likely to keep legions of programmers very busy for a long time to come. Phasing in the euro will bring plenty of challenges. Currently, many companies need only deal with their national currencies, but even small, locally focused companies will have to phase in or switch to euro systems sooner or later. And the systems range from cash tills and computer keyboards with euro symbols all the way up to powerful number-crunching programmes handling corporate accounts. IBM calculates that the cost to companies doing business across the Continent will be in the region of US$175 billion. Fortunately, the banking industry is ahead of the pack in its preparations for the euro, which are thought to cost around US$100 million for big banks.

And the euro shift won't touch only countries in the first wave of euro adopters. The European Union is the main trading partner for Britain, and while the British government is holding to a 'watch from the wings' line, British companies doing business with the mainland will probably find it pays to go euro sooner rather than later, since big Continental companies will be going for it. *Business Week* reports that Anglo-Dutch consumer products giant Unilever and many UK headquartered banks are among the companies that plan to start operating in euros at the birth of the new currency on 1 January. They're sure to bring legions of suppliers and customers along with them.

Nonetheless, a survey by accounting firm Grant Thornton of London indicated that some 37 per cent of European companies haven't even started thinking about the euro. It's a fair bet that a considerably higher proportion of the cash-wielding public is even farther from incorporating the euro into their plans.

## The Euro Dream

It shouldn't take Europeans long to experience the benefits of the euro – which, among other things, will allow one to compare prices in different countries. The variations in price are sometimes big, and with no border controls between many EU countries, we can expect a sharp increase in cross-border shopping trips.

Despite the darkest suspicions of die-hard eurosceptics, the single currency isn't being introduced to confuse people and make life more difficult. It's part of a policy designed to remove the obstacles to doing business between European countries, creating a unified trading zone with a GDP to match that of the US. One likely consequence, posits the *Economist*, is that the euro could become a real alternative to the US dollar on a world scale, which would make it harder for the United States to run unlimited current-account deficits and to exercise unchallenged leadership of the international financial system.

Entry requests were reviewed at a summit meeting in May 1998, and the G-11 were officially named; Britain, Denmark and Sweden have chosen not to join the euro at this time – and Greece didn't make the cut. At the same meeting Wim Duisenberg, a Dutchman, was named as head of the Central Bank, making him every bit as powerful as America's Alan Greenspan, head of the Federal Reserve Bank.

In any event, focusing on the EMU entry criteria has spurred countries to greater budgetary sobriety across Europe and in turn helped drive interest rates down – all good news for investors. On the corporate front, the introduction of the euro should cut the cost of transacting cross-border business in Europe. Companies won't have to give their banks the spread on foreign exchange transactions, and they won't have to pay for currency hedges to lock in their prices. Moreover, the euro should stimulate cross-border efficiencies, allowing companies to expand, consolidate, restructure or relocate without regard to currency differences. No wonder investors are getting excited.

Banks, insurers and finance houses are expected to be among the first companies to go regional with cross-border product offerings in the single currency, which will make for greater consumer choice and

mobility within Europe. Right now it's theoretically possible to take out
a mortgage in one currency to buy a property in another, but the foreign
exchange risks are daunting for the average consumer. With the euro,
that risk is eliminated. The increasing pace of preparations for Y2K
and the euro are making software houses an irresistible investment
opportunity, too.

With zero hour approaching, things are suddenly falling into place
for the euro. Against expectations, European economies started picking
up in 1998, after almost a decade of sluggish performance which threat-
ened to scupper the currency's introduction. What's more, the *Economist*
reports that European Commissioner for Monetary Affairs Yves-
Thibault de Silguy thinks that the spending on preparations for the
euro, coming on top of Y2K spending, will give Europe's economies a
further boost.

## Borders, What Borders?

For cross-border travellers in Europe, things are just returning to where
they were a century ago, when it was possible to wander across the
Continent without a passport. Only recently have border controls
between many European countries been dropped (under the EU's
Schengen agreement), but already some countries are wondering what
they have let themselves in for.

Since October 1997, flights between Italy, France, Germany, the
Benelux countries, Portugal, Spain, Denmark, Sweden and Finland
have had domestic status, while land border controls are virtually non-
existent. The big worry now is that there are no secondary lines of
defence to pick up illegal or undesirable immigrants – once they have
made it into one of the countries, they can travel unimpeded to any of
the others with little fear of being caught at border crossings.

Europeans and their governments are already daunted by the prospect of innocent economic migrants and asylum seekers turning up on
their doorsteps from Africa and the near East. Many refugees in 1997
and 1998 were Iraqi or Turkish Kurds, who have been arriving in
increasing numbers and applying for political asylum. EU countries are
afraid things could get worse: recent years have seen sudden influxes
from Albania and Bosnia; and the risk of mass migration from the
countries of North Africa is ever present, particularly with Algeria virtually in a state of civil war.

But much more worrying are the activities of organized criminals who now make big money smuggling illegal immigrants, as well as the more traditional contraband of drugs, guns and money. According to Professor Ernesto Savona, director of Italy's Transcrime research institute, the Albanian Mafia has now grown so powerful that it has already chased the Italian Mafia, once its patron and big brother, right out of the lucrative business of trafficking migrants. 'Albanian-organized crime has its foot in the door, which is Italy, and this means people, prostitution and drugs.'[1] It will be tough for EU countries to hold on to the Schengen ideal of free movement of people without more stringent immigration and asylum laws.

Expect Europe's open-borders policy to come under a lot of pressure within the Schengen group, while the UK looks on smugly.

**Immigration** If you're looking for a hot-button topic in Europe, immigration has long been a reliable choice and is likely to stay that way well into the next millennium. Recently deceased British politician Enoch Powell made his name thirty years ago with his notorious 'rivers of blood' speech on immigration, while in France the National Front party of Jean-Marie Le Pen now commands around 15.2 per cent of French votes on an anti-immigrant platform of 'France for the French'. It's all about culture (with a small c), jobs, and welfare. The presence of immigrants who are really, seriously different can create huge culture shock, especially when they are there in large numbers and form their own self-contained communities. For instance, Germany, Europe's biggest receiver of immigrants, has around 7 million immigrants out of a population of 82 million.

Every European country has its unique immigrant population profile – which itself begs the question of how many generations it takes for immigrants to be classified as locals. The UK, France, Belgium and the Netherlands have people from their former colonies, Germany has Turks and Eastern Europeans, most northern European countries have people from southern Europe, and southern Europe, which used to lose migrants to the north, is now having to deal with the unaccustomed problem of absorbing immigrants from Africa and the Balkans. Apart from the smells of unfamiliar cooking and the sound of strange languages, the big fears are either that the immigrants will work, taking the jobs of local people and driving down pay levels, or that they won't work but instead will live on benefit payments.

Slow-to-change communities are feeling the effects of the economic upheavals that are sweeping the world and devastating traditional industries, leaving legions of unemployed. It's all too easy for bewildered Europeans to point the finger of blame at immigrants, who are often concentrated in areas where the hardest-hit local people live too. And it's all too tempting for extremist parties to play on voters' fears, forcing even moderate politicians to take a harder line on immigration.

For example, the left-wing government of French Prime Minister Lionel Jospin caused a furore among its own supporters as it examined residency requests from 140,000 illegal immigrants. The government is aiming to modify tough immigration regulations passed by previous conservative governments under pressure from the far-right National Front, which wants to send all immigrants home. Jospin's new law is easier on immigrants who have French-born children or who have been in the country for many years, but is tougher on recent arrivals and bachelors.

All across Europe, governments will have a tough job balancing conflicting factors. On one hand, they wish to stay true to their humanitarian traditions and tackle the practical task of integrating new arrivals. And on the other hand, they are mindful of the risk of social conflict that is likely if they overstretch the capacity of local people to absorb newcomers.

So far, the immigration debate has been conducted largely in terms of rights and responsibilities, of economic burdens, of redistributing an economic cake that is assumed to be of fixed size. But in the early years of the coming millennium, we can expect to see the focus start to shift towards finding ways to help immigration contribute to the economies of receiving countries.

The fact is that Europe needs immigrants. Birth rates across Europe are low and the native populations of most European countries are ageing and shrinking. As people live longer and the demographic bulge of baby boomers starts heading towards retirement, Europe will increasingly need the work and the taxes of immigrants to keep its economies humming.

## You Are What You Speak?

So, in much of Europe in the year 2000, you'll be able to cross borders without noticing them and you'll only need to carry one type of currency, the euro. But what language will you speak? More and more, it's likely to be English. Increasing numbers of Europeans are deciding that if they have to invest time and effort in learning a second language, it may as well be one that can be used as widely as possible in Europe and beyond.

Like so much else in Europe, there is a precedent for Europeans sharing a common tongue, a *lingua franca*. For well over a thousand years, into the early centuries of the present millennium, educated people across the Continent spoke variants of Latin, the language imposed by the Romans. Modern French, Italian, Spanish, Portuguese and Catalan are direct descendants of Latin.

For much of the present millennium, Europeans spoke a huge variety of local dialects. It was only with the establishment of modern nation-states and public schooling that the idea of standardized national languages took hold, enabling people in different parts of the same country to communicate with each other. But the problem with language is that it's not only a means of communication, it's also a repository of national culture, identity and pride.

When the European Community was founded French was the predominant language until the UK joined in 1972, when English began to pose a threat. Since the admission of the Scandinavian countries in 1995, English has been even more widely used; an article in the *Electronic Telegraph* noted a recent survey of more than a billion pages of EU documents that confirmed that English has taken the lead. Although there are eleven official EU languages, European Commission meetings take place in just three tongues: English, French and German.

The smaller EU nations, such as the Scandinavian countries and the Netherlands, take it for granted that their languages are of domestic interest only. Even Italy and Spain apparently have no international aspirations for their languages. Not so Germany and France, where the national languages are seen as flagships of the national culture, to be promoted with government backing to stop the insidious slide towards English.

More than half the Germany foreign ministry's cultural budget is devoted to promoting German language and culture abroad in 180 German schools with 2,200 teachers and specialists. Nearly 170 government-supported Goethe Institutes employ 750 people in seventy-eight countries to champion the cause.[2]

France takes its language very seriously indeed and is trying its best to stem the tide of English. It has a highly respected body, the Académie Française, to rule on correct usage, and has placed legal restrictions on the use of English in public communications. France even runs an international forum of forty-nine Francophone countries, which held its seventh summit, in Hanoi, Vietnam, last year. Earlier this year, France lodged an official protest with the European Commission about the way English is supplanting French as Europe's prime working language. As part of its campaign, France has made it clear that it will block the appointment of the next president of the EC if he or she does not speak fluent French.

But, for better or for worse, English is becoming the 'industry standard', in much the same way that VHS became the videocassette standard and MS-DOS, Wintel and TCP/IP have become computer standards. Perhaps it's the fact that English developed as a melting pot of the major European languages. Or maybe that it's an 'open standards' language – accessible to all, and not owned by any one country.

Sonja Huerlimann, account planner at Advico Young & Rubicam Zurich, predicts that English will become the first foreign language taught in Swiss schools. The *New York Times* reports that young French people are flocking to Britain to improve their English-language skills, which are appreciated in much of Europe but considered a threat to the primacy of the French language back home. The Netherlands has successfully touted the English language skills of its people to promote itself as an ideal location for multinational companies to set up their European headquarters.

Paradoxically, even as Europeans increasingly choose to adopt English as their 'trading language', many find themselves more able than ever to slip back into their minority languages and dialects back home – linguistic diversity is thriving in Europe. In Spain, young Catalans, Basques and Galicians have grown up being allowed to talk languages that were banned under General Franco. In Italy, it was recently discovered that Italian had not been officially registered as the national language. While amending this oversight, legislators took the opportunity to register eighteen regional dialects and languages.[3]

Despite its reputation as being English only, the Internet is providing a low-cost medium for minority language speakers dispersed across Europe and beyond to network in languages ranging from Albanian to Welsh. Visit http://www.partal.com/ciemen/europe.html for a sample.

In the coming millennium, expect Europeans to apply global–local thinking to language. For functional global communication, English is bound to emerge as the best option. For local, personal and cultural purposes, local languages will continue to be the entrance tickets to parallel worlds. The losers in this process will be those poor souls who speak only English.

## What's Next in the UK

The United Kingdom – what's next even for just those two words begs a lot of questions. Namely, how far into the new millennium will the country still be a kingdom, and how much longer will it remain united?

But starting this section on a negative – or even a questioning – note would run counter to the spirit of the times for the UK. The country is on a roll, Cool Britannia, fêted by feature writers the world over, once again regarded as a world-class style capital. And it's been lauded not only as a style leader, but also as being ahead of many other European countries in terms of its preparedness for the New Economy. 'The UK is seen in some quarters as a model for a more commercial, entrepreneurial Europe,' says Adrian Day, of leading brand consultants Landor Associates, based in London.

The buzz has spread all over the world, but probably the sweetest satisfaction comes from changed perceptions close to home. France has tended to regard Britain with amused and slightly bemused hauteur – a trendy tourist guide of the eighties was entitled *London, 100 Years Behind and 10 Years Ahead.* But many French are now seriously wondering whether Britain is leaving them behind. Unprecedentedly large numbers of young French people are crossing the Channel to find work in Britain and polish their English – some 60,000 of them are in London's financial district alone, according to *Le Figaro.* Even the leader of the French parliament, Laurent Fabius, recently lavished his charm on Britain's Prime Minister, according to a report in the *Financial Times*: 'We are curious about you, dear Tony Blair, your personality and style, which have made more than one of us feel old-fashioned.'

Who would have expected it? Through the late 1980s and much of the 1990s, Britain seemed to be suffering a hangover from the Thatcher Revolution. The eighties boom peaked in 1988 and was followed by gloomy years of waiting for the return of the elusive 'Feel Good Factor', a buzzword used by the Conservative government of John Major (who succeeded Mrs Thatcher). House prices languished, homeless people were everywhere and politicians faced incessant accusations of corruption and wrongdoing – the so-called Sleaze Factor. Ironically, the Feel

Good Factor only returned at the landslide victory of the re-engineered 'New' Labour Party under Tony Blair in May 1997.

Postwar Britain has been characterized by boom-and-bust cycles, and time will tell whether the latest upswing will fall into the patterns of the past or break them. New Labour has certainly declared its intention to change the country. Much of the spadework was done by successive Thatcher governments in the 1980s; they were responsible for breaking the power of the labour unions, abolishing restrictive working practices, privatizing state monopolies and forcing the notions of good housekeeping and profitability on both the public and private sectors. And New Labour's macroeconomic thinking is not a million miles from Mrs Thatcher's.

Blair's honeymoon period has extended well beyond 100 days, although some of his high-profile showbiz supporters (e.g. the Gallagher brothers of Oasis) have already deserted him to protest against reforms of the welfare system. And there must be some doubts as to whether the Cool Britannia aura will survive untarnished until the new millennium – after all, fashion is fickle.

But, as Landor London affirms, the British at large have a sense of optimism, believe that the country is changing and that New Labour is modernizing it. So Tony Blair and the British people may well still find themselves on an extended honeymoon when the millennium turns. In any event, with a landslide majority behind him, Blair is one of the few current world leaders who can be confident of being in his job when the year 2000 dawns. For Britain, it's a fair bet that the years straddling the turn of the millennium will go down in history as 'The Blair Years'.

**United? Kingdom?** For the first time in many, many years, there is a real prospect of London handing over or 'devolving' powers to Wales, Scotland and Northern Ireland, provided that mutually acceptable formulas can be devised. In the case of Northern Ireland, it would be a truly millennial achievement to leave behind violent civil conflict and find a formula acceptable to both the Republicans, who want the province to join the Republic of Ireland, and the Unionists or Loyalists, who want it to remain part of the United Kingdom. The early years of the next millennium are unlikely to see any substantial alteration in the sovereignty of Wales and Scotland. Any change in the composition of the United Kingdom will come with Northern Ireland.

As for the monarchy, the tragic death of Princess Diana in August 1997 triggered a heated debate about her estranged in-laws, the Royal Family and the continuing loyalty of the British to the monarchy. Polls at the time showed a marked cooling off of feeling towards 'the Royals' and their relevance to modern British life. (Then again, this is an era in which the Royals are reputed to employ paid spin doctors whose remit goes far beyond that of the traditional press secretaries, and in which the Blairs appear to be professionally styled prior to major appearances.) On a less emotional tone, would-be constitutional reformers used the occasion to renew discussion about whether it is appropriate for the people of a modern, postindustrial nation to be 'subjects' rather than 'citizens'.

The future of the monarchy, at least for the first half of the next century, is likely to be decided by emotional criteria. Public discussion of the Royals – meaning street level rather than media – tends to focus not on constitutional issues, but on personalities and, occasionally, on money. Recent polls have indicated that Prince Charles has recovered a lot of the ground he lost at the time of his ex-wife Diana's death, while Prince William has inherited his mother's good looks and goodwill. According to a report in the *San Francisco Examiner*, 'Recent polls have shown that about 60 percent of Britons want the monarchy to continue. In the aftermath of Diana's death, support for the monarchy dropped to between 40 and 50 percent, the lowest level in modern times. Analysts note that William's father, Prince Charles, has been able to take advantage of the public's affection for William and his younger brother, Harry, to restore at least a portion of his own image, heavily damaged by his stormy divorce from Diana and his admitted affair with Camilla Parker Bowles.'

So, provided the Royals perform well for the media (think showbiz dynasty) and provided they are discreet with their money, they can probably count on the sort of public goodwill that will keep the monarchy show running and running, and keep the K in UK. On the other hand, media editors must be drooling for the day when the young prince starts dating and, inevitably, screening for a wife. The precedents don't bode well.

**Identity and Change** Some world powers are the product of revolution – France, the United States, Russia, China, India. Others have recast themselves after the turmoil of war or civil conflict – Germany, Italy and Japan being obvious examples. Almost alone among the world's great industrial nations, Britain has no 'Independence Day' or 'Liberation Day' to celebrate.

Modern Britain is the product of evolution, not revolution. The British have never had a violent break with their past, never had to sit down together and write out a constitution or think up a completely new way of governing themselves. The legal system goes back centuries, with sedimentary layers of laws and modifications of laws. The British way has been to look to the past and tweak what worked before, rather than undertake a radical makeover.

This approach seemed to pay dividends for a long time. Over the centuries, the country amassed an empire that spanned the globe. Older Brits still recall nostalgically school atlases in which every continent had large areas of pink to mark British possessions, an era when 'the sun never set on the British Empire'. But all that changed with World Wars I and II, which depleted the country and for ever loosened its grip on its colonial possessions.

Over the last fifty years, Britain has been forced to rethink itself, to abandon some cherished tenets of its self-mythology and to allow a new identity to emerge. The process has been long and painful, but it's irreversible. In the mid 1990s, then Prime Minister John Major tried to stem the tide with a call for a 'Back to Basics' approach, along with a dewy-eyed evocation of old maids on bicycles and cricket on the village green. The country ridiculed his vision and voted him out at the next opportunity.

The British seem increasingly prepared, or perhaps resigned, to face a harsher future in which old maids won't ride around on bicycles and the state won't try to provide for all needs. 'In the UK, a sea change is occurring,' reports Gavin Heron, former strategic planning director at TBWA London, now based in Hong Kong. 'People are moving from a dependency mindset to that of personal responsibility or control. They no longer believe the government will provide for them as it used to. The millennium is acting as a catalyst for a break with the past. It represents the future as now.'

**Embracing Foreigners** Britain is in the process of consciously becoming a multicultural country – a huge change from the days of the empire.

The United States forges its nationhood in schools with the pledge of allegiance to the flag. In France, immigrants are expected to put aside their origins and 'assimilate' French ways – as happened in France's former colonies. The British, in contrast, have never expected foreigners to become British, so they were pretty much left to retain their own ethnic identities, as used to happen in British colonies. In Britain, immigrant groups have tended to retain their own ethnic flavour as they have found their way into society.

Absorbing immigrants has gone against the grain for many British people. Racial issues have been debated hard for many years and the anti-immigrant National Front enjoyed a brief spell of limited support in the 1980s. But an indication of the progress made can be seen in Mike Leigh's award-winning feature film *Secrets and Lies* (1996), in which a working-class English woman is tracked down by the daughter who was taken from her at birth. The fact that the daughter is black and the mother is white is barely mentioned and has little relevance to the story, which is about family relationships and is virtually colour blind. Had the film been made ten years earlier, it would probably have been about race.

Much of Britain's self-mythology has been about a plucky little country resisting foreign attempts to invade it – the Spanish in the sixteenth century, the French under Napoleon in the nineteenth century, and the Germans under Hitler this century. The country's history of military and imperial success bred a feeling that Britain had little to learn from foreigners.

This British sense of effortless superiority has been severely eroded and even turned on its head. Over the last fifty years, as Britain has slipped down world rankings in all sorts of areas – GDP, income, standard of living, nutrition, education, sport – many British people began to acknowledge that maybe foreigners knew a thing or two after all.

A willingness to learn from foreigners is perhaps what distinguishes New Brits most from previous generations. A measure of this willingness is the fact that some of Britain's most chauvinistic and reactionary clubs have thrown their doors wide open to foreigners. Britain's football clubs – flush with cash from new TV deals – now field players from all over the globe. Even more surprising is that some of the top clubs have hired foreign managers – a radical development for the country that claims to have invented the game.

# Big Next: an Independent Asia

One hundred years ago, vast tracts of Asia were under colonial rule or foreign domination. Powerful industrialized countries controlled the destinies of many millions of Asians – in the region, only Thailand and Japan could be regarded as sovereign nations. And so it continued for almost fifty years more, through and beyond the Second World War.

Now, as the twentieth century draws to a close, the continent can look back over several decades of extraordinary changes and rapid development. Many Asians enjoy levels of education and affluence that surpass even those of the old colonial masters. The last vestige of foreign dominion was removed at midnight, 30 June 1997, when Britain returned Hong Kong to China, thereby ending what many Chinese described as '150 years of shame'.

Asians now control their own destiny. The region's response to several big issues will be crucial in shaping that destiny and determining what sort of century the next one will be.

## Economic Adjustment

It is a great pity for the region that the Hong Kong handover celebrations on 30 June were almost immediately overtaken by months of headlines about a regional economic crisis that grew and grew, just as forest fires in Indonesia burned out of control and blanketed much of south-east Asia in choking smoke. The sobering effect of the crisis has led to widespread fears that the hard-won economic gains of the last decades may be lost in some countries and that the twenty-first century may not after all turn out to be 'the Asian century' as had been so widely predicted.

At the time of writing, the ramifications of the regional economic crisis are still working themselves through. Many analysts have come to the conclusion that the crisis was caused by structural problems, which the region is now being forced to tackle. According to this analysis, a good shakeout will help the countries of the region to discard unproductive practices and get themselves into shape for the next stage in their development. Lower currencies will provide an extra edge in export markets for manufacturers in the region who ride out the storm.

'Structural,' however, may be too pat an explanation, and if accepted at face value could deflect the deeper analysis and problem-solving necessary to restore the tigers' roar. Rampant over-investment in icons such as office buildings, hotels and airports soaked up billions of dollars that may have been better invested in future productivity. Over-reliance on traditional relationships as the basis for business, at the expense of a truly open market, led to many self-interested decisions. And a natural business cycle was at play here, too. Boom to bust, expansion followed by recession, has been the hallmark of the twentieth century. No one should have believed Asia was immune.

Not all countries in the region were affected. The Philippines barely merited a mention in the frenzied media coverage. Perhaps it should have. Its growth period started later (having been held back by the Marcos years), so it had less far to fall, but it did fall . . . and hard. In contrast, Vietnam only recently hooked into the global economy (when the US trade embargo was lifted in 1994) and its currency, the dong, isn't convertible, so its exposure to the storm was limited. As a highly placed resident Westerner put it, 'We haven't seen much of the economic crisis here. Vietnam is still trying to sort out a local problem – Stalinism.'

China's experience of the economic storm came mainly through Hong Kong, which is exposed to regional economies through its finance sector. Unlike in other countries in the region, Hong Kong bank authorities managed to defend the Hong Kong dollar against the pressure of the foreign exchange markets. Its peg against the US dollar is widely expected to hold, thanks to the dollar reserves of the city and the pride that's at stake – for the Hong Kong dollar to weaken so soon after the departure of Britain would mean a terrible loss of face for Beijing. The main Hong Kong casualty of the Asian crisis to date is Peregrine Investment Holdings, which collapsed largely as a result of its exposure in Indonesia.

As for the rest, Taiwan appears confident that it can continue its steady economic growth, and the effects of the Asian economic crisis have barely been felt in China, although the warning has not gone unnoticed. Dentsu Young & Rubicam (DY&R) Guangzhou reports that 'there is much fear in China given the recent drop in economy in the region and the talk of devaluing the yuan or the renminbi'. China gives the region cause to hold its collective breath. If the renminbi were to fall, it is likely to take the rest of the region's currencies down with it.

As many commentators have pointed out, the only foreseeable major threat to the region lies in the social consequences of the economic crisis and the adjustments that the region is going through. For the last twenty years Asia has been largely stable and peaceful. Only a very small minority of Asians has been concerned with political freedom and social inequality – South Koreans routinely take to the streets to do battle with the authorities – as the majority has been more interested in working hard for material prosperity. However, any setback to rising standards of living could prompt social unrest, as was seen in Indonesia in late 1997 and early 1998. Indonesia has emerged as one of the most deeply troubled economies, with its authorities apparently reluctant to take the sort of action that has the potential to salvage the situation in other hard-hit countries, such as Thailand and South Korea.

DY&R Korea reports cautious optimism there as people tentatively hope for a return to Korea's previous record of growth. South Korea is no stranger to the vested interests and cosy behind-the-scenes deal-making that have characterized Asian economies in recent years, but it has taken the IMF's strictures very seriously. With the country's recent record of solid achievement as an economic power, and its national determination to out-do neighbouring Japan, the economic crisis could strengthen South Korea in the long run.

Although China has been barely affected there are fears that even the current process of economic change there could lead to problems. As DY&R's Sharon Lee in Shanghai put it, 'If the income gaps between rural and urban centres are not narrowed, there may be tremendous social upheaval.'

*The Journal of Business Ethics* spelled out the issues: 'In the transformation of the employment system and the opening of labor markets, there are nearly one hundred million potentially unemployed people in rural areas, and ten million in state-owned enterprises. If the enterprises continue to employ the latter, the reforms in the enterprises will fail and the new enterprise cannot bear such heavy burdens. Moreover, it is easier for rural workers to find jobs in cities because they are willing to accept lower wages than urban workers . . . Shanghai has two million unemployed workers but four million and sixty thousand jobs are offered to the non-local workers.'

The factors that were expected to make 'the Asian Century' on the whole still apply: large, dynamic populations eager to work for prosperity (and to work for less than many of their 'developed market' counterparts); belief in education and training; belief in market economics along with respect for collective values; social stability; growing self confidence; and huge, largely untapped markets for growth-minded multinationals. The region has already established a track record for realizing its potential, and there is clearly still more potential to be tapped in the twenty-first century.

## Asian Consciousness

National boundaries are internationally established, but regional boundaries are in the eye of the beholder. For example, what Westerners think of as 'the Middle East' is called 'West Asia' in the Malaysian media. For our purposes, the Asian countries covered in this section are those in the Asia Pacific region, with shorelines washed by Pacific Ocean waters. Even within this definition, Asia is a vast and diverse region, stretching from the highly seasonal north of Japan down to the equator and beyond, including the year-round tropical heat of Indonesia. The religious landscape is similarly varied, ranging from Confucianism in the north, Catholicism in the Philippines, through many varieties of Buddhism and growing devotion to Islam in the south, with a recent overlay of Marxism in China and Vietnam.

Talking with people in the region, there seems to be little clear agreement about what makes them 'Asian'. For some, it's a certain gentleness and graciousness of manner that contrasts with the more abrupt style of Westerners. For others, it's the central place that rice growing and eating have had in shaping the cultures of the region, or it's a question of geographical proximity and unity, even though the vast majority of people in the region have never travelled abroad. Still others cite the much-touted 'Asian values', meaning respect for authority and age, and a willingness to put the interests of the group before the interests of the individual.

In the final analysis, being Asian may ultimately be a question of choice, a question of identifying with the issues, interests and sensibilities of other people in the region, and making common cause with them. Unlike in Europe, where a similar process is taking place, most Asians are fortunate in not having recent memories of war to overcome as they forge links with their neighbours. Although memories of Japanese occupation linger long for some older Asians, there are fewer people old enough to remember the war.

The development of Asian consciousness, and with it Asian power, will come not just from trading goods, but also from sharing ideas and culture. While Asia is a powerhouse exporter of manufactured goods,

it continues to be a big importer of entertainment and style products
– Hollywood films, popular music, designer fashion wear, computer
software, sports. Consumers in Asia, and indeed around the world,
would have no hesitation in buying electronic goods or domestic appliances made in Asia, but the same cannot be said for 'intellectual copyright' products. The region has its own products in this area, but the
audience is barely regional, let alone global.

As Steven Lyons, of Burson-Marsteller Hong Kong, said, 'Lifestyles
and values will continue to be altered by Western media and product
developments. Asia will have to work hard at maintaining its cultural
identities. Rural areas will be the last bastions of traditional cultural
and family values.'

The emergence of Asian confidence and creativity will be a key factor
in the maturing of the region. The turning point will come when Vietnamese soap operas top the TV ratings in Indonesia, when Indonesian
pop stars play to packed stadiums in Thailand, when a Thai fashion
designer sells like hotcakes in Shanghai, when a Chinese feature film
breaks box office records across Asia.

## Getting Schooled

One of the cornerstones of 'Asian values' is emphasis on the importance
of education. In societies without social security, children are a sort of
pension plan. It used to be smart to have lots of children to spread the
risk. These days, the emphasis has switched from having lots of pairs
of hands to having a few well-educated brains. Family sizes are shrinking, and parents are investing in putting their children through higher
education.

The pressure to get educated is being felt by children of all ages, all
the way down to preschoolers. Steven Lyons expects 'serious education
to start at increasingly younger ages (three to four)'. Our colleague
Stuart Harris, a market research practitioner in Kuala Lumpur, reports,
'My son Ruben got his first school report in Kuala Lumpur at age
twenty-one months!' As DY&R Shanghai observed, 'The pressures from
their parents are tremendous, to the point where children are given
little time to enjoy themselves – most of it is spent studying or learning
new skills, such as computer, piano, painting, etc.'

Rapidly expanding economies need skilled and educated people at
every level, which has resulted in a severe labour shortage in some of
the faster growing economies of the region – and has provided a bon-

anza for overseas universities, particularly in Australia, Britain, the United States and Canada. But the sharp devaluation of some currencies in the region, and the risk of devaluation hitting other currencies, is making students look closer to home for their education. 'There will be a major drop in Asian students being sent abroad,' predicted Han van Dijk, of DY&R Singapore.

Two key education factors will be crucial in determining the shape and success of Asia in the twenty-first century.

The first is how education is imparted. Obedience and respect for authority are deeply instilled in Asian children. Unquestioning rote learning is the norm, and not only for Chinese and Japanese children, who need to memorize hundreds of complex characters just to be able to read. While the top-down, memorizing approach produces socially responsible youngsters who apply themselves diligently to their studies, some people are beginning to worry that it doesn't foster the personal qualities that Asia needs to make quantum leaps into new economies of the next century.

Already Japanese employers are complaining that university graduates are not up to speed for today's workplace – the *Economist* reports that unemployment among graduates and school leavers is two to three times higher than the national average. The government has introduced changes to take the emphasis off exhaustive examination. However, as the *Economist* reported separately last year, parents may welcome the idea of more liberal, creative education, but they fear changes may damage their children's chances of employment.

Nevertheless, DY&R Tokyo thinks the country is likely to see greater emphasis on teaching analytical skills, with more attention paid to the personal development of children, while in China, DY&R Shanghai forecasts that education will become 'more focused on guiding children, bringing out their potential instead of forcing them to memorize everything that they may not even understand. The whole examination system will be changed. Grades are still important, but will not mean everything ten years later. More students will be accepted in universities as the system will be based on potential/talent rather than just examination grades. In addition, there may also be more private universities available.'

The second key factor will be the development of regional centres of educational excellence. High-quality establishments already exist, but they tend to draw students from their local markets. Ambitious students study either locally or in the West, with few considering study in other countries in the region.

Television and Internet chat will help to build relations between young Asians, but there is no substitute for the bonds that are created when people from different countries meet face to face and study together.

## Dealing with China

How to deal with China is an issue for all countries in Asia, including China itself. The sheer size of the place, its 1.2 billion population and its diaspora make it impossible to ignore.

Chinese culture and thinking continues to have an impact on all countries in the region. Throughout the centuries, Japan adopted and adapted hugely from China – Japanese writing is based on the Chinese system, even though the languages are totally different. Countries sharing borders with China have felt the need to assert their own identity while developing a modus vivendi for living with such a huge neighbour.

Chinese emigrants have established themselves throughout the region, often achieving great success in business and arousing local envy in the process. So-called 'Overseas Chinese' number some 57 million worldwide, with an estimated 53 million of them in Asia Pacific, according to John Naisbitt in *Megatrends Asia*.

Since the beginning of recorded history, China has been a massive presence in the Asia Pacific region, a country with a manifest belief in its status as 'the Middle Kingdom'. As the century draws to a close, China has emerged from years of turmoil and hardship, and is looking forward to taking its place among the wealthy superpowers. 'Deng Xiao Ping created the blueprint of a brilliant future for Chinese people. The next millennium will be a great era for China, a continuation of the new future that has been created,' says Sharon Lee, of DY&R Shanghai.

China's pride and ambition have far-reaching implications for the Asian region, and indeed for the Chinese themselves. Being virtually isolated for much of the twentieth century has limited the impact of China's vast population on the rest of the world, but China has increasingly opened up with the reforms masterminded by Deng.

It used to be said that if all the people in China jumped up and down at the same time, the world would shake. Probably not literally true, but it's the sort of thought that naturally comes to mind when contemplating a population of 1.2 billion people, most of whom currently don't travel, don't own cars, don't have central heating or air conditioning, don't have a telephone or life insurance policies, etc. But relatively few of those 1.2 billion potential customers live within geographical or financial reach of consumer heaven; for the moment that privilege is enjoyed far more by the 100 million or so urban dwellers along the coast. During the first decades of its existence, the People's Republic of China tended to exert its will by military means. The new economically liberal China being guided by President Jiang Zemin is finding a very effective lever in its economic power and the prospect of granting or denying access to China's vast and potentially lucrative market.

Three of Asia Pacific's great success stories are Chinese: Singapore, Hong Kong and the island of Taiwan, which the People's Republic officially regards as a renegade province. As China's economy grows and opens, the links between them will strengthen, forecasts DY&R Taiwan: 'Following an improved relationship with China, "The Great China Economic Circles" will gradually take shape.'

The rise of these Chinese economies, and the prosperity of overseas Chinese, is likely to raise some serious questions in non-Chinese countries of the region, particularly with regard to their Chinese immigrant minorities.

In Indonesia, social tension always risks spilling over into anti-Chinese sentiment and even blood-letting. As many as 500,000 people were suspected of Communist sympathies and killed in the coup that brought Suharto to power in 1965, and anti-Chinese sentiment has been evident in Indonesia's latest troubles.[4] In neighbouring Malaysia, the government is mindful of local resentment. It regards the very large Chinese community – about 32 per cent of the population – as economically advantaged and has implemented a pro-Malay affirmative action programme for the last twenty years.[5]

In future, will a powerful and prosperous China continue to stand by if its overseas cousins are persecuted for being Chinese? Will the huge and pervasive influence of China prompt non-Chinese (e.g., Malays in Malaysia) to assert their own culture and identity more vigorously? Will China be seen as a welcome Asian alternative to Americanization/Westernization? Or will Asians look even more to the West to counterbalance Chinese influence?

# 3

# Globally Speaking, What's Next?

## Millennium Countdown

Although the new millennium doesn't strictly speaking begin until 1 January 2001, the year 2000 packs the bigger psychological punch – and people in some parts of the world are getting hit hard. 'It feels like something big is about to happen,' writes Danny Hillis in *The Millennium Clock*. 'Graphs show us the yearly growth of populations, atmospheric concentrations of carbon dioxide, Net addresses, and Mbytes per dollar. They all soar up to form an asymptote just beyond the turn of the century: The Singularity. The end of everything we know. The beginning of something we may never understand.'

Living in this time of enormous change – a period that spans the second and third millennia – fosters a sense of historical importance that leads to an increased drive to leave one's 'mark' on whatever field or endeavour one is involved in. Individuals will assess their lives in the twentieth century, making pacts with themselves for changes that will be brought about in the twenty-first – the ultimate New Year's resolutions. For the eve of 31 December 1999, reservations already have been made to ring in the new year on the QE2, on the international dateline and in New York City's Times Square.

## Cause for Celebration?

'The actual celebration of the arrival of the next millennium isn't as important in the East as it is in the West. While looking forward to the onset of the next millennium, the current economic situation has put a damper on expectations. The overall attitude is one of hope,' reports Yoshitaka Abe, CEO & president of DY&R Tokyo. But, he adds, this business climate spells angst. 'The economic downturn is at the forefront of businessmen's minds. The 'millennium bug' is a worry for computerized companies. New Year's Eve [of 1999] is looked forward to, but not being made as big a deal of as in the West.'

Stuart Harris, a market research practitioner based in Kuala Lumpur, explains: 'Overall, the millennium is a European milestone (including honorary Europeans in the Americas) and is an imported concept in much of Asia. The Chinese think of their history in terms of 6,000 years. Buddha's followers may well have his birth time (around 500 BC) as their reference point, and Muslims (most of Indonesia and half of Malaysia) haven't yet reached 1,500 years since the birth of the prophet. So, although they're all counting our years too, I would suspect that they don't feel it so deeply.'

While part of what's next is very definitely a sense of globality, reaction to change, including the change of centuries in the West, is deeply local. Millennial angst isn't the same everywhere. 'In Canada, consumers' concerns about changes in the new millennium tend to centre on changes to their personal situation,' reports Laurence Bernstein, an account planner at Y&R Toronto. 'They will be older and, therefore, more dependent on government assistance in the form of pensions (which they believe won't be available) and healthcare (which they believe will be severely cut). Younger people are concerned that when they enter the workforce, they will not be able to find employment or their chances for advancement will be limited due to people retiring later. Therefore, there is some concern and darkness in their view of the postmillennium society.'

'People in interactive entertainment see the next millennium as a golden Digital Age,' says Sven Meyer, managing director of Psygnosis, Germany. 'Most people in this industry see the year 2000 and beyond as an almost unlimited hunting ground for business opportunities.' Around the world, businesses are rushing to register names associated with the changing century. Companies are getting creative, coming up with such catchy names as 'nu.millennia inc.', chosen by a San Diego-based publishing house. In cyberspace, a host of millennium-oriented Websites has been constructed, and many more are in development. Search engine Infoseek currently offers links to more than 50,000 such sites (search term: millennium).

## A Mixed Reaction

In the popular square in front of Paris's Georges Pompidou Centre, a digital clock has been counting down to the millennium since 1987. Yet currently, the mood across most of Europe seems to fall a long way short of eager anticipation. Only the UK, Denmark and, possibly, the Netherlands are looking forward to the big click-over with optimism.

The remaining countries are certainly anticipating change, but for many it's something to be endured rather than embraced. Even the changes countries have actively pursued, such as the single currency and the European Union, are now viewed with less optimism than they were just a few years ago. In short, many Europeans fear that life won't be as good for them in the next century.

Edward Appleton, managing director of Y&R GmbH Frankfurt, reports that unemployment continues to be the big headache for Germans, who were previously accustomed to steadily rising living standards. In 1998 the Germans decided change was in order, electing as Chancellor Social Democrat Gerhard Schroeder, who has his own website, and whose youthful charisma prompts comparisons to Bill Clinton as well as Tony Blair. Despite this outcome, Helmut Kohl goes into history as the politician who reunited East and West Germany, and brought Europe on track for one European coin.

Citizens of Sweden and Switzerland fear that their cosy prosperity will not last into the new millennium. Katarina Varenius of Hall & Cederquist/Y&R Stockholm anticipates the collapse of Sweden's comprehensive social security system, while Sonja Huerlimann, an account planner of Advico Y&R Zurich, reports widespread consternation in Switzerland, which is located in the middle of the European Union but is not a member: 'The overall attitude at the moment is fear, uncertainty, and instability, largely caused by the explosive rise of unemployment, which nobody was aware of a few years ago. Globalization also worries the Swiss people.'

France, too, is entering a period of self-doubt. The centralized structure of authority which has existed since the Napoleonic era, and a widespread sympathy with socialist principles, has led the French to expect the state to sort out their problems and provide for the future. Yet the state has proved powerless in the face of stubborn unemployment. Account planners Dominique Missoffe, Françoise Weishaupt and Claire D'Hennezel at Y&R Paris report a depressed social climate, a sense that things are stuck and increasing numbers of people looking for individual solutions and individual autonomy. The big question for many is whether the country will get behind this reforming, self-help trend and celebrate it in time to use the turn of the millennium as an emotional springboard into global next.

The Spanish are famed for their capacity to celebrate a good 'fiesta', which they did for many years following the death of General Franco in 1975 and the restoration of democracy. But as Lola Gonzalez, consumer research director of Y&R Madrid, reports, anticipation of the new millennium is 'contaminated' by the fact that in 2002 Spain will enter the EMU (Economic and Monetary Union) with consequent economic, social and labour-market effects. There is also fear that the European Union subsidies will dry up as the EU switches development resources from southern European to eastern European countries.

Italians have long been enthusiastic supporters of the European project, partly out of gratitude for development funds and partly in the hope that Brussels would give them better government than their own politicians. Y&R Milan believes that the country is approaching the millennium with a mixture of fear and optimism. Italians feel poorer than in the recent past and fear that the future will not be better as technology and cheap labour abroad will threaten jobs. On the other hand, these fears are balanced by some positive developments that few would have imagined possible just a few years ago – low inflation, public debt under control, a stable government, agreement on institutional reform and some healthy, big companies.

All in all, the mood of Europe at the turn of the millennium is likely to depend very much on economic news and the progress of the single currency project which begins 1 January 1999. If all goes well, it could well be party time across the Continent, with optimism and millennial energy spilling over into the next century and driving forward Europe's essential reforms and restructuring.

## The Biggest New Year's Celebration?

In contrast to its Continental cousins, the UK is one of the places in the world in which the dawn of the new millennium is most eagerly, and anxiously, anticipated.

The Scots are famed for their boisterous celebration of New Year's Eve – Hogmanay – and over the years, the rest of the UK has absorbed their traditions and enthusiasm for the occasion. If it's important to celebrate properly on a normal New Year, then for many it will be vital to celebrate the turn of the millennium memorably. The big concern, according to Jim Williams, director of strategy & research, Y&R Europe, is not to be left out, not to be one of the sad souls living through the great moment at home alone.

Preparations for a truly memorable event are well under way, especially on the site of the Millennium Dome, a vast and controversial edifice being constructed in the heart of London's Docklands. For the time being, the focus of British attention is on New Year's Eve 1999 itself, rather than what lies beyond, according to Landor's Adrian Day, senior executive director.

## What's on the Horizon

Whatever we claim to think of the impending millennium, most of us in the West are at least a little curious about what lies around the corner. We've grown up with futuristic novels and movies set in 2001 and beyond, and we can't help but be somewhat anxious about how our lives will be altered by the period of rapid change we're currently experiencing.

Now that we've laid out the Big Nexts that will help shape life next, we'd like to share with you our sense of what other key trends are lying in wait. The implications of these trends will not be quite so broad as those of the Big Nexts, but collectively they indicate the direction in which today's trendsetters are moving our lives.

### Next: A Din of Small – and Not So Small – Voices

Think of Drudge – as in Matt Drudge, author of the online 'Drudge Report' – as the symbol of a small voice roaring. He is America's most famous Internet personality, a cyber-gossip who has now been signed by Rupert Murdoch's Fox TV to transfer his yack from the on-line world to network television. Armed only with a computer and modem, he has managed to build himself into a media mogul online. While his online report hasn't yet reaped major profits for him, it has provided a daily audience for his views and 'news' reports – one that is far larger than would have been accessible to anyone outside the major media prior to the birth of the Internet.

As with any form of mass media, the Internet wields great power. The difference between the Internet and TV or radio is that the Net allows two-way communication and gives as much potential power to a thirteen-year-old computer geek as to a corporate CEO or government leader. 'Power' online is based solely on the ability to draw in an audience and communicate with it in a persuasive manner. It can be utilized to bolster the rank of a political party, to form a fan club for a favourite celebrity, or to sell products and build one's brand.

Voices outside traditional 'news' organizations are being heard in other media as well. A most interesting development in recent years in the US has been the video news release (VNR, which is routinely substituted for 'hard news' without warning to viewers that the footage was created by, for, and about a brand, a company or an organization – by anyone with the money to make and distribute videocassettes with edutainment value. Clearly, this is a consequence of the proliferation of twenty-four-hour news services and of the subsequent hunger for programming. (Imagine how much more programming is demanded by the Net.)

As brands make themselves heard at news stations worldwide, one needn't take a very large step to consider the viability of branded news on TV. With iconography that has come to serve as a universal language (think Nike swoosh), numerous global brands are well on their way to creating the credibility they need to offer up believable 'news' and feature coverage.

## Next: Arm's-Length Communion

Caucuses, coalitions, militias, networks. By any name, such groups are all the rage. But 1998 is not a year for joiners. It's a year in which followers sign on for brief respites of participation for the sole purpose of being recharged by the power of community: join a church for the monthly potluck supper; sign up for a half day of volunteering rather than commit to a long-term project; tuck a membership card from a political action committee into your wallet – no need to attend a second meeting. Informal networks are in; rigid institutions are out.

## Next: Brands 2000

As a number of twentieth-century powerhouse brands battle to retain market share, new industries are springing up as if from nowhere to create power brands for the next millennium. Examples include Boston Market, creator of the home meal replacement industry; Starbucks, which turned coffee into a retail experience; and America On-line (AOL) which made the proverbial back fence a twenty-four-hour/seven-days-a-week opportunity for neighbourly chat and captured a share of coach potatoes' minds and eyes from the networks. More trends to watch: convergence, as manufacturers and programmers of the boxes that run home and office create ever more indispensable products; edutainment, as we strive to make the next generation (and ourselves) more competitive; and relaxation as we pursue relief from the stresses of modern-day life.

## Next: A Branded Existence

The world populace soon will have an all-too-clear understanding of the adage 'everything communicates', as marketers extend their reach beyond the usual platforms. Already in the testing phase: advertisements delivered via ATM and sampling offers based on smart-card purchasing patterns. Just as urban infill will eventually lay claim to every vacant lot in the urban landscape, so, too, will 'brand infill' ensure that every experience, thought, place and product is marketed to its utmost potential. As with marriage, some unions will be for life; others will be brief, even foolhardy. The unstoppable James Bond marketing machine – *Tomorrow Never Dies* drove high-speed visibility for BMW. Ericsson and Heineken, among others – is a ready reminder of the opportunities.

## Next: In Praise of Parenthood

The death of eight-month-old American Matthew Eappen at the hands of his British au pair sparked heated debate about his mother's choice to continue her professional career – albeit in a part-time capacity – rather than stay home to care for her children. The debate over 'choice' will no longer revolve solely around abortion; instead, more and more women will be faced with the need to defend their 'choice' to work outside the home – particularly when that home is in an upmarket community. Parenting will be touted as the most important profession of the next decade.

## Next: Redefining Desirability

The new age of heightened desirability is thirty-six – the age at which Princess Diana will forever rest, frozen in time at the height of her sensuality. The fashion industry will continue to push parallel images of the heroin-chic sixteen-year-old model, mature beyond her years, and her counterpart: the youthful and innocent coquette. But the older, wiser, and much more sexy Diana archetype will prove a compelling alternative. Mature woman/young stud relationships will make headline news, supplanting the Jennifer phenomenon of the eighties, when twenty-something trophy wives were hunted and mounted by fifty-something tycoons. Look for Leonardo DiCaprio to partner with Sharon Stone, for the Francesca Annis–Ralph Fiennes romance to be duplicated again and again. Mid-youth now runs until the onset of menopause, with thirty-six marking the absolute age of power and those over forty-two still regarded as 'hot', bringing to relationships experience, enthusiasm, and – thanks to new fertility tricks – even the prospect of children.

## Next: Greener Approaches

As this planet gets more crowded, consumers are recognizing their impact on the world, the world's impact on them – and our communal responsibility to future generations. So far, the 'pure consumer' has embraced such green products as natural cosmetics, eco-friendly fabrics and organic food. Interest in sustainable architecture – with its emphasis on energy conservation, long-life materials, and environmentally friendly building techniques – is on the rise. And electric vehicles and their gas-and-electric-powered cousins, the hybrids, are poised to usher in an era of 'green' automobiles. Toyota, for one, expected to sell 12,000 models of its hybrid, the Prius, to Japanese consumers in 1998. As green thinking migrates from left to centre, consumers will increasingly demand environmental accountability from product and service providers.

## Next: Aggressive Health Maintenance

Technology is coming that will ensure less invasive, more civilized and more humane ways to prevent, detect and treat disease. Ten years ago, magnetic resonance imagining (MRI) was an innovation which provided a radiation-free alternative to X-rays. The potential of this innovation will be extended far beyond testing for neurological disorders. MRI scanners will become far more accessible, and even primary-care practitioners will have direct access to such machines, enabling them to do everything from detecting breast abnormalities to determining the extent of knee and spinal injuries. At the same time, CT scans – which produce cross-sectional images by computing, using small doses of radiation – will facilitate virtual examinations of the lungs, bowels and other organs, without painful and dangerous invasion of the human body.

There is a yin and a yang to most trends, though, and this one is not without bad news. As disease screening becomes more prevalent, and more sophisticated, people deemed to be predisposed to particular diseases might be subjected to unnecessary medical procedures. Already we're seeing healthy women submit voluntarily to radical mastectomies, simply out of the fear that a 'high risk' label creates in them.

As the health field grows ever more technical, and as patient choices continue to expand, expect to see a growing cadre of 'medical advocates' – professionals hired to guide individuals through the jungle of medical literature, 'alternative' medicines and medical options. In many ways, it will be these people who become the new 'family doctor' – despite the fact that they are not practising physicians.

## Next: Them and Us – Left vs Right

In the short time before the new millennium, expect a major global clash between the left/liberals and the right/conservatives akin to the one associated with capitalism vs/communism and socialism. This new Cold War will be fought with particular intensity over family values issues. The superwoman of the 1980s has been killed by innuendo and a backlash against feminism and the gains of the women's movement. Next on the right's seek-and-destroy list are those who want abortion available on demand. The overarching goal: to return religion to the centre of public life.

Throughout the Western world, where family life has been a lesser priority than issues such as economic expansion, taxation and even education, expect social clashes to erupt, with women – particularly working women – bearing the brunt of the blows. Immigrants and minorities also will be the object of increasingly violent debate, as global fears pertaining to everything from job shortages to the loss of national identity and culture fuel the fears of those who face an uncertain future in an entirely new millennium. Fundamentalist Christians and Muslims, ultra-Orthodox Jews, and other factions on the religious right will gather force as the millennium approaches, many of them using the Internet as a tool for recruitment, proselytization and denouncing the sins of the world.

## Next: Desperately Seeking People Like Me

As a byproduct of this schism between left and right, expect more and more investors and businesses to seek partners with compatible political and social (even religious) points of view. Whether it's Shell Oil being scrutinized by potential investors or home contractors incorporating scripture into their advertisements, business relationships will be based on far more than the bottom line.

The same sentiment holds true for people who are simply looking for a network, a connection to others like them. In the coming years, geography will become far less important than shared attitudes, beliefs, experiences and values. The Internet ensures that whoever we are and whatever our passion, we have a very good chance of connecting with 'virtual neighbours' who will support and sustain us. This trend can be benign (at-home dads forming support networks) or it can be truly dangerous (already White Power activists, conspiracy theorists and holocaust revisionists are gaining strength on the Net). As people become more adept at harnessing the power of cyberspace, these unions will have the potential to change the world, for good or evil.

## Next: Privacy is Dead

Of all the pre-millennial fears we face, loss of privacy is perhaps the most common. The truth is privacy is dead. It's been taken away by the microchip, and it's not coming back. One interesting side-effect of our lack of privacy is that it will spell freedom for many people. Instead of being ashamed of what we might consider our perversions or 'unnatural' impulses, we'll see more and more just how many people think and behave the way we do. And once we realize that our indiscretions, big and small, are never secret for very long, we'll be encouraged to allow our wild sides out of the closet a lot more often.

So, while the right will grow stronger and far, far more outspoken, we'll also see an increased indifference to scandal (how scandalous can something be when 'everyone' is doing it?). From infidelity to bondage, from foot fetishes to businessmen wearing women's undergarments, we'll see an 'assumed blindness' develop to one another's underbellies, along with a sense of futility regarding efforts to keep humans from being human.

## Next: Am I Normal?

Getting inside the heads of ordinary people is an international craze. We now expect every guest who appears on a talk show to bare his or her dirty laundry – and very soul. And the fascinating thing is, just about all of them oblige us! There's even a family in Sweden that has mounted a camera inside their refrigerator so visitors to their Website can monitor the family's eating patterns.

Is this trend simply a movement toward exhibitionism? We think it's much more than that. What we're seeing is a deep-seated desire for confirmation. We want to know that what we're doing, thinking and feeling is normal, and we're looking to an audience of strangers to reassure us that no matter how bizarre our actions or attitudes, there's someone else who's far stranger. And as a result of our own loosened tongues, we're angrily rejecting everyone else's right to be discreet. (Just consider the backlash against Britain's Royal Family when their mourning of Diana's loss didn't meet the public's new standards of grief.)

A surge in typeradio – online chat with a moderator-announcer controlling the flow of the dialogue – and online support groups and discussion forums will be one of the more obvious offshoots of this trend. In the political forum, we'll be willing to forgive every mistake, indiscretion or even crime – as long as we are privy to a detailed and heartfelt public confession or even an angry denial of wrongdoing. What we won't forgive is the sin of silence.

## What's Next? Trend Bytes for Tomorrow

The remainder of this chapter is filled with trend bytes, our prognostications regarding new products, services and ways of working and living that will develop in the next few years. Some of the ideas may strike you as unfeasible or ill-conceived; others may be exactly in line with your vision of the future. Even the authors disagree as to which of these observations and postulations are most significant. What we all do agree on, however, is that each of the following entries makes for intriguing fodder in our continued effort to discern the possibilities – and, ultimately, the probabilities – of life in the next millennium.

## Lifestyle

**Simple Pleasures** Sewing, quilting bees and other activities from times past will emerge as an antidote to today's chaotic lifestyles. Look for a revival of such crafts as candle making, wood carving and paper making.

**Hobbyist Cooking** Staying at home to prepare a full meal will no longer be a customary practice in many households; instead, cooking will be seen as more of a hobby, a way to entertain one's friends or spend time with one's family.

**Dinner Clubs** In some families, dinners will become a bigger priority as parents struggle to connect with their kids and as busy days leave no time to enjoy a relaxed breakfast or lunch. Groups of neighbours will form 'dinner clubs', whereby each household is responsible for providing one dinner a week to all five participating families.

**Silicon Sex** In an age in which real-world sex has become risky, to say the least, many are turning to the relatively safe and frequently anonymous world of silicon sex. Options range from cybersex (in which partners – or groups – engage in explicit, real-time online communication, including chat and/or video) to online pornography, from computerized sex toys to the forthcoming 'sexbot'. Tomorrow's schools will incorporate cybersex and online sexual content into their sex-education lesson plans.

**Co-parenting** Working parents will seek more assistance in raising their children from childless (or 'childfree', depending on one's point of view) relatives and friends. Gay couples unable to adopt children will be among those who co-parent. Retirees will serve a greater role in the lives of young children, not just as caretakers for their own grandchildren, but – on a paid or unpaid basis – as surrogate grandparents and field-trip organizers for kids whose own relatives live too far away.

**Experience Collection** As excesses are increasingly recognized as such, expect people to place greater emphasis on acquiring (and giving) experiences rather than things. Diamonds may well be forever, but they don't have the conversational value of an African safari. Dinner at a favourite restaurant, day spa treatments and even movie rentals will become increasingly common 'gifts' – replacing a host of unwanted 'things'.

**VRTV** Virtual reality headsets will let viewers 'walk through' TV shows.

**Pop & Pulp** Providing a brief respite from info overload, enormous value will be placed on activities that allow one to temporarily switch the brain to 'off', such as sports, simple TV programmes and comics – anything that doesn't require deep thought.

**Healthy Cults** New tribes of kindred spirits (e.g., parents who home-school, organic gardeners, mothers who perform community service, upwardly mobile professionals who bowl) will become the healthy cults of the twenty-first century. Cataloguing these hyperlocal associations will allow marketers to target such groups with products and pitches designed especially for them.

**Easing Up** As the true costs of stress (physical, financial and emotional) become more commonly known, look for companies to monitor and attempt to reduce the stress levels of employees. We'll see everything from on-site aromatherapy centres and healthful cooking classes to all-expenses-paid, company-planned vacations.

## Surroundings

**Rebirth of the Big City** We'll see a backlash against country living as word gets out that the rural lifestyle is actually less healthy than living in metropolitan areas – this is already true in the UK. Telecommuters especially will stay in or return to the cities in an effort to retain a sense of connectedness to the world at large.

**Members Only** Parents concerned about their children's safety will buy memberships in local 'safe havens' for kids. Look for an increase in members-only beaches and parks, zoo groups and museum clubs. Small neighbourhood parks will increasingly require electronic-passcard entrance.

**Appliances Smarter than You** Intelligent refrigerators will track consumption of staples, printing a shopping list on demand or transmitting it electronically to a home-delivery service; smart stoves will 'know' how you like your eggs; 'energy management systems' will supervise the activity of major home appliances, enabling homeowners to take advantage of off-peak pricing.

**Wide World of Walls** Intelligent fabrics, including wallpapers, will turn every flat surface into an art gallery one moment, a TV/computer screen the next. Virtual aquariums or scenic vistas on flat screens will add interest to the family room wall.

**High-tech Homes** We will control lights, phones, curtains, alarms, media unit, climate, etc. with the touch of a button – and we'll soon take it all for granted.

**Custom Living** Home builders will see an increase in requests for 'special purpose' rooms, from sewing rooms and hobby shops to wine cellars and prayer rooms.

**Tea Parlours** Hot and cold, caffeine-laden and herbal, medicinal and simply comforting, tea will stake its claim as the all-purpose beverage of the millennium. Tea parlours will challenge coffeehouse culture.

## Services
**Nutrition on wheels** Companies will deliver an assortment of nutritious frozen meals to busy households once a week. Meal trucks will circle through neighbourhoods at dinnertime each day to offer a selection of entrées and extras.

**Community PAs** Harried homeowners will pool resources to hire community personal assistants to do the things they no longer have time to do for themselves (e.g., dry cleaning drop-off/pick up, grocery shopping, pool maintenance, 'handyman' repairs).

**Mail-order Genetics** With the rise in infertility and with more older couples wanting to have children, mail-order catalogues will provide details about egg and sperm donors, allowing prospective parents to shop for genetics in the comfort of their homes.

**It-ain't-my-fault Insurance** Look for insurance policies that cover the cost of divorce and others that protect parents from financial responsibilities caused by their children's misbehaviour.

**Media Menus** Not satisfied with over a hundred cable channels and pay-per-view options? Look for on-demand movies and TV episodes, downloadable via your computer or PC/TV.

**Friendship Finders** Computer-generated friendship circles will identify those around the world with whom you have the most in common. On the face2face level, paid agents will unite people interested in forming friendships with other like-minded individuals.

**Four-legged Security** In our increasingly security-conscious world, we'll see the growth of a rental market for trained dogs: bomb-sniffing attack dogs patrolling corporations, guard dogs for homeowners on vacation, 'security' dogs for people jogging alone or working late at night, etc.

**Holiday-in-a-box** Busy families will turn to 'packaged' holidays and other celebrations to cut down on stress. Even middle-class consumers will hire entrepreneurs to decorate their homes for Christmas, using either the customer's decorations or rental adornments from the company. Expect to see an increase also in packaged holiday meals, either delivered to the door or picked up at high-class hotels, restaurants or supermarkets.

**'My' Big Brother** Soon after mourning the loss of their personal privacy, consumers will begin using Big Brother's arsenal to their advantage. After all, he is part of the family. Net-based private eyes will be employed to check up on the criminal, financial background and medical records, etc. of a potential mate or employee; satellite technology will enable anyone to purchase a photo of a celebrity wedding, a competitor's top-secret facility or a spouse's indiscretions. Parents of young children will insist on having visual access to their little darlings at daycare, and parents of latchkey kids may extend camera-surveillance systems to their own homes.

**Automatic Gift Transmission** A growing number of companies (e.g. florists, wine merchants, speciality food stores) will offer personal shopping – in advance. Customers will fill out a form at the beginning of each year, indicating what should be sent to whom. The process will be carried out automatically at the appropriate times, with shipments billed to your credit card as they're sent out.

**Digital Signatures** Unique to the individual, digital signatures will be as important in the coming decade as PIN numbers are today.

**Dial-a-geek** The increase in home offices will escalate demand for on-site emergency computer diagnostics and repair.

**Gene Screen** We can expect an increase in genetic discrimination, as dates, job applicants and club members are screened by intellectual aptitude.

**Triple Play** Daycare and elder-care initiatives will increasingly bring together three groups currently in need of companionship: children, the elderly and pets.

**Personal Shoppers** Migrating from department stores to supermarkets, personal shoppers will be retained by busy consumers to plan a week's worth of meals and deliver the necessary combination of raw ingredients, frozen foods and prepared meals. Menus will be tailored to family food preferences, dietary needs, lifestyle and weekly schedules.

## Gadgets and Gizmos

**Sleep Channels** Sleeping machines will be used either to produce restful sleep or provoke intense dreams. In development: Nova-Dreamers, a technology that combines eye masks and circuitry to promote dreaming. Alarms awaken the user moments after the dream has ended so he or she can make a record of the dream.

**Robotic Lawn Mowers** Mowing grass within a specified boundary and programmed to avoid obstacles such as bushes and children's playthings, these time-savers will be an increasingly common sight in suburban backyards.

**Digital Nutrition-Analysis Kiosks** Plug in age, family medical history, lifestyle, etc. for printout of recommended vitamins, herbs, supplements, food choices, plus discount coupens.

## Personal Appearance

**Insta-makeovers** Inspired by TV talk shows, makeovers will be an increasingly popular form of self-indulgence. Full-day sessions will incorporate hair redesign, makeup lessons, clothing consultation and a complete new outfit, teeth whitening and, as an option, makeup tattooing (permanent eyeliner, etc.) Longer stays at spa facilities will include such things as outpatient plastic surgery and etiquette courses.

**Big as You Wanna Be** The fat-acceptance movement is growing, and will only increase as baby boomers head into their fifties and sixties. One result will be better style options for larger women, as well as continued growth of such publications as *Mode*, designed to help women live healthfully and happily, regardless of size.

**Functional Fashion** Allowing for the ultimate personalization of the wardrobe, fabrics of tomorrow may include stress-relieving, massaging fabrics; fabrics that emit favourite and/or aromatherapeutic scents; and fabrics containing personalized, printed messages and wearer-created designs. Nanotechnology will allow fabrics to be embedded with tiny computers, sensors and micromachines; possible applications include cooling and heating systems, periodic self-cleaning and self-repair.

**Embracing 'the' Look** Twin movements towards customization and simplification will lead consumers to purchase a few essential (and perfectly suited) items of clothing rather than waste money on extensive wardrobes that take up precious storage space and rarely see the light of day.

**Male Beauty** An increasing number of all-male beauty salons (already common in Paris) will provide a variety of head-to-toe treatments.

## Mindset

**Big Brother in the Sky** An anti-satellite backlash will grow as consumers and businesses grow more concerned about invasions of privacy.

**Smart Stays Sexy** Don't be surprised to hear of a new unisex fragrance called Brainy or Intellect, or of orgasms grounded in mind fucking, with no physical contact, just the power of the mind to lead us beyond cybersex (i.e., mutual masturbation) into something more heady and esoteric. The elusive g-spot is above the shoulders.

**Brains over Brawn** An extension of the current trend of 'geek chic', modern-day heroes in popular culture will rely less on muscles than on brains – and computer know-how.

**Global Gung-ho** Small-world realities have made us more aware not only of each other's fashions and preferences, but also of each other's passions and plights. Accompanying this awareness – as already evinced by such worldwide organizations as Amnesty International and Greenpeace – will be a deepening sense that one can truly 'think globally' and 'act globally'.

# 4

# Global Culture Swap

In today's global society, consumers can't help but be aware of cultural icons and influences from other nations. Countries are swapping products and fads in a cross-cultural frenzy. Who has graced the cover of America's *People* magazine more times than any other? Diana, the late Princess of Wales. A year or so ago, the US club scene was in a frenzy over 'foam parties', a novel form of entertainment brought over from London via the island of Ibiza, Spain. America's slacker grunge craze even gave way to a new UK invasion: Mod's third wave, a movement marked by such British pop artists as Blur, Elastica, Oasis and Sleeper and by such American fashion designers as Anna Sui and Marc Jacobs.

To the dismay of many, trends and icons emanating from the US are also leaving their mark around the world. And the results can be incongruous, to say the least! What's the biggest tourist attraction in Romania today? The painted monasteries of Bukovina? Dracula's castle? Guess again. The biggest attraction is Southfork Ranch, a US$1 million replica of the homestead made famous by TV's night-time soap opera *Dallas*. The centrepiece of the Hermes Vacation Park in the city of Slobozia, Southfork drew more than 2 million visitors in its first year of operation. Explaining the Texas-based TV show's popularity in his country, owner Ilie Alexandrov told the *St Petersburg Times* (Florida), '[*Dallas*] was a bridge to the West for us. The average Romanian could only fantasize about such beautiful cars, a ranch, nice clothes. It was a kind of paradise.'

Trends emanating from the US (courtesy of MTV, global marketing efforts, the Internet and the like) range from hip-hop to snowboarding to gun culture. In addition to buying US$100 plastic replicas of guns, some Japanese have travelled to the US for 'gun tours', featuring opportunities to hold and shoot a variety of firearms. 'It's become a fad, a cool thing, to like guns,' security company employee Michiko Nagashima told the *Washington Post*. 'This is a bad import from the West.'

Another current rage among Japanese youth is *chapatsu*, or tea hair. Dyeing one's hair brown is considered an act of individuality and rebellion, akin to American and European hippies growing their hair long during the sixties. Japanese schools have responded by banning dyed brown hair, and many major companies are refusing to hire brown-haired applicants.

## Trend Filters

Though many of today's trends start in the US and Western Europe, the way they are translated around the world varies considerably. Key to the evolution of trends are the 'gatekeeping' cities within each country, those places through which trends enter and are then spread throughout a nation.

In China, according to Mila M. Marquez of DY&R Guangzhou, trends start in the key urban centres of Guangzhou, Shanghai and Beijing. Typically, these trends are primarily brought about by an influx of Western influence – media penetration, tourists and so on. Marquez notes: 'Guangzhou in the southern part of China is heavily influenced by Hong Kong because of its proximity. This is also the seat of the yearly China Trade Commodities Fair, so a lot of European, Japanese and American traders pass through. Most of the multinational companies have their marketing and manufacturing offices in Hong Kong, so the presence of expats dictates the fast development or evolution of people and culture. Going forwards, Hong Kong's influence will continue to be evident in fashion, music and lifestyle. Beijing will remain the seat of politics, while Shanghai will be the fashion and lifestyle trendsetter and the centre of finance.'

Sachin Talwar, of Burson-Marsteller Roger Pereira Communications, Mumbai (formerly Bombay), tells us that trends in India also tend to originate in the US, but don't spread throughout the country until they've been filtered through such gatekeeping cities as Bombay, New Delhi and Bangalore. 'All three cities share several characteristics,' notes Talwar. 'They are relatively more Westernized, they are cosmopolitan, they host many more foreigners and foreign enterprises, Indians edu-cated abroad are more likely to find jobs there, and these cities have better schools and colleges – particularly among those that teach through the medium of English.'

The role the English language plays in trend adoption is particularly evident in India. 'The trendsetters in this country are not necessarily the rich,' explains Talwar. 'In fact, Bombay and New Delhi have vast numbers of the nouveau riche but they do not set trends. The trends are set by people the industry calls the "English medium types" (EMTs). Their schooling has been at elite schools – both day and boarding – that teach in English. Traditionally, the sons of professionals, executives and bureaucrats have been to these elite institutions of learning. They are not all wealthy, but most belong to the upper middle class. On the other hand, there are the "Hindi medium types" (HMTs). At school, they have been educated in one of the Indian languages. Many of them would have also learned English but . . . their familiarity with the language would be more limited. In the big cities a large number belong to the trading classes and are wealthy. Yet, they are looked down upon by the EMTs. Worse, the HMTs often display an inferiority complex. While they are wealthy, they wish to emulate the EMTs in their social behaviour. They tend to wait for the EMTs to adopt a trend before feeling confident about adopting it themselves. HMTs often send their children to elite schools to climb the "emulation" ladder. While this is often successful as far as the child is concerned, it leads to strains within the family as the elders often find it difficult to accept the changed lifestyle of their child.'

Talwar continues: 'The trendsetters, in the main, emulate whatever is happening in the US. Thus, most trends in the US appear in India after an interval of time – in some cases the time is short; in others, it can be quite long. In areas such as music and clothing, the trends come to Bombay very fast indeed. Yet, in areas to do with sexual mores, trends take a very long time to travel to India.'

## New World Capitals

How long will the United States continue to drive trends around the world? Laurence Bernstein of Y&R Toronto doesn't see this changing anytime soon: 'Unless the next stage of the development of the European Community is a cultural unification – which is unlikely given traditional language and cultural differences – major trends will probably continue to emanate from the US,' he says. 'It takes a monumental, culturally homogeneous society to lead deep-seated trends (ideas and fads can come from anywhere; trends tend to rise up from the essence of the people). Asian developing countries, some of which may have the size and cultural strength needed to be leaders, are currently too focused on American values to explore themselves and develop their own trends in the near to mid-term. Furthermore, until such time as the American stranglehold on the media is replaced, it is hard to see how non-American cultural values will permeate the world.'

Lucinda Sherborne, senior planner at Y&R Auckland, has a different perspective on the situation: 'The next few years will continue to see key lifestyle trends being filtered out of the UK and the US,' she says. 'However, we see these trends and the uptake of these trends speeding up as the world gets smaller and smaller due to increasing effectiveness of technology and the breakdown of global boundaries. The increasing ease of travel, immigration, technology, the Internet and mass media communications will drive these trends, also providing different channels for different ones. I believe the opening up of the world will also allow other countries to generate trends, possibly bypassing traditional trendsetting countries.'

We, too, believe that we'll see an increase in the influence of trendsetters from other countries in coming years. The Internet will have a big hand in this. The simple fact is that as the world grows ever more interconnected, the influence of any one sector will be felt more readily in other sectors. This global interconnectedness levels the playing field in many respects, because it affords those outside today's trend centres access to a broader forum.

One of Marian's colleagues, a Colombian based in Cali, sent Marian a note recently that said, 'Trends develop more and more in less commercial economies where newness is creative expression versus a reaction to a new product that enters the marketplace with a large budget.' She pointed to student enclaves and market towns as two likely enclaves for trendsetting next.

We're already seeing shifts in centres of cultural influence around the globe as baby boomers have regained their position at front and centre (edging out those upstart media darlings, the Xers). They brought with them a renewed emphasis on the biggest cities, the cultural centres.

Herewith are our predictions for trend centres next, those cities that will dictate what we wear, watch and listen to in the decade to come.

## Destination Next: *Gemütlich* Places/Global Villages

Just as cosier, genuine people are today more desirable than those who are arrogant or aloof (think Elton John and Chelsea Clinton vs Earl Spencer and Kate Moss), so, too, are cosier, genuine places more desirable. They embody *gemütlich*, a German term that conveys a combination of all that's hospitable, homey and sane. Antwerp, a mini-Paris with such designers as Dries Van Noten, is in; Brussels is out. Capetown is in; Johannesburg is out. Of all such places, those that are global villages are trendiest, because they afford the ultimate combination of cosy lifestyle against a backdrop of blended world cultures.

In the West, two *gemütlich* cities, both global villages, are Amsterdam and San Francisco. Interestingly, these are also the digital capitals of Europe and North America, respectively. San Francisco has long been a melting pot of alternative lifestyles and creative expression; in the past decade, it's also emerged as a centre of digital creativity. Across the Atlantic, thanks to the Channel Tunnel, IT hot-shots and Web designers can ply their trade in London during the week, then hop on a train to Amsterdam on Friday evening and enjoy a weekend of laid-back vice and virtue. Recreational drug use and daring parties all within easy walking or bicycling distance, no language problems, prices for every pocket, no pretensions – just come as you are and do your own thing.

As the world becomes increasingly wired, the cybersavvy duo of Amsterdam and San Francisco will command an even greater share of the spotlight. Expect *gemütlich* positioning – cosy marketing – to be *the* successful positioning for products ranging from consumer electronics to home meal replacements or remote banking.

## Destination Next: Gateways

Berlin and Prague, gateways east, are very much global villages next. Though they belong to Xers, these cities bear the mark of older generations, who, as elsewhere in Central and Eastern Europe, preserved traditions in the face of cultural oppression. Prague was the setting of the 1989 Velvet Revolution, the romantic transition that restored democracy to Soviet-controlled Czechoslovakia. It was also home to a hipper, rock music-influenced counterculture that venerated anarchy and produced playwright-as-president Vaclav Havel. The most untrendy aspect of modern Prague is American expatriate culture, with its new-style commercialism. While the first post-revolution invasion brought art-seeking, antimaterialistic young Yanks, Prague now is global in the truest sense, down to its multiplex cinemas. And yet the city sustains a quirky balance; its ancient culture co-exists, even blends, with the commercial culture of perpetual newness, a strong wind that blows across Central Europe.

Back in the heart of Germany and the heart of Europe, Berlin has been there before (think Christopher Isherwood and *Cabaret*). It has everything – fine buildings, huge public spaces, a romantic/tragic past, more than a hint of low life – it is the gateway to the East or West (depending on where you're coming from), and now the nation has decided to make it the crowning glory of a country reunited at such cost. The former Eastern Bloc countries still tend to see Germany as their natural partner in the West, which makes Berlin a natural for all those eager easterners keen to brush up on their German. And Sony's decision to build a new film centre in the new city centre is certain to be a magnet for trend leaders. On top of that, Berlin's 'love parades' are an attraction, sometimes pulling in more than a million people. The message: love, peace, happiness. Drugs such as ecstasy are an important part of the scene.

The most threatening cloud on Germany's horizon is the rise of the new right (neo-Nazis), whose surprisingly strong showing in the last election reflects the unrest of a populace increasingly dissatisfied with the byproducts of their new democratic order: namely, the record levels of unemployment that result when a state-controlled industrial economy enters the free market. The new enemy: everyone not German (all foreigners replace the Jews as the neo-Nazi target).

## Destination Next: Music Meccas

Because innovative musicians find a following in places that support creativity, we look to music meccas for signs of what's next. Chicago's Wicker Park boasts a music scene that includes Liz Phair, Urge Overkill and Veruca Salt. Clubs and studios in this once-downtrodden neighbourhood thrive alongside such megalabels as Drag City, Touch and Go and Wax Trax. In England, the small port city of Bristol is the birthplace of three influential bands: Massive Attack, Tricky and Portishead. It was Portishead, creator of 'trip-hop', that landed Bristol on the places-to-watch list. (Trip-hop, an underground dance style, draws on reggae sounds and incorporates torch singing and even nostalgic film scores.)

## Destination Next: Port Cities

Sydney has long been the trendsetter capital of Australia, but its role as Olympic host in the year 2000 will ensure its influence is felt far beyond those shores. Increased tourism means more 'messengers' will visit Sydney, returning home with a catalogue of experiences from a city in which styles are set by the gay community, a highly educated creative community and 'new money' entrepreneurs. Other ports to watch: Genoa, Marseilles, Rotterdam and Hamburg. The latter two are among the edgiest, each with a noteworthy fashion and music scene.

## Destination Next: Cities with an Edge

For hardier souls who like their trends a little edgier, there are alternatives: most notably, Moscow/St Petersburg and Naples.

**Moscow/St Petersburg** In a Europe where everything is coming together, Russia will give adventurous Europeans the chance to experience something very different – an advanced, industrialized European country living in the raw, close to the edge. As Zoya Ivanova, account executive at Y&R Europe, Moscow Representation, sees it, life in Russia will get harder but more interesting as people fight with their brains rather than guns. This will be a thrilling and disturbing experience for cosseted young Europeans – far more exotic than trips to more distant destinations. It will also give them some new angles on things they take for granted.

**Naples** For adventurous Europeans who can't face the chill of Russia, Naples offers the experience of managing chaos under azure skies. Without the tourist hordes and self-consciousness of many Italian cities, Naples will be the place to observe old Italy head-to-head with the twenty-first century – rapier-sharp native wit and invention devising strategies to handle high-tech and regulations. Marco Lombardi, planning director at Y&R Italia Milan, notes that Naples is today a dramatization of Italy's good qualities and faults: 'When you are there, you can feel in the air a positive tension, a mood of *statu nascenti*, which is best expressed through the music of the people coming from *centri sociali* (self-managed young communities).'

## Destination Next: New Asian Hubs

After centuries of bigger-is-better nationalism around the world, it's easy to forget that some of the most influential and successful human enterprises have not been huge countries, but rather city states – Athens, Florence, Venice to name but three from history. In Asia, Hong Kong and Singapore have proved the value of small concentrated units, increasingly rivalling each other as regional hubs – meta-capitals, acting as magnets both for their hinterland and for overseas entrepreneurs looking to do business in the region.

The scene is set for other influential hubs to emerge. Shanghai already has a glorious heritage from its pre-revolutionary days and will act as a focus for talent to rival Hong Kong and Guangzhou. In a recent America Online interview, Pete Engardio, a *Business Week* staffer covering the region, said that China's coastal provinces are so economically dynamic that they could absorb about five cities like Hong Kong, although Hong Kong is likely to retain the unique advantages of a legal system, a free press and a corruption-free society.

Meanwhile, emerging nations such as Singapore, Malaysia and Vietnam are jockeying for position in the regional and international community. Malaysia, which aims to oust Singapore as the cornerstone of South-east Asia, is busy developing a vast high-tech enterprise zone, the Multimedia Super Corridor, with the aim of leap-frogging Malaysia into the Information Age. Vietnam is focusing less on technology and more on its unique cultural heritage. DY&R's country development manager predicts great things for Vietnamese artists and creators, both in the field of plastic arts and in TV and advertising, and foresees a vogue based on Vietnam's traditional womenswear: 'Western women will start to wear the Vietnamese national dress, the "ao dai", or Western fashion designers will adapt it for Western women to wear. The dress is too feminine, too "sexy" for designers to pass up.'

# 5

# Living in the Digital Age

'There is no reason for any individual to have a computer in their home.' Ken Olson, then chairman of Digital Equipment, in an address to the World Future Society, Boston, 1977

A couple of years ago, Richard Eastman of Billerica, Massachusetts, who managed a genealogy forum on online access provider Compu-Serve, noticed some odd messages from one of about twenty computer users during a regular weekly gathering of their 'cybercommunity'. A message from the Reverend Kenneth Walker indicated that he wasn't feeling terribly well, and the reverend soon began transmitting messages with gross typographical errors. Another member of the cybercommunity, a nurse from Long Island, New York, immediately began asking Reverend Walker for his symptoms. At one point, according to a report from Reuters, Walker wrote, 'By keyboard it melting . . . I jest nuut.' Minutes later, he typed, 'Helo . . . have broblemd . . . thimk I am waying stroke.' Eastman then started asking him for his phone number. After six attempts, he finally got the number, called a telephone operator, and found himself talking to a police officer in Scotland. The police forced their way into Walker's home minutes after Eastman called, and took Walker to a hospital.

Walker, who said doctors believe he may have suffered an epileptic attack, called Eastman to thank him. 'This wasn't any great heroism,' Eastman said. 'The only thing different in this case is that it was online.' Eastman, who has written a book about genealogy, and Walker, considered an expert on Scottish records and archives, have since found they have many things in common. 'It's kind of an interesting thing how two lives 3,000 miles apart get wrapped up,' Eastman said. 'Obviously, we share a common interest. There is a kinship, if you will.'

Welcome to the global neighbourhood.

## The Human Faces of Change

For those who have become 'plugged in', the Internet offers a world of new people, new ideas and new information. It opens up avenues of communication that allow us access to places we otherwise might never have gone. It's becoming increasingly evident that the Net also will alter the path that trends take around the world. Today, online communication is taking place primarily in English (an estimated three-quarters of all Internet sites are located in English-speaking countries.) As the Internet attracts a more global audience, however, there is a mounting effort to broaden the appeal and usefulness of the Net by taking down the 'English only' signs, thereby enabling and encouraging people to communicate and collaborate in their native languages.

The number of multilingual Websites is growing. The Internet Society and Montreal-based Alis Technologies have established Babel (http://babel.alis.com:8080/), a site aimed at internationalizing the Web by promoting the use of languages other than English. Babel will eventually be available in approximately ten languages. Dynalab (http: www.dynalab.com.), a Taiwanese font manufacturer, is marketing GlobalSurf, a utility that provides fonts in twenty-three languages, including Arabic, Chinese, Japanese, Korean, Thai, Hebrew and most European languages. The product solves the common problem of garbled type resulting from double-byte Asian characters by using fonts that support Unicode. Web pages can now correctly display these foreign language characters on any browser that supports Unicode.

As the online population gradually falls more closely in line with global realities, we can be sure that cross-cultural influences will no longer emanate primarily from Western trend capitals. In the past few years, the online community has evolved beyond 'technogeeks' to encompass the thought and opinion leaders who – with close, smart tracking – can serve as important barometers of how, when and whether particular fads, trends and styles will evolve from the 'mindspace' of

the Internet to the 'marketplace' of the face2face world. It's these pion-
eers of next who will reshape the world of marketing communications
and commerce for the future.

## Cybercommunication

In watching the evolution of communication online, it's been interesting to note how cybernauts have resolved the problem of the lack of
body language in this medium. As any Internet user can tell you, an
entire code has been developed to convey the human emotions that
one cannot see in cyberspace. These typed symbols – most commonly
called emoticons or smileys – give a degree of life and individuality to
online expression.

To view a Western smiley, tilt your head to the left. Among the most
common examples:

:-)      Basic smiley (shows humour/happiness)
;-)      A wink (shows you're being a flirt or sarcastic)
:-(      A frown (means you're sad, depressed, or have hurt feelings)
:'-(     Crying
:-D      Laughter, or a really big grin
:-*      A kiss
:-P      Sticking out your tongue
:-x      'My lips are sealed.'
:-0      Astonished

In contrast, here's a sampling of Japanese *kao maaku* (face marks)
which are meant to be viewed straight on:

(ˆ_ˆ)        Happy face
(;_;)        Weeping face
\(ˆ_ˆ)/      Banzai smiley (arms raised in a traditional cheer)
(*ˆoˆ*)      Excited face
(ˆ;)         Cold sweat
(_o_)        'I'm sorry'

The Internet is also creating its very own language, one that steals
from everyone, from stenographers to street kids. Many of us have
become adept at the standard abbreviations of the Net: using BTW
instead of writing out 'by the way'; IMHO, for 'in my humble opinion';

POV instead of 'point of view.' We've also usurped shorthand made popular by urban black youth in the US: dis as a stand-in for 'disrespect'; 24/7 to mean twenty-four hours a day, seven days a week'. As Europeans and Asians establish more of a presence in Internet chatrooms and newsgroups, we suspect Euro and Asian slang will infiltrate commonly used cyberlingo. At the same time, we'll be seeing cyberlingo begin to infiltrate language offline. Already, our former Dutch colleagues are using BTW and ITRW (short for 'in the real world') in everyday conversation. And just as African-American slang has pervaded American language in the 1990s (courtesy of rap music), geekspeak has pervaded the jargon of business life in the US.

## Wired World?

### Europe Online

So, just how long will it take for the Internet to become a truly global medium? At present, the Internet is dominated by North Americans, as is apparent from the chart below.[1]

Western Europe is an affluent, educated continent with a high penetration of high-tech appliances and good telecommunications infrastructure. So how come it's so far behind the United States with regard to Internet adoption?

To be fair, there are exceptions. Northern Europe in general has many more computer and Internet users than does southern Europe. In fact, the far away Finns, famous even amongst themselves for being people

## Who's Online? April 1998
### World Total: 115.75 Million

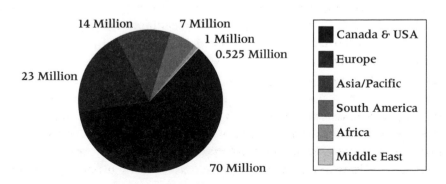

14 Million

7 Million

1 Million

0.525 Million

23 Million

70 Million

Canada & USA

Europe

Asia/Pacific

South America

Africa

Middle East

of few words, boast the world's highest per capita proportion of Internet servers and users, and 'greater Scandinavia' is easily the world's best-connected region, according to a new compendium of Net-related statistics called the *Internet Industry Almanac.* The study found that Finland has 244.5 Net users per 1,000 people. Its northern neighbours also rated high. Norway second (231.1), Iceland third (227.3), Sweden eighth (147.3) and Denmark tenth (125.6). The United States clocked in at fourth, with 203.4 Net users per 1,000 people. The worldwide user rate is 16.9.[2]

In contrast to the Scandinavians, not even 1 per cent of the loquacious Italians use the Internet, according to Marco Lombardi, planning director at Y&R Italia Milan. Italian marketing consultant Giancarlo Livraghi (http://gandalf.it/netmark/) blames this poor showing on technophobia and fears about the dangers of the Internet: 'Families (as well as politicians and teachers) are bombarded every day with sensationalism and misinformation that makes them uncomfortable and scares them away.'

Climate and social customs probably play a part, too. Long, dark, hard winters force northern Europeans to spend many months of the year indoors – ideal for developing computer skills and networking with other people online. As Katerina Varenius of Hall & Cederquist/Y&R Stockholm puts it: 'The trend is that we will see less of these people out in the garden, since they will be sitting in front of the computer. The computer is a fully legitimate place to be – you don't have to explain to anybody whether you do something useful or not.' By the same token, the long, fine summers of southern Europe just invite pavement café and beach life – why shut yourself away with a computer and modem when you can go out and socialize in the sun?

Language is cited as an obstacle to non-English-speakers using the Internet – the vast majority of websites are American and many non-US sites have English-language versions. Yet the Internet hasn't yet caught on big time in the UK, which obviously has no language problem. Some analysts speculate that the British predisposition for 'tradition' has in some ways hampered their embrace of this new medium. It will be interesting to see whether Richard Branson's Internet venture, Virgin Net, will succeed in galvanizing Britain into becoming more of a force in cyberspace. Judging from the success of past Branson ventures, such a scenario is likely.

In some respects, France was ahead of the European pack with France Telecom's Minitel system, a screen-based dial-up information and communication system launched in 1984. The equipment was provided free on demand and as many as 6.5 million subscribers used it. Yet some industry analysts think that having Minitel may have inclined many French people to dismiss the Internet as unnecessary for their needs. Minitel is certainly well entrenched. France's major national daily papers *Le Monde* and *Le Figaro* are on the Web and even offer search facilities, but their archives cannot be accessed through the Internet; it's Minitel only.

Nevertheless, in early February 1998, Prime Minister Lionel Jospin became the first French leader ever to appear on a podium with a technology guru when he welcomed Microsoft founder William H. Gates III at a technology conference. Jospin's government has vowed to embrace the Internet, even if its *lingua franca* is English.

Part of Europe's problem is that computer penetration is a lot lower in Europe than in the United States and it's growing at a less rapid pace in Europe than in North America and Asia. Sweden has developed an innovative socialist–capitalist approach to address this situation: Lands Organisationen (LO), the country's largest labour union, has negotiated a special bulk lease-purchase deal for its members, resulting in a huge increase in business for PC makers. Just four months after it was struck in 1997, the LO deal with PC manufacturer Hewlett-Packard accounted for more than 30 per cent of all home PCs sold in Sweden that year. Also, Swedish tax breaks are making it easier for employers to supply their workers with cheap PCs. Expect more deals of these types to drive higher computer sales in other countries over the coming years.[3]

But even for computer owners with Internet access, relatively high telephone charges discourage the sort of long online sessions that enable users to develop Internet interest and skills. The deregulation of European telecoms markets that took place in January of 1998 is likely to increase competition and drive down prices. But the case of British Telecom in Britain shows that entrenched monopolies aren't dislodged overnight – it takes quite a while for serious competition to be established.

Y&R feedback about the Internet from around Europe is pretty consistent, along the lines of 'there's lots of hype, it hasn't had much impact here yet, but people are very interested and expect it to change the way they do business'.

The most concrete expectations come from Katarina Varenius: 'The change to expect, I would think, would be the closure of retailer branches of all sorts, due to the shift from visiting a physical location to visiting it on the Internet. Post offices, banks and food stores will close down their 'bread and butter' stores, and focus their competence and one-on-one service on flagship stores . . . The number of smaller businesses has increased. The high unemployment level has caused a need for job creation, and one way is to start your own business. The Internet has made it much easier to succeed, due to the low costs involved in presenting your idea and your business to the market.'

Sus Røedgaard at Y&R Copenhagen reports similarly upbeat thinking about the Internet: 'Internet is not only for technology freaks anymore. A lot of Danish institutions and cultural organizations are on the Net. The Ministry of Culture in Denmark has sponsored a site called "Kulturnet Danmark" (http://www.kulturnet.dk/) that has links to all cultural institutions on the Net. Kulturnet also helps cultural organizations to get on the Net by helping them program their homepage. Even the Royal Danish Theatre is online, and so is the Danish Royal Family.'

There's little risk in predicting that Western Europe is not going to take the world lead in cyberspace in the foreseeable future. The old continent has its share of digerati, but Europe looks a long way from reaching the critical mass of popular usage that will encourage and sustain a real range of local Internet initiatives. The United States will lead the race well into the next millennium.

Within Europe, it's hard to imagine the southern countries doing anything other than playing catch-up – at best – for years to come. For European leads on the Internet, it's worth watching the Nordic countries. They've been tinkering with the Internet for some time now, and the Swedes in particular have proved that they can put together marketing concepts that cross borders easily – Abba, Ikea and two distinctive car marques (Volvo and Saab).

Watch out for the Netherlands, too – the Dutch are rapidly adding to their Internet server count, which per capita in Europe only lags behind the Scandinavian countries and Switzerland. Given their great talent for languages, the Dutch have no problem jumping into the Internet mainstream and holding their own. And with astute trading bred in the bone, the Internet is just the thing to stimulate Dutch commercial use, with everyone from Royal Dutch Airlines to porn merchants offering their services.

## Asia Online

For most Asians, the Internet is more of a future promise than a present reality. Cybercafés are springing up all over the region, making the Internet more accessible, but usage is generally limited by the low level of computer ownership overall and tight government restrictions in China and Vietnam.

Asian governments are pretty bullish about the Internet. Even Vietnam, with one of the most censorious and information-restrictive governments in the region, celebrated an official 'Vietnam Internet Day' in November 1997. The occasion marked the awarding of licences for four Internet service providers (ISP). Signing up costs around US$36, with US$4 per month access charges – not for everyone in a country in which the average annual wage is US$300.

Surprisingly, the most technologically advanced country in the region, Japan, has proved to be pretty slow in making use of the Internet. MIT Media Lab chief Nicholas Negroponte has posited that the adoption of personal computers, and hence email, by the Japanese was held up by the invention of the fax, which permitted handwritten telecommunication. Using the QWERTY keypad to input Japanese characters is certainly less convenient.

On the other hand, Chinese characters are equally difficult to input, yet Taiwan has 1.26 million Internet users, according to last year's survey by Internet Information and Intelligence. And that number is expected to climb to 3 million by the year 2000. The popularity of the Internet has boosted consumer acceptance and usage of Web shopping sites. Taiwanese consumers can even report tax by Internet.

Several years ago, Singapore declared its intention to become a fully wired state, with a connection in every household. Initially the government tried to control its citizens' Internet usage by routing traffic through an official gateway and barring access to sites deemed unsuitable. It quickly realized, though, that controlling even Singapore's bit of the Internet was a losing game.

Neighbouring Malaysia, as mentioned earlier, is determined to become the IT centre of the region, with its Multimedia Super Corridor enterprise zone and cyberlaws guaranteeing digital freedom – a U-turn from the government's previous stance. News broadcasts routinely show government ministers consulting the World Wide Web, and approximately one million ordinary citizens are thought to do likewise. DY&R Kuala Lumpur reports that the Internet has had a tremendous impact on the working and personal lives of its users. It has meant better access to information, and connectivity, allowing users 'to be in touch with the world anytime you want'.

Perhaps the biggest surprise – and the biggest paradox – in the wired world is India. It has just one ISP, a government-controlled company that provides access at charges, according to DY&R Mumbai, that are far beyond the means of ordinary Indians, and yet it has spawned a thriving IT services sector that is taken very seriously around the world. A selection of Indian software companies looked far from out of place at the 1998 CeBIT, the world's biggest IT trade fair, in Hanover, Germany.

Thanks to modems and satellite links, big foreign companies can call on the talents of highly qualified Indian IT specialists in such cities as Bangalore and Pune for data processing, programming and other skilled work. Many Indian software houses are focusing on helping overseas companies deal with the millennium bug problem – a labour-intensive and, therefore, costly process of auditing code, fixing date-compliance problems and then verifying the fix in a dry run.

# Internet 2010

At present, the world's widely disparate adoption rates have to do with a number of factors, ranging from limited phone lines to repressive governments, from excessive telephone charges to cultural separations between work and home. All of these barriers to adoption will fall as the Internet continues to invade our lives at work and home. Why are we so convinced of this? Perhaps the most compelling reason is that computers are no longer about technology. They're about something far more important: community and communicating.

## Computers + Community + Communicating

When the telephone was invented, it was initially a tool of commerce, controlled by men in the workplace. Gradually, its value as a means of connecting with friends and family was discovered, and it found its way into the home. Like most 'intrusions' into our personal bastions, the telephone was initially relegated to the home's 'public space', most likely on a 'conversation bench' in the hall. Today, who among us sleeps without a phone within reach? And when was the last time you thought about the 'technology' associated with the device? All we know is that with the right number combination, we can access our party of choice on the other end of the line. How does it work? Who cares?

Thanks to the Internet, computers are currently making a similar transition from technology to communications tool – although the transition has been far simpler in North America than in other parts of the world. One reason for the apparent reluctance of consumers to log on in many parts of the world is the much firmer line that's drawn between work and home. In the States, the workforce has no problem with the notion of being 'on call'. From the telephone to the answering machine to the beeper to PCs, we are using new technologies to blur the line between work and home, allowing us to merge our two lives. We've even developed entirely new workstyles – including home offices, telecommuting and virtual offices – to take better advantage of the opportunities new technologies present.

In most parts of Europe and Latin America, by contrast, when one closes one's office door, one is closed for business. There is no expectation that one should be able to conduct commerce beyond traditional work hours. This sharp delineation between work and home makes it far easier to understand why home PCs fall way down the list of 'must haves' in some parts of the world. In fact, research shows that in many countries, the home computer market is driven primarily by a focus on raising competitive children, rather than a desire to extend professional productivity or connect to new media.

Like other barriers – including today's near monopoly of English-language content online – consumer resistance to in-home computers will decline. In tradition-bound Latin America, we're seeing significant growth in online access, with users in Colombia, for instance, having quadrupled in the past year. Our colleagues in Y&R offices in that region tell us that the 'killer app' for most Latin Americans won't be online research or shopping or gaming; instead, it will be online chat – a natural outlet for cultures that stress social interaction.

## Technology and Tradition

Since a meaningful component of our thoughts about change revolves around new media and emerging technologies, it's not surprising that when the authors were working together within TBWA, our unit decided to conduct a global study regarding consumers' attitudes towards the technologies that are changing their lives. ('Unabomber'

Ted Kaczynski may be the world's best-known Luddite, but he's far from alone with regard to his fear of technology.)

In 1996 the two of us hypothesized that people living in more 'traditional' cultures – for instance, Italy and Spain – would be more fearful of new technologies than those living in such 'modern' cultures as the US, the Netherlands and Sweden, where digital convergence is a reality for the average professional. We couldn't have been more mistaken. Responses to our study – from more than 2,000 households in thirty countries in Europe, North America, Asia and Africa – indicated that it is, in fact, people who are already 'plugged in' to the Internet and other technologies who are most wary of what the future might hold (including information overload, loss of privacy, and so on). In contrast, consumers who are not yet plugged in are far less apt to express such concerns.

Some of the findings of the 'Technology+Tradition' study are set out below.

Consumers are future-oriented, but the past remains extremely relevant to many:

- 56% agree: 'I look ahead to the future, but I derive a good deal of comfort from looking back at the past.'
- 39% agree: 'I'm a very modern, future-oriented person; I look ahead, not back.'
- 2% agree: 'I'm much more interested in the past than the future.'

Traditionals seem divided between wholehearted futurism and the draw of the past, while Moderns are decidedly more likely to look ahead while deriving comfort from the past.

| Attitude/% agree | Traditionals | | Moderns | |
|---|---|---|---|---|
| | Italy | Spain | US | Denmark |
| Very modern | 45% | 50% | 29% | 11% |
| Look ahead/derive comfort from past | 40% | 50% | 71% | 89% |
| Past-oriented | 15% | 0% | 0% | 0% |

Despite growing reliance, technology is not considered all-important: 83 per cent agreed: 'Composing music will always be more important than writing great computer software' and 20 per cent agreed, 'I'm excited by new technologies.' The excitement of both Traditionals and Moderns is hampered by concerns about technology's impact:

|  | *Traditionals* | *Moderns* |
|---|---|---|
| Concerned that technology will dehumanize us | 89% | 81% |
| Concerned that new technologies will invade people's privacy | 84% | 72% |

But, Moderns are made far more nervous by new technologies (30 per cent) than are Traditionals (18 per cent), and Moderns are more concerned (60 per cent) than are Traditionals (50 per cent) that they won't be able to keep up with technology's pace of change. The nervousness expressed by Moderns is probably rooted in experience (e.g., marketplace shifts, digital convergence), as well as the fact that Moderns are more apt to be 'on call' all the time. No wonder they're more cautious about endorsing high-tech lifestyles.

|  | *Traditionals* | *Moderns* |
|---|---|---|
| Own telephone answering machine | 51% | 76% |
| Own personal pager/beeper | 51% | 68% |
| Own cellular phone | 15% | 20% |
| Own cordless phone | 45% | 54% |
|  | *Traditionals* | *Moderns* |
| Very interested in telecommuting | 50% | 31% |
| Somewhat interested in telecommuting | 33% | 42% |
| Not at all interested in telecommuting | 11% | 19% |
| Telecommute (part- or full-time basis) | 2% | 5% |

The Internet was rated the most impressive modern-day technological device/advancement (26 per cent agree):

- 'Global communications available cheaply for all.' (Australia)
- 'It's accessible to everybody – it's like inventing the telephone all over again.' (Chile)
- 'It has levelled the world playing field.' (UAE)
- 'It connects all parts of the world, whether for business or pleasure.' (Lebanon)

## There's No Pulling the Plug

Despite fears regarding such things as information overload, slow rates of in-home PC adoption in some parts of the world and the cost of connecting people in remote corners of the globe, the authors are convinced that Internet usage will become commonplace in virtually every part of the world within the next decade. For those of us whose lives are already deeply embedded in the Net, there simply is no going back. And in our global economy, when corporate leaders in North America and parts of Asia and Europe are connected to the Net, you can be sure would-be customers, suppliers and competitors will come online, too – and they'll bring consumers in their countries along with them.

Once that happens – once the Internet becomes *truly* global – fads and trends from Latin America, Africa, Australasia and Europe will make their way onto the computer screens of fad-hungry early adopters across North America, and vice versa. We'll see a trend-swapping free-for-all that will forever change the cultural power bases around the world.

# Next: A Prescription or a Travelogue?

## The Continuation of Your Journey

The remainder of this book is organized around three subjects: How We Live; How We Work; and How Commerce and Media Work Us. As you move through these chapters, your journey will be made more meaningful if you keep the following three concepts in mind:

### Key Concept 1: Age Redefined

Throughout the world, one's place and year of birth have always had a great impact on one's expectations, outlook and even capacity to note and digest the meaning of change. While that remains true even today, we must also recognize the degree to which chronological age is becoming somewhat less important than 'attitudinal' and 'experiential' age. A thirty-year-old who travels broadly and is plugged into new technologies and information sources has had a far different life experience from a next-door neighbour of the same age who has explored the world neither geographically nor electronically. So, too, is a seventy-year-old who has embraced new technologies living a far different life from one who has chosen to cling to the 'old ways'.

### Key Concept 2: The New Haves and Have Nots

Economic status is more important than ever before, for one simple reason: money buys technology, and technology is the driving force that's changing the landscape of planet Earth. Moving forward, the

chasm between those who do and do not have access to new technologies (particularly the Internet) will be far more significant than separations caused by age, geography, sex or lifestyle. Already, we're seeing
technology haves beginning to live and work in two parallel universes:
face2face and cyberspace. Those who aren't wired will be blocked from
an entire universe of information, communication and community.

## Key Concept 3: Convergence Is Inevitable

The unprecedented pace at which the world is changing makes blurring
inevitable. Convergence is about much more than PC/TV; it's also about
home/office, global/hyperlocal and news/marketing. This book is
intended to help you decode these new links, since it is at the point of
convergence that opportunity lies.

# How We Live:
# Next Style

## [6]

# Rites of Purification: Body and Soul

New beginnings bring out the human urge to clean up and start afresh. With the start of the next millennium just around the corner, it's a fair bet that this urge will become pretty strong in societies that measure time by the Western calendar.

Major religions have their own ways of body, mind and spirit purification, often involving fasting or abstaining from certain types of food. Muslims observe the fasting month of Ramadan, when they mustn't eat or drink between sunrise and sunset. For Christians, the pre-Easter forty days of Lent have traditionally been a time of frugality, preceded, in many countries, by the excesses of Mardi Gras (Fat Tuesday) or Carnival.

Early industrial man had purgatives to eliminate unwanted substances from the body. For late-twentieth-century man, purification means 'detoxification'. In the last quarter century or so, the urge to purify has grown stronger due to a rise in the number of harmful substances, a growing inclination to worry about them and – fortunately – more ways for concerned individuals to take action for themselves.

Approaches to purification vary, but the underlying belief is that the combination of faith, the right actions and perhaps a few well-chosen commercial products and services will enable the individual to restore him- or herself to a natural, pristine state in time for the new beginning of year 2000. This final stretch prior to the next millennium will give new meaning and impetus to the spirituality and health trends of the last couple of decades.

# Readying the Soul: in Search of Spirituality

## Next: Something to Believe In
In response to an increased sense of isolation, a disconnectedness from the natural world and even fears related to the millennium, Westerners (particularly baby boomers) are turning for solace and insights to the mysticism and spirituality of Eastern and New Age religions.

In the UK, for instance, while the number of monks and nuns in traditional Catholic orders is in steady decline, there is now a six-month waiting list to join the Buddhist *sangha* (community) of monks and nuns at Samye Ling in Scotland, according to the *Telegraph* magazine. The Hindu population in the US has grown from about 70,000 in 1977 to 800,000 today. And Buddhism, the fastest-growing Eastern religion in the US, has an estimated 750,000 adherents.

Though only 20,000 Americans claim New Age as their religion, 23 per cent believe in reincarnation and 12 per cent believe in astrology. And gurus such as Marianne Williamson and Deepak Chopra are raking in followers and cash at a dizzying pace. Chropra estimates his annual gross at US$15 million; his nineteen books have been translated into twenty-five languages. The New Age category sold 10.5 million books in the US in 1996.

The ancient tradition of Kabbalah, a Jewish mysticism, is also attracting enthusiastic students around the world, including such American celebrities as Madonna, Roseanne and Barbra Streisand. Mysticism is the answer to 'a hungry, thirsty, bottle-of-water-in-the-desert need for connection with transcendent meanings', United Jewish Appeal officer Alan Bayer told *Time* magazine.

The mix of ancient religion with modern-day icons can be discordant, to say the least. While sitting in a Berlin café, we noted how small our world has become: the waiters were Milanese, the bartender Albanian, and the music was supplied by none other than Barbra Streisand, singing the most holy Jewish prayer. What was intriguing is that the music was piped through this space as nothing more than song, as entertainment.

What's next? Evidence of a more diverse spiritual culture will become more common in our daily lives. Greeting card lines, for example, will expand to incorporate New Age sentiments, interfaith celebrations and 'alternative' holidays such as winter solstice. Interfaith households will come to represent an important niche market, driving increased demand for products and services geared to their specific needs. (A 1990 survey found that one in three American Jews was living in an interfaith household, as were 21 per cent of Catholics, 30 per cent of Mormons, and 40 per cent of Muslims.)

Spirituality's increased prominence in daily life will be reflected in such things as summer spirituality camps for kids and week-long retreats for adults, both intended to infuse participants with spiritual rejuvenation and growth.

## Focus: Islamic Europe

An increasing majority of Europeans no longer practise any religion other than consumerism. Not so for the followers of Islam, Europe's fastest growing religion. The scene is set for Islam to become a major factor in Europe's political and social life in the coming millennium as second-generation Muslim immigrants figure out how they relate to their host cultures and more Muslim immigrants arrive.

The Muslim population has risen to around 3 million in Germany (mainly Turkish), over 2 million in France (mostly North African), and around 1.5 million in the UK (mainly from Pakistan and Bangladesh), with sizeable Muslim communities also in the Netherlands and Sweden. Fresh legal and illegal arrivals, especially from nearby trouble spots Algeria and the Balkans, are likely to swell the numbers and make Muslims an even more visible part of Europe's patchwork. Already, according to the *Electronic Telegraph*, Britain has around 3,000 makeshift places of Islamic worship, with 160 purpose-built mosques and another 80–100 scheduled for completion by the millennium.

Britain's Prince Charles has made a point of getting close to Muslim community leaders, but for many Europeans, having large numbers of Muslims in their midst is taking a lot of adjustment. Muslims in Europe are in fact far from being a new phenomenon. Muslim Moors ruled Spain for 700 years until 1492, developing one of the most advanced cultures in Europe – the Spanish language still bears a strong Arabic imprint. The Turkish Ottoman Empire ruled Greece for 400 years until the early nineteenth century and twice narrowly missed conquering Vienna (1529 and 1683). In former Yugoslavia, Muslims lived alongside Catholics and Orthodox Christians until just a few years ago. Conversely, France ruled Algeria for 130 years until 1962.

Unfortunately, Europe's dealings with Muslims have left a legacy of mistrust that will be difficult to overcome. Both Christianity and Islam have been militant, proselytizing religions fighting each other for territory and converts, and most Muslim immigrants in Europe come from countries that were colonized or militarily defeated by European powers. Resentments linger.

Europe's support for Israel since its foundation, defence of Salman Rushdie's *Satanic Verses*, the Gulf War and failure to stop the massacre of Bosnians have all been readily interpreted by some Muslims as confirmation that Europeans are anti-Islam. Insecurity is further exacerbated by the rhetoric of anti-immigrant parties such as France's National Front, by arson and other attacks on immigrants and by news media coverage that tends to play up the wild-eyed fanatic elements of Islamic fundamentalism.

Flare-ups will no doubt continue on both sides, but new developments are likely in the early years of the new millennium:

- More Euro-Muslims will achieve wealth.
- The Internet will encourage more networking and solidarity between different Muslim communities across borders.
- Euro-Muslims will increasingly use their numbers to exercise political pressure on governments in matters of concern, e.g., Middle East policy.
- Islam will become a cultural heritage rather than a religious practice for many second-, third- and fourth-generation Muslims – much as Christianity is for many Europeans today.
- Elements of Muslim culture will be adopted as counterculture platforms by rebellious and spiritually thirsty Europeans.

A little further into the century, we can look forward to seeing Europe become a cradle for progressive Islamic thinking as educated young Euro-Muslims re-evaluate their beliefs and culture from a Westernized standpoint – which would be difficult in Islamic states where questioning of religious orthodoxy can be life-threatening.

## Spirituality in Everyday Living
**Home as Spiritual Sanctuary** In North America, an increasing number of homeowners are requesting amenities tailored to specific religious and cultural practices. As reported in the *Wall Street Journal*,

the movement includes the Chinese practice of feng shui; Zen gardens for Buddhists; side-by-side kosher kitchens for Jewish families; and homes oriented towards Mecca for Muslims.

Suntosh Village, a 130-home retirement community being built near Orlando, Florida, will feature an optional prayer room for Hindus. The rooms, built on the east side of houses to take advantage of the rising sun, feature arched and ceramic-tiled walls, a marble floor and storage cabinets for prayer items. 'Almost all people of East Indian origin will have a space, if not a room, designated for prayer,' says project spokesperson Vince Desai. 'What we're doing is preparing a room for this use from the beginning.' Loosely translated from old Sanskrit, *suntosh* means contentment.

**Pilgrimage 2000** Travel that also fulfils a spiritual quest is on the rise. A decade ago, according to a report in *Utne Reader*, fewer than 4,000 people annually followed El Camino de Santiago, Spain's fabled pilgrimage route. In summer 1996, 95,000 made the trek. In Taize, France, Gen Xers from around the world converge each week to pray and sing repetitive chants, known as the songs of Taize. In 1994, the Taize monks' trek to Paris attracted over 100,000 pilgrims.

**Spiritual Healing** Once derided by practitioners of modern medicine, faith healing is gaining legitimacy. Ninety-nine per cent of 269 doctors interviewed at a meeting of the American Academy of Family Physicians said they're convinced religious belief can heal. Three-quarters believe the prayers of others can help a patient's recovery, and 38 per cent think faith healers can make people well. Recent studies linking faith and healing have led an increasing number of doctors to prescribe prayer and meditation as a complement to regular medical care. In fact, some have begun incorporating prayer into their treatments: they will prescribe meditation rather than medication, positive thinking rather than Percocet. In a backlash against the daily rigours of a twenty-drug breakfast cocktail, patients are turning to the simple comfort of spirituality for support – and a cure.

**Spirituality-based Spending** Entrepreneurs catering to religious sensibilities will offer an expanded range of products and services. For example: Oklahoma-based long-distance phone service provider Lifeline, founded in 1990 as an 'alternative that stands for biblical values', has more than 900,000 customers, with billings in excess of US$14 million a month.

## Next: Bodies As Temples

The urge to detoxify and 'purify' our bodies (and our environment) has been widespread ever since Rachel Carson's *Silent Spring* raised the alarm in 1962. In the past few years, though, the alarm has rung far louder, as headline news warns us of everything from mad cow disease to mysteriously falling male fertility rates and the possible dangers of electromagnetic emissions.

In the popular lexicon, *chemicals* used to be the catch-all word for manmade substances perceived as undesirable or dangerous. The term of choice is now *toxins*, a far more powerful concept that covers not only manmade but also naturally occurring substances ranging from snake venom to bacterial and fungal by-products. Confirming their place in modern demonology, toxins are featured as one of the hazards in 'Doom', one of the world's best-selling 'shoot-em-up' computer games.

In the past, eco-health concerns stirred high-profile collective action in the form of pressure groups such as Greenpeace. But the self-help, take-charge-of-your-life spirit of the late nineties is now prompting millions of ordinary individuals around the world to develop their own eco-health strategies – via combinations of avoidance, combatance and elimination.

**Body Beautiful** Modern consumers do not distinguish between wellness and health and fitness; the tendency is to equate feeling good with looking good, and vice versa. In Japan, for example, wellness and fitness blur together in terms of consumer perceptions of the gym or fitness club. Similarly, today's beauty-selling industry has seen lust and sensuality pushed into a corner as elements of 'allure', while 'total wellness' – encompassing mind, body and spirit – has taken centre stage as the more powerful, and more convincing, modern-day aphrodisiac.

**Alternative Therapies** *Asia Inc.* reports that after years of using modern medicines, Asian executives are returning to ancient healing techniques, including massage and acupuncture. 'We're in the unusual position of reintroducing old techniques to young Asians,' commented Nancy Bekhor, managing director of Hong Kong's Vital Life Centre. Rather than psychological stress, Asians tend to complain about a loss of physical and emotional energy. One popular healer who caters to the business crowd offers US$45 sessions that include soft music, vigorous rubbing – both on and above the body – and a lecture on channel-healing and the spiritual world.

Workers with tension-filled necks and shoulders are keeping masseuses busy. In the US, the number of massage therapists has increased 8–15 per cent in each of the past ten years, reports the American Massage Therapy Association. What used to be considered an indulgence is increasingly seen as a form of therapy. In response to survey results from its 1.5 million members, Oxford Health Plans, an American health maintenance organization (which serves as a health insurance plan for members), has added to its New York regional network approximately 1,000 alternative medicine practitioners, including massage therapists, yoga instructors, acupuncturists, nutritionists and chiropractors.

To fight back against toxins, consumers are turning to a variety of methods and products aimed at assisting the body's natural cleansing systems. Fasting diets, for instance – which can range from water-only fasts to a diet made up solely of whole foods – support detoxification by releasing into the body stored, fat-soluble toxins, which are then broken down by cleansing organs and excreted. For those who want faster results, health-food stores sell a variety of herbs reputed to aid detox efforts. Gaia's Supreme Cleanse Internal Cleansing Program (US$34.95), for instance, is billed as a four-part, two-week programme that yields a full-body cleanse.

In the future, expect to see a greater number of artificial environments dedicated to 'natural healing'. The Alpha Health Environment Capsule, which premiered in 1990 in Tokyo, is one such example: as reported in *Business Daily*, the capsule, which is equipped with a dry heat sauna, massage vibration, aromatherapy, germicidal lamp, ionized face air, calorie indicator, ultraviolet light, brain wave therapy and stereophonic sounds (New Age music or nature sounds), is intended to make users 'look, feel, and live better'. The capsule's 'passenger' relaxes on the machine's contour comfort bed, while wearing special lightshield glasses designed to put his or her mind 'in meditative ease'. Already very popular in Korea, Japan and China, Alpha capsules are beginning to make their way West. Two new machines from Sybaritic Inc. that promise to be equally popular are the Sunspectra (featuring a domed hood and special colour light effects to enhance treatments) and the

Weitrol 123 (specifically targeted for weight loss through natural metabolic stimulation).

**Day Spas** Once upon a time, a trip to the spa meant a minimum of a week to ten days of relaxation and rejuvenation. Such an investment (in time and money) is too much for many of today's consumers, who opt instead for some quick r&r at a day spa. Six years ago, according to the International Spa & Fitness Association, there were approximately 30 day spas in the US, representing a US$50 million industry. Today, more than 600 spas bring in a total of US$250 million a year. The best spas manage to provide a taste of the destination spa experience at a fraction of the cost. The Yamaguchi Salon and Coastal Day Spa in Ventura, California, for instance, evokes a Zenlike tone with scented candles, steaming cups of herbal tea and mini-sculptures of water falling on stones. The spa's Day of Beauty (US$265) includes a light organic breakfast, massage, facial, pedicure, manicure, scalp massage, colour consultation, hairstyling, makeup, lunch and spa gifts.[1]

Shopping malls are becoming particularly popular sites for day spas, whether as stand-alone units or as part of an upscale department store. Harried shoppers can choose from an assortment of beauty and relaxation treatments. A six-hour package offered by Maximus Total Beauty Day Spa Deluxe in Long Island, New York, for instance, consists of a facial, full-body massage, spa manicure and pedicure and lunch. Priced at US$300, it's the perfect way to finish off a day of credit overload.

**Gentle Exercise** Endorphins earned through twenty miles of serious running are rarely worth the effort, not to mention the surgery later in life to replace damaged ligaments and cartilage. For a more beneficial 'high', a growing number of stressed-out Westerners are escaping to the Eastern practices of yoga and t'ai chi.

The general aim of yoga is to increase oxygenation of the blood, stretch muscles, and increase suppleness. This, in turn, increases concentration and helps reduce toxin levels, a key source of skin problems and stress-compounding mood swings. It is also reputed to stimulate internal organs, particularly the heart and lungs, and slow the ageing process. In the UK, yoga is regularly practised by a quarter of a million people and is expected to grow by 20 per cent in the next year. Roper, a market research company and pollster, estimates that 6 million Americans are regular yoga participants.

In addition to using yoga as a means of staying fit (half an hour of power yoga uses the same number of calories (300–350) as jogging for the same length of time), adherents are turning to yoga as an alternative medical technique. Jon Kabat-Zinn, PhD, founder of the Stress Reduction Clinic at the University of Massachusetts Medical Center, combines yoga and meditation in his standard eight-week programme. And Columbia Presbyterian hospital, in an effort to reduce post-surgical stress and depression, speed up recovery and prevent further heart problems, is experimenting with a battery of alternative healing methods, including yoga, hypnotherapy, Swedish massage and therapeutic touch.[2] Companies with stressed-out workers are also taking note of yoga's healing benefits. *Newsweek* reports that CMP Media, Inc., in Manhasset, New York, sets aside a conference room for one hour each week for yoga. An instructor conducts a class that's been modified for the varied ages and conditions of participating employees.

In recent years, the centuries-old art of t'ai chi has made its way from China to many parts of Europe and North America. A growing body of scientific evidence has found that this 'internal' martial art – intended to build body strength and qi (pronounced 'chee'), one's energy or life force – can be effective in improving overall health, decreasing blood pressure, increasing muscle mass, lowering levels of body chemicals related to stress and even reversing the frailty of old age. T'ai chi classes can now be found throughout many Western cities, in such places as senior centres, neighbourhood parks and rehabilitative programmes. Even some companies are getting in on the action. European American Bank, for instance, hired Jesse 'Two Owls' Teasley, a poet and medicine man, to teach employees the principles of t'ai chi.[3]

**A Breath of Fresh Air** Among products seeing increased sales are home air-filtration systems and vacuum cleaners that use a water-filtration system rather than a bag for collecting house dust. Also available at premium prices are microfiltration dust bags intended to limit dust dispersion. The enemy: airborne allergens such as dust-mite particles.

Residents of smog-ridden cities such as Mexico City, Tokyo and Beijing turn to oxygen booths for a respite from those cities' high pollution levels. As reported by alt.culture.daily (http://www.altculture.com), a more upscale version of this fad, the oxygen bar, has taken hold among health-conscious Americans and Europeans. In 1996, former competitive swimmer Lissa Charron opened the first North American oxygen bar in Toronto, the O2 Spa Bar, where masked patrons 'gas up' on pure or flavoured oxygen. Spin-offs soon followed in Reno, Los Angeles and New York. True believers insist that regular shots of oxygen not only increase one's energy, but also relieve maladies ranging from allergies to hangovers. Although professional athletes inhale oxygen before competition to boost energy levels, there is little scientific evidence as yet to substantiate benefits claims. (In fact, some doctors warn that too many trips to the oxygen bar could result in oxygen toxicity and/or cellular abnormalities.) Aside from bars, oxygen has become a staple at day spas and health resorts, where the range of treatments now includes oxygen pills, oxygen-enhanced drinks and oxygenated skin creams. Oxygen-snorting celebrities are said to include Jeff Goldblum, Ben Stiller, Kirstie Alley and Woody Harrelson, who opened an LA yoga centre with adjoining oxygen bar in 1997.

**Water, Water Everywhere** Consumers put off by artificial colours and flavours in soft drinks are opting for healthier choices. Fruit beverages, ready-to-drink teas and sports drinks are growing in popularity, but the number one seller in an estimated 1.4 million hotel minibars worldwide is none other than bottled water.

At the height of the recent south-east Asian haze scare, authorities advised citizens to stay indoors and drink plenty of water to flush out the toxins contained in the smoke. The idea of flushing out harmful substances seems to be intuitively right for the human psyche. While 'plain water' clearly does the job adequately, there will be increased opportunities for products that offer an enhanced cleansing action. A number of French mineral waters have long claimed to promote action of the kidneys, and in West Africa, where many people believe in flushing out malaria from the body, beer drinkers value brands that are reputed to cause increased urination.

Bottled water infused with nutrition supplements (ginkgo biloba, ginseng, multivitamins, etc.) is a certain next. Watch for the development of special-use water, bottled and marketed for specific environments. For instance, a particular brand's Type A might be perfect for 'everyday' use, Type B for après exercise and Type C for entertaining. For consumers taking baby steps towards better health, there's already Water Joe, a caffeinated water product promoted as 'a caffeine alternative in a healthier format'. A half-litre bottle packs a caffeine equivalent of one cup of coffee.

Look for more consumers to invest in in-home water purification systems. According to *Time*, American homeowners bought more than US$450 million worth of water-treatment systems in a recent year. At least 12 per cent of US households treat their water in some manner, despite the fact that the US has one of the best water-supply systems in the world. Consumers' primary concerns are to remove lead, bacteria, arsenic and other contaminants that affect the water's taste and safety.

**Organic Eats** 'Give me spots on my apples, but leave me the birds and the bees,' sang Joni Mitchell almost thirty years ago ('Big Yellow Taxi', 1970), in one of the earliest pop laments for ecology. Consumer demand for organic fare has since grown steadily in the developed world. Organic food is grown without pesticides, hormones, antibiotics, or herbicides; meat is reared without additives, and the animals are kept in more humane conditions. Genetically-engineered food is also taboo – and the opposite of the organic food that is valued by many.

Despite a cost that's typically 10–15 per cent higher than for conventionally produced food (due to higher production costs), US demand for organic food was estimated in 1996 to be growing at a rate of 20 per cent per year. In Britain, business increased 55 per cent in 1996 for Organic Farm Foods, Britain's largest organic food supplier (the company sells more than 600 tons to supermarkets each week). Managing director Peter Segger told the *Observer*, 'Until last year, there was a steady growth of interest in organic foods, but since BSE, there has been a fundamental change. People are thinking a lot more about where their food comes from.'

On the Continent, organic food is becoming a priority for a growing number of companies and governments. As reported in the *Guardian*, 10 per cent of all food sold in Denmark in 1997 is believed to have been organic, 'and the government is revising its goal upwards to 20 per cent; ditto Finland, Sweden, and many German provinces'. Thus far, in the fifteen member states of the EU, 63,000 farmers have gone organic, representing 0.75 per cent of all farmers and 1.1 per cent of farmed land, reports *The Times* (London). Top performers are Sweden and Austria, with 8.6 and 8 per cent of their land, respectively, now organically farmed. Swedish policy is to convert 10 per cent of all farms within three years. In France, the organic food market is set to double by 2000. In hopes of claiming a 10 per cent market share, French retailer Carrefour has launched forty-eight organic products, ranging from flour and oil to chocolate and jam. *Eurofood* reports that products in the Carrefour Bio line cost 10–30 per cent more than non-organic products, but 20–30 per cent less than branded organics.

Consumers' hearts may warm to the idea of fruit and vegetables grown 'the natural way', but the less-than-perfect appearance of much organic produce is a turnoff for many. Now choice is widening for consumers in search of produce that is pleasing to eye and palate. Two pesticide-free alternatives: hydroponic and aeroponic products, which are grown in controlled, enclosed conditions that don't require pesticides; and genetically manipulated plants, with an in-bred resistance to pests that renders chemicals unnecessary.

**Vegetarianism** While people adopt vegetarian lifestyles for many reasons – ethical and environmental among them – the current surge in vegetarianism seems most closely linked to the desire to live more healthfully. As early as 1993, *Beef Improvement News* of Australia noted 'widespread vegetarianism' among teenage girls aged 14–17. And a single mention of the US based Vegetarian Resource Group in America's *Parade* magazine a few years ago generated an estimated 3,000–4,000 inquiries.

According to *The Vegetarian* (May 1995), the incidence of vegetarians in the following countries (expressed as a percentage of the total adult population) is as follows:

| | |
|---|---|
| Western Germany | 4.5% |
| The Netherlands | 4.4% |
| United Kingdom | 4.3% |
| Italy | 1.25% |
| France | 0.8% |
| Switzerland | 0.75% |
| Poland | 0.2% |

Today, an estimated 12 million Americans consider themselves vegetarian, including 25 per cent of teens. In response to demand for meatless food, manufacturers have introduced 'meat analogue products' with names such as 'Foney Baloney' and 'Fakin' Bacon'. Anticipate increased vegetarian fare at mainstream fast-food venues, as well as the development of vegetarian-only establishments.

**Functional Foods** Leaders in medicine, nutrition and high-tech are collaborating to create a new class of products known as 'functional foods', 'medical foods', or 'nutraceuticals'. By any name, these foods have been engineered to impart health benefits beyond basic nutrition. It's far from a fringe movement. Dr Stephen DeFelice of the US-based Foundation for Innovation in Medicine recently told the *Guardian* that 'every major food and pharmaceutical company out there has a nutra-ceutical task force'. Campbell Soup, for example, has introduced a line of meals clinically proven to combat high blood pressure, high choles-terol and diabetes. Frozen meals (three meals and one snack per day) are delivered weekly at a cost of US$79.95. Designed in conjunction with the American Heart Association and the American Diabetes Associ-ation, Intelligent Quisine is promoted as a convenient way to make healthful food choices and reduce one's intake of medications.

Dr DeFelice predicts that consumers soon will be equally likely to seek cures for what ails them at the supermarket as at the pharmacy. 'The main advantage of medical foods over drugs is that they contain naturally occurring products – even if they weren't made naturally,' said DeFelice. 'Their main medical effect will be to shift emphasis from curing illness to preventing illness.'

'Enhanced foods' are modified and/or fortified to promote health benefits. In Japan, drinks with added 'polyols' have been introduced to reduce the risk of dental cavities, and Coca-Cola has launched a controversial adolescent soft drink containing DHA, an essential fatty acid said to promote learning ability. Sales of the fermented milk drink Yakult, available in Japan since 1935, now total more than 23 million units a day in some sixteen countries worldwide. The product contains 6.5 billion lactobacillus casei shirota bacteria, which, taken daily, are said to promote 'positive intestinal flora'. Since 1992, Japan has approved more than seventy-five products as 'Foods for Specialized Health Use' (FOSHU), including protein-modified rice for people with allergies and phosphate milk for those with kidney disorders. Labels on FOSHU products include a recommendation from a Japanese nutri-tional foods association and a reminder to eat a balanced diet.

At Sainsbury's in the UK, women considering pregnancy can pur-chase bread fortified with folic acid (known to prevent spina bifida in babies). Those concerned about cholesterol levels can purchase loaves with oat fibre, and the 'omega loaf' adds fish oil for a healthy heart. European scientists also have bred a tomato with about four times the normal level of beta-carotene, which the body uses to make vitamin A, and twice the level of lycopene, which may reduce the risk of some cancers.

Certain natural foods, free of alterations and additives, are also being recognized and promoted for their functional qualities. Bruce Ames, professor of biochemistry at the University of California-Berkeley, reports that dietary antioxidants slow down or limit the metabolic processes that damage cells, thus reducing the risk of disease and helping people live longer and healthier lives. Ames' example: the quarter of the US population that eats the least fruits and vegetables – rich in antioxidants – are deficient in folic acid, vitamin C and carotenoids. Rates 'for virtually every kind of cancer' in this group are double those for the quarter of the population that eats the most fruits and vegetables. In the US, oatmeal is one of the few foods that can claim official government sanction for health benefits. The all-natural, low-fat food has been proven to lower cholesterol and may reduce the risk of heart disease; it will soon carry a supporting label approved by the Food and Drug Administration. Scientists are studying garlic, soy, cranberries, broccoli and red wine to determine if similar FDA health-benefits labels are deserved.

When genetic research succeeds in pinpointing each individual's predisposition to specific illnesses, people will be able to use an appropriate combination of functional foods to ward off illness. Parents will be among the first true believers, using food profiles to plan their children's diets.

**Supplements** Vitamins and herbs are increasingly being added to the arsenals of those intent on keeping their bodies pure and healthy through natural means. Vitamin C, in particular, is touted as a combatant of free radicals (highly reactive chemicals suspected of being carcinogenic), but Vitamin E is fast gaining prominence. Citing recent information that Vitamin E is effective against certain cancers, cardiovascular disease and even Alzheimer's disease, *Food Processing* magazine labelled Vitamin E 'the nutrient of the year for 1997'.

The market for herbal products is skyrocketing in the US, having grown from US$500 million in 1992 to more than US$3 billion in 1998. Consumer interest in alternative medicine has fuelled this growth, as did passage of the Dietary Supplement Health and Education Act of 1994, which defined herbs as food supplements and set limits of government regulation far below that required of pharmaceuticals. According to a Gallup survey, Americans' use of herbs increased nearly 70 per cent in 1997.

The *Atlanta Journal and Constitution* reported that the top-selling herbs in the US in 1997 were as follows:

1  Ginseng (relieves fatigue)
2  Garlic (reduces blood cholesterol)
3  Ginkgo Biloba (may improve circulation, memory)
4  Echinacea (helps maintain immune system)
5  St John's Wort (antidepressant)
6  Saw Palmetto (helps maintain urinary tract function in older men)
7  Echinacea/Goldenseal (may boost immune system)
8  Pycnogenol/Grape Seed (antioxidant)
9  Goldenseal (antibacterial)
10 Evening Primrose (relieves PMS, arthritis, breast pain)

**Lite/Lowfat/No-fat**  As consumers take a more active role in monitoring their health, lite/lowfat/no-fat products will constitute a grocery category worldwide. Importantly, qualifying products are apt to be marketed to consumers as a 'healthful choice' rather than a weight-loss product. The most dominant trend in the German food industry over the past two years has been the change in diet away from traditional fatty foods and rich meats toward light, healthful foods. While Germans used to consume large amounts of steak, pork and sausage, these meats have recently lost out to such 'lighter' foods as poultry and fish. A recent study indicates that when American consumers look at the nutrition label on a food product, 74 per cent are looking for fat content information. This exceeds those that are looking for the number of calories (58 per cent), cholesterol content (56 per cent), sodium content (51 per cent) and serving size (41 per cent).

As expressed by Steven C. Anderson, president of the American Frozen Food Institute (AFFI), 'The frozen food industry has led the rest of the food industry in making not only convenient and high quality products but products that are low in fat, which is what consumers are looking for today.' Currently, the US$3.3 billion frozen-entrée category is dominated by ConAgra's Healthy Choice. To avoid being pushed out of the market, H. J. Heinz is repositioning its Weight Watchers frozen dinners, emphasizing health first, vanity second. Among other steps, the company has signed deals with insurers such as Independence Blue Cross Inc. of Philadelphia to give rebates on life-insurance premiums to members of the Weight Watchers programme. Celentano's Great Choice line of reduced-fat entrées appeals to the same market as Healthy Choice.

**Culinary Freshness** Consumers also are placing renewed emphasis on quality and freshness and manufacturers and governments are responding. Nissin Gourmet Beef of Osaka, Japan has patented a method to 'quick freeze' fish and meat, keeping it tasting fresher longer. This has important implications for restaurants, which often serve 'fresh' fish that is six to ten days old rather than its frozen counterpart, which generally is soft and tasteless as a result of cell membranes having been broken by ice crystals. The new process is so fast that ice crystals don't have a chance to form. The result is a product, 'Trufresh', that tastes fresher than most never-frozen fish. Trufresh fish isn't sold in super-markets, since the daily defrost cycle most freezer cases have would cause the fish to thaw out and refreeze the slow way. Expiry dates on perishable goods may become obsolete. LifeLines Technology of New Jersey has developed 'smart' labels that change colour to indicate when the food may have gone bad by keeping tabs on the temperatures to which the product is exposed. A frozen-food package that has been left unrefrigerated for too long, for example, would alert the consumer that the food may have spoiled despite not having reached its expiry date. To emphasize the quality of their product, frozen food manufacturers have taken to referring to it as 'temperature controlled' or 'fresh frozen'. Until recently, US inspectors only looked at, touched and smelled ani-mal carcasses when inspecting meat. Under new rules, inspectors will scientifically test samples.

Malaysian company Halim Mazmin Bhd is targeting thirteen coun-tries for distribution of frozen halal food (food sanctioned by Islam). In addition to Islamic countries, target markets include Britain, China, South Korea, Taiwan and the US. 'There is a high demand for halal food from various countries regardless of religion as halal food is known for its hygiene and is widely consumed even by non-Muslims,' claims Executive Chairman Halim Mohammed. Similarly, non-Jews are taking greater interest in kosher food due to the perception that it is somehow 'cleaner' than non-kosher products.

The field is wide open for a food manufacturer to establish its identity as the 'safety' brand, providing a non-religious 'seal of cleanliness and safety'.

## Next: Pure Products

Consumer interest in natural products stems from simultaneous desires to minimize our impact on the environment and to limit the impact of the environment on us. While Crystal Pepsi was a failure when it was launched in the early half of this decade, the trend toward clear products – another outgrowth of the green movement – has moved well beyond new-age beverages to encompass deodorants, shampoos, dishwashing liquids and toiletries. Regardless of the actual ingredients used, consumers continue to regard these products as being somehow purer, more natural and more healthful for them.

**Going Natural**  In the health and beauty industry, the appeal of natural (versus synthetic) cosmetics ingredients is reaping profits for makers of everything from botanical shampoo to herbal toothpaste. For example, since 1978, when it began selling plant-based shampoos, Aveda has grown into an international, US$100 million industry powerhouse, and has recently been bought by industry giant Estée Lauder. Today, more than 30,000 salons stock several hundred items bearing the Aveda name. Taking some cues from the UK's Body Shop, Origins Natural Resources, an environmentally friendly line of cosmetics and aromatherapy products, has grown into a US$45 million business in only six years. The fastest growing division of Estée Lauder, Origins currently has nineteen freestanding stores and forty 'stores within stores' in the US, Denmark, England, Germany and Japan. And Tom's of Maine, long a staple of health-food stores, has begun to win shelf space in drugstores and supermarkets in the US. It's all-natural (no additives, dyes or sugars) herbal toothpaste now accounts for annual sales of approximately US$20 million. The company sells roughly 250 all-natural products, including deodorant, shampoo and mouthwash. (http://www.toms-of-maine.com/). Purity sells, so even manufacturers unable to make claims of being 'all natural' may instead point to such 'pure' characteristics as being 'hypoallergenic' or 'not tested on animals'.

**Chemical-free Kids**  Keeping our babies chemical-free is becoming a fast-growing industry. Baby clothes made from organically grown cotton, for example, are being touted as healthier for babies because there are no pesticides or chemical residues to be absorbed through the skin. Likewise, companies that sell organic baby foods, such as Earth's Best Baby Food in the US, are beginning to win shelf space from such industry giants as Heinz, Gerber and Beechtree. Also in response to parents' concerns, Hasbro's Playskool toy line has launched a line of children's products and toys featuring Microban antibacterial protection. The intent is to protect the toys – and by extension, the children who use them – from the growth of germs and bacteria. Older children and adults can also purchase a new product called No Sweat, a sweatband that adheres to the inside of one's baseball cap. The charcoal-activated hat liner with a bactericide absorbs moisture when the user sweats.

## Next: One-World Consumerism

In an effort to ensure that the healthful life continues to be a 'choice' on Planet Earth, people are embracing one-world consumerism – the vote-with-your-dollars acknowledgement that 'what goes around, comes around'. As we live with the results of our centuries-long promiscuous waste of planet resources, the environmental mantra 'reduce, reuse, recycle' becomes that much more meaningful.

As recently as 1985, less than 1 per cent of all merchandise produced in the US was marketed as being 'environmentally friendly'. By 1995, that percentage had increased to 20. In Germany, the Green movement is so strong that Hans Tietmeyer, president of Deutsche Bundesbank, has predicted that '[In the long run] only those companies that consider environmental protection to be an integrated and natural component of management, development, production and even the products themselves – rather than viewing it as a bothersome appendage – will be successful and have a chance at surviving on the market.'

Though consumers in Europe and North America generally continue to stress quality and price over environmental concerns, more and more large retailers are beginning to stock 'green' items and make 'green' decisions. US company Patagonia, known for its upscale outdoor clothing, has announced plans to use only organically grown cotton. Its spring 1996 catalogue pointed to the fact that 'the process of growing conventional cotton involves the heavy use of chemicals that toxify the soil, air, and ground water'. (In the US alone, 20 million pounds of pesticides are used to grow cotton every year.) In Germany, the central travel agency removed short-trip Concorde flights from its programme, acknowledging undue pressure on the environment. (Concorde uses five times the energy required by a normal jet.)

**Renewals** Consumption next will be about reusable, multipurpose items that limit strain on the environment. A study conducted at the Milan Furniture Fair points to a growing interest in upgradeable furnishings, flexible pieces that can be added to or adjusted as one's needs change and one's finances permit. IKEA, for instance, now offers modular kitchen cabinets set into wood frames that can sit on the floor or be fastened to a wall. The idea is that young people can invest in a few simple pieces at first and then add more units as their families and incomes grow.

Already in demand is everything from America's modestly-priced Castro Convertible couches (sleep sofas) to roller skates that convert to in-line skates when Johnny is ready to move from bumps and scratches to more serious injuries. Parents fed up with shelling out money at every age and stage of their children's lives are fuelling demand for all manner of children's products that 'grow' with their kids. One can now purchase nursery mobiles that turn into toddler activity centres, which then become art units for older children. Also popular are bassinets that become cribs, then toddler beds and, finally, glider benches. Some furniture makers are even producing tables with multiple sets of removable legs so parents can adjust the height as their children grow.

# Loving and Lusting

Sexual harassment. Sexual addiction. Homosexuality. Cybersex. In one form or another, the once-taboo subject of sex has emerged as a leading topic of conversation – and debate. Why all the interest in what's happening in the world's bedrooms? For many people, sex and sexuality are moral issues. They perceive the rise in out-of-wedlock births, the fight for gay rights and the depiction of sexual acts on television and in the movies as evidence of the steady decline of society. Others decry the small-minded intolerance they feel has turned an act of love and/ or passion into something 'dirty'.

The authors of this book are interested in sex for a slightly different reason. We are students of the art of the sexy sell. We find it intriguing that sex is used to market everything from lingerie to automobiles, perfume to CDs. And we understand that society's ever-evolving sexual attitudes have a tremendous impact on the ways in which products are sold.

Among marketers, it's common knowledge that sexual messages can be far more explicit in Europe than in the US. America's 'puritanical bent' very often becomes a factor when advertising and television or movie content attempts to cross the Atlantic. Witness the fact that Adrian Lyne's *Lolita*, depicting a man's sexual interest in a twelve-year-old girl, ran across Europe but still has not found a distributor in the US. (At last word, it has only been shown on cable TV's Showtime.) A similar situation developed when American TV star Roseanne announced plans to produce a US version of Britain's *Absolutely*

*Fabulous.* The network decreed that the producers would need to tone down the characters' sexual promiscuity (and alcohol and drug use) in order to meet network standards and attract advertisers in the States.

In past decades, differing standards have not posed a major problem for advertisers. In today's global market, however, some analysts are warning companies such as McDonald's and Pepsi that if they want to attract consumers in overseas markets, they'll need to inject a bit more sexuality into their ad campaigns. At the same time, European multinationals must heed social – and sometimes even legal – constraints in other parts of the world. The fact of the matter is that the success of cross-border marketing efforts continues to be contingent on satisfying each market's desire for excitement and stimulation without offending the sensibilities of consumers in other targeted countries. Not an easy task given the widely variant attitudes toward sex in Europe vs the US vs Asia vs Islamic countries, etc.

And it's not just differing social mores which must be taken into account. That which is deemed sexy, erotic and/or romantic also differs according to country and culture. Harlequin, publisher of romantic novels, recently conducted a survey regarding what women around the world do to make themselves feel more romantic. In analysing the responses of some 6,200 women in twenty-one countries, Harlequin found the following:

- Women in France, Germany, Greece, Turkey and Norway are most likely to listen to romantic music.
- Women in Argentina, Finland and Holland prefer to watch a romantic movie.
- Respondents in Canada and the US are most likely to opt for a bubble bath.
- Women in Russia and Hungary are most apt to read a love story.

As you review the global nexts that follow, keep in mind the existence of such local distinctions. For when it comes to matters of the heart (and libido) cultural differences can spell opportunity – or disaster.

## Next: Sex Redefined

To a certain degree, sex is sex. The act itself hasn't changed over time. Sure, there are interesting variations, but we can be certain that everything that can be done in that department has already been done.

Nonetheless, we're seeing a redefinition of sex today, as new attitudes and new technologies begin to alter the ways in which we look at – and even engage – in sexual acts.

**The New Intimacy** Those who prefer to couch conversations about sex in euphemisms sometimes refer to sex as 'being intimate'. But just what does it mean to 'be intimate' these days? Does intimacy involve bodily contact or simply personal knowledge? Can one be intimate with someone one has never seen? The definition appears to be changing: the new understanding of adultery, as defined in *Newsweek*, is that it's 'a sin of the heart and mind as much as – or even more than – the body'. The essence of an affair, according to American psychiatrist Dr Frank Pittman, is the secret intimacy between two people that must be defended with dishonesty. 'Infidelity isn't about whom you lie with,' he says. 'It's whom you lie to.' Proponents contend that 'emotional adultery' is committed when a person other than one's spouse becomes more central to one's thoughts and fantasies than one's partner.

In the Digital Age, one needn't ever have met one's partner (much less had face2face sex with him or her) to be 'intimate'. In an age in which real-world sex has become risky, to say the least, the relatively safe and frequently anonymous world of cybersex has proven a viable alternative. The real-time communication supported by online services and Internet Relay Chat enable people to live out their sexual fantasies with virtual strangers, albeit online. On AOL, the most chat-friendly online service, people can engage in group conversations in sexually oriented public chatrooms, create private chatrooms for a little 'one on one', or get down and dirty via 'instant messages'. Swapping genders is a popular activity among members of both sexes, as is a general tendency to lie about any and all other aspects of one's body and one's life.

In an interesting trend, electronic intimacy – whether via online chat, email, or cell phone – increasingly is being considered the 'real thing'. In a letter to American advice columnist Ann Landers, one cyberlover wrote: 'I met my girlfriend on the Net. She is Canadian. I live in Illinois. We have gotten together, face to face, only once, but over the last few months, we have ... fallen in love.' Another American, from New Jersey, sued his wife for divorce, alleging that her racy computer messages to a man she had never met constituted adultery. A judge didn't agree – this time. Any remaining doubts about the true nature of an electronic relationship were dispelled by a sensational case that unfolded not too long ago in the US: An enraged man killed his wife upon learning that she had received flowers from a man she had 'met' online.

**Silicon Sex** New technologies aren't just being used for cybersex, they're also playing a role in bringing couples together, spicing up sex lives, even providing 'alternative' partners.

In the Netherlands, Philips Electronics plans to introduce a 'singles chip' that's designed to unite compatible lovers. The chip, which is small enough to be concealed in an earring or tie pin, can be programmed with such information as likes, dislikes and personality traits. To be used in a singles bar, nightclub or other social arena, the chip is designed to scan the room for other singles chips and beep if it locates a compatible profile.

People who prefer computer screens to the real-world singles scene can employ online personal-ad services such as Match.com. In addition to being convenient and open twenty-four hours a day, these sites have the added advantage (according to some of their operators) of having a clientele – simply by virtue of being on the Internet – that is more affluent and better educated than the average population.

In the software realm, a new genre of sexy titles – including 'Interactive Sex Therapy', 'Anne Hooper's Ultimate Sex Guide', 'The Joy of Sex', and 'Dr Ruth's Encyclopedia of Sex' – is being promoted as therapeutic self-help for those hoping to improve their sex lives. As might be expected, much of the content focuses on sexual enhancement (making sex last longer and making it better). Searching for entertainment rather than enlightenment? There's always 'Virtual Valerie' and 'The Penthouse Photo Shoot'.

Online sex has been around since the infancy of computer bulletin boards in the early 1980s, when entrepreneurs discovered people would pay to download suggestive pictures and engage in lewd talk on electronic message boards. Modern offerings are much more diverse. In Britain, when the Adam and Eve film channel found it difficult to gain permission to broadcast on television throughout the day, it sidestepped this regulation by running its erotic films around the clock on the Internet. And Adam and Eve aren't alone: at present, there are more than 10,000 sexy Websites.

A range of adult products is also available to cybershoppers, including everything from sexy lingerie to instructional videos. Forrester Research estimates that online sales of adult merchandise in the United States reached US$51.5 million last year, or about 10 per cent of all consumer goods sold over the Internet during that period. That number doesn't include revenue from subscriptions or per-minute video sex charges, which account for the majority of many online sex companies' sales.

Speaking of video sex: Yahoo now lists more than 300 Websites that offer the equivalent of phone sex with pictures. Customers of virtual strip shows pay up to US$10 a minute to talk to a stripper via computer and watch a live video performance. Customers of Las Vegas-based Virtual Dreams, which claims to be grossing close to US$1 million each month, pay US$5.99 a minute to watch and direct a personal stripper or as little as US$2.99 a minute to tune into other customers' fantasies. The average call lasts twelve minutes, but some customers run up tabs of several hundred dollars. Of those dialling Virtual Dreams' video-conferencing service, 75 per cent are in the US. The company is in the process of setting up deals with independent studios in such places as Amsterdam, Sweden and London to create a global network of inter-active strip shows. Seattle-based Internet Entertainment Group, which operates one of the larger sex businesses on the Internet, runs at least a dozen Websites that sell subscriptions, digital phones, adult videos and other merchandise. But IEG is best known as one of America's biggest proprietors of video phone sex. All told, company revenue could top US$20 million this year.

In coming years, *The Futurist* predicts the availability of a broader array of e-pleasure alternatives. Robots that provide sexual companion-ship are deemed likely to become common in the future, and prototype models already have been reported in Japan. The so-called 'sexbots' will have humanlike features and will be soft and pliant, like the latest dolls for children. Vibrators will provide tactile stimulation and sound systems will provide 'love talk'.

## Next: New Standards of Desirability

The definition of what's sexy also is undergoing change. As we discussed on page 43, today's optimum age of desirability is far older than that of Lolita. Today, it's Ivanka Trump versus Ivana Trump, and mom Ivana is closer to her peak. In the US and Europe, celebrity women over forty are posing in the buff, inspiring both desire and curiosity. There's no question that the pictorials sell magazines: the December 1995 issue of

*Playboy*, which featured fifty-year-old covermate Farrah Fawcett, sold 2.5 times the average. Such layouts successfully sell the image of middle-aged women as not only beautiful, but sexy. While this is hardly news to Europeans – consider the long-standing appeal of Catherine Deneuve, Simone Signoret and others – America has long been home to the so-called 'cult of youth'.

Slimness is another beauty standard being called into question. Egypt's top sex symbol, Laila Alwi, admits to 140 pounds, but the public estimates her weight as high as 220. Egypt's *Radio and TV Magazine* recently noted that the country's film and TV stars 'fluctuate between obesity and plumpness', and suggested they adopt the slogan, 'Down with slimness!' Local advertisers acknowledge they now seek a decidedly full look in their mass marketing.

Though thin is still the beauty ideal in the US, there's evidence that Americans are beginning to accept the larger woman: Ms Average American stands five feet, four inches tall and weighs 144 pounds. A growing number of magazines that target large-size women, including *Big Beautiful Women* (*BBW*), *Radiance* and *Mode*, are growing in popularity. Their message: you don't have to be thin to deserve great clothes and a happy lifestyle. A plethora of books advancing the 'don't diet' message have hit the shelves, including Glenn Gaessner's *Big Fat Lies*, Richard Klein's *Eat Fat* and Barbara Altman Bruno's *Worth Your Weight*. And recognizable and respected fashion designers have finally added bigger sizes to their lines to accommodate the clothing needs of the estimated 65 million larger women previously not catered for. The list includes Ellen Tracy, Emanuel Ungaro (under the label Emanuel), Dana Buchman, MaxMara (Marina Rinaldi), David Dart, Carole Little, Liz Claiborne (Elisabeth) and Tamotsu. The Ford Models 12-plus division has some fifty women on its roster, including Emme (named one of *People* magazine's 50 Most Beautiful People in 1997).

Extending the redefinition of physical beauty even further, a North American marketing campaign for high-tech wheelchair company Colours broke with the traditional advertising tendency to portray the disabled as asexual/passive. With the intent of drawing attention to the disabled as sexual beings, the 'People of Colours' campaign included such images as a near-naked, quadriplegic pregnant woman in a wheelchair, and a couple embracing on a bed with a wheelchair off to the side. The ads are credited with sparking an openness among the disabled and society in general. 'The disabled community is coming of age,' Tony

Coelho, chairman of the US President's Committee on Employment of People with Disabilities, told the *Toronto Star*. 'A lot of folks in advertising and the media continue to portray us as being incapable of having these feelings. This has been very educational. It shows everyone that the disabled have sexual feelings, they're sensuous and they have an interest in their bodies, just like anybody who isn't disabled.'

## Next: Re-emphasis on the Art of Seduction

In the area of love and lust, we're seeing both a rise in silicon sex and a return to the romantic gestures of a slower time.

**Romantic Revival** In *Last Night in Paradise: Sex and Morals at the Century's End*, American author Katie Roiphe argues that young people are floundering in an attempt to give sex meaning again. 'We have all this freedom and an unprecedented amount of equality between the sexes, and we aren't happy,' she explained to a *New York Times* interviewer. Roiphe attributes the popularity of nineteenth-century British author Jane Austen, whose novels *Emma* and *Sense and Sensibility* have been adapted for recent big-budget films, to a nostalgia for romance and a world in which the rules of courtship are clear.

Today, in the States, romance novels are responsible for close to 50 per cent of mass-market paperback sales, generating annual revenues of approximately US$775 million. African-American, Asian and Hispanic women make up about one-third of romance readers, making multi-cultural romances one of the fastest-growing subsets of the genre. As the market has broadened, so, too, have the plot lines; only a fraction of the romance market is composed of the historical or 'period' bodice-rippers of years past. In line with movies and television, romance novels have turned to the nitty-gritty of modern-day life, focusing on such subjects as alcoholism and illiteracy.

The genre is also moving away from such violent images as maidens being ravaged by swarthy pirates and other rogues. In the nineties romance heroines are rarely brutalized. As noted by *US News & World Report*, 'Long attacked by feminists as mind candy for oppressed housewives, the books now are being hailed as happily and unapologetically subversive by a growing group of women scholars.' The typical romance heroines have satisfying jobs and find wonderful men with whom they have consensual and pleasurable sex. While they sometimes struggle, the women always win!

In the fashion world, romance emerged as the overall theme of both haute couture and ready-to-wear collections in 1997 – and continues into 1998 as well. The romantic revival included ruffles, flounces and florals. Period films have fed the frills trend, from empire-waisted *Emma* dresses to the gauzy, ethereal gowns and scarves worn by Kristen Scott Thomas in *The English Patient.* 'It's a little nostalgic,' French designer Agnes Trouble told the *Chicago Tribune.* 'Fear of the 21st century,' she contends, has inspired lovely fantasies of the past as an alternative to the uncertainty ahead. 'We may do the Gap and Banana Republic every day,' says Richard Martin, curator of The Costume Institute at the Metropolitan Museum of Art in New York, 'but we occasionally want something special, some element of fantasy and distinction. Romance is it.'

**Mainstream Erotica** Erotica is all the rage these days, as erotic products are increasingly being embraced by couples turned off by hard-core pornography but whose sex lives need a bit of a jump-start. Products range from videos (*The Voyeur, Cabin Fever*) to audiotapes (*The 10 Commandments of Pleasure: Erotic Keys to a Healthy Sexual Life*) and books (*The Erotic Edge: Erotica for Couples, Real Moments for Lovers,* the *Sleeping Beauty* trilogy from Anne Rice). In fact, the number of erotica books published increased 324 per cent in the first six years of this decade, according to *Subject Guide to Books in Print,* while the overall number of books published increased only 83 per cent. The genre has subdivided itself into everything from first sexual experience erotica to sadomasochistic erotica and vampire erotica. A clear sign that erotica is gaining mainstream acceptance: collections of women's erotica are now available from the Book of the Month Club catalogue.

In an article in the *San Jose Mercury News,* writer Melinda Sacks said erotica 'is all part of the move toward what is being called "hot monogamy" – the idea that people can stay in one relationship for years and still have passionate sex'. Susan Page, author of *Now That I'm Married, Why Isn't Everything Perfect?,* explains, 'Since the sexual revolution, there's been a tremendous increase in our expectations about pleasure. We know it's possible and we have been given permission to seek it out. The alternative to that is to say, "Oh, I'll never have really good sex again; too bad," once the infatuation wears off.'

By indulging in erotica, couples open doors of communication that allow them to share their sexual fantasies and preferences. The genre also serves as an instruction manual, giving couples ideas for new or improved techniques. 'Instead of just groping our way along,' Los Angeles sex therapist and psychologist Dr Susan Block told the *Mercury News*, 'this gives us a chance to observe and learn.'

Sexually speaking, Germany is taking a leadership position. As put by a reporter for the *Daily Telegraph*, 'Leather, rubber, bondage, homosexuality, bisexuality or sado-masochism: You'll never feel the odd one out in Germany – unless you happen to have a wife and two children and are into straight sex.' Theresa Orlowsky and Dolly Buster, Germany's top hard-core porn stars, are household names and appear regularly on TV talk shows. One of Germany's leading public television networks recently commissioned twelve leading film directors, including Nic Roeg, Ken Russell and Susan Seidelman, to make half-hour erotic films and showed them to large audiences on weekend evenings. And nearly every German city and large town has a Beate Uhse store selling an array of pornography, sex toys and lingerie. Owned by Germany's seventy-seven-year-old millionaire of the same name, the stores have sprouted in other countries across Europe, racking up annual sales of more than US$80 million. In January 1996, in celebration of her fiftieth anniversary in business, Uhse opened the Erotic Museum in Berlin. Located on a prime piece of downtown real estate, the museum fills three floors and contains more than 3,000 items.

**Sexy Lingerie** Challenging every woman to seduce herself first, such companies as Victoria's Secret have convinced the female population to upgrade its utilitarian 'underwear' to 'lingerie'. What used to be received as a gift is, today, a purchase made with pride. The UK (long a bastion of sensible undergarments) is among the countries experiencing an explosion of interest in lascivious lingerie. According to the *Daily Telegraph*, even that standard bearer of respectability, Marks and Spencer, 'cannot fight the commercial invasion of sexy underwear, nor the consequent awakening sensuality of British women'. The hottest lingerie colours in Europe? The shock-value palette: scarlet, deep purple and black.

And this trend isn't confined to the West. In China, where advertising of lingerie was banned until recently, items once considered decadent are now eagerly welcomed. In fact, demand for lingerie has been increasing 20 per cent a year in such cities as Shanghai and Beijing and even faster in smaller cities. While many women are used to paying as little as US$2 for a cheaply made bra, German undergarment maker Triumph International estimates that a US$12 bra should be affordable to women making US$100 a month, about an average worker's salary. The market potential is vast: China is home to nearly 400 million women aged fifteen to fifty-five.

In India, the latest fad is the designer bra. Munish Tangri, who runs a thirty-year-old family business in undergarments, told *India Today* that until five years ago, having twenty bra designs in stock was 'more than enough'. Today, even seventy styles is 'too little'. A bra boom occurs in the summers, says Tangri, when young girls seek strapless, deep-cut and well-designed bras to wear under off-shoulder or transparent dresses.

'Silk teddies, satin nightgowns, and lacy two-piece wonders are taking the Arab world by storm,' according to an article in *Business Monthly*, the journal of the American Chamber of Commerce in Egypt. As elsewhere in the Muslim world, an Egyptian woman's daytime fashions are conservative. But in the privacy of her bedroom, a married woman can wear whatever she chooses in front of her husband. Sevel, one of Egypt's best-known companies, began making lingerie in 1986 under licence to the French company Valisère. The *Washington Post* reports that the company saw annual sales climb from US$177,000 to US$3.26 million over the course of 1997.

Evidence of lingerie's crossover to daytime fashion is seen in the slip dress phenomenon. With its slinky suggestion of lingerie, the silhouette has become the profile of the late nineties. Consider what is perhaps the most famous dress of 1996: Carolyn Bessette-Kennedy's wedding gown. Even sexier and more wispy is a definite next.

**Seductive Scents** *Elle Decoration* recently reported that getting in touch with one's sensual side is imperative for maintaining physical and mental health. '50 Ways to Make Your Home a Sensual Haven' notes that humans can identify more than 10,000 different smells. After seven hours of sensory deprivation, the mind slows down and begins to generate its own stimulus: anxiety. In extreme cases, hallucinations and delusions result. The relationship between sexuality and sensuality and scent is being exploited at record pace.

While scented candles long have been a mainstay in homes, those said to have aromatherapeutic properties are grabbing an increasing share of the market. Proponents believe the essential oils (plant extracts) found in such candles alleviate a variety of ailments, from headaches to tension. Some, with such names as 'Seduction' and 'Sensuality', are even touted as aphrodisiacs and 'mood setters'. 'It's part of the growing trend toward pampering [ourselves],' says Susan Rogers of Crabtree & Evelyn. 'People want to be able to indulge themselves in a way that's healthy and stress-free.' Also growing in popularity are fragrances claiming to 'centre the body and mind'. Chakras, for example, is a collection of unisex fragrances that are said to adjust to an individual's body chemistry and induce the various sensations for which the scents are named. Available scents include 'Attraction', Bliss' and 'Fulfillment'.

In coming months expect mainstream status for aromatherapy for men. Already marketed in the UK are such manly mood mixes as 'Aahhh!', 'Brrr!' and 'Woah!', male-oriented treatments designed to tackle stress, promote relaxation, or create a positive attitude.[1] In the men's fragrance market, anticipate the migration of sampling efforts from the department store into such places as high-traffic commuter venues and sports events.

Which leads us to another next . . .

## Next: the New Man

Meet the new man. He works out. He's attentive to his choice of clothing. And he may well patronize a beauty salon, makeup counter or plastic surgeon's office. Make no mistake: this is no girlie man. He simply enjoys looking good and feeling sexy, and appreciates the very tangible rewards that come with each. Increasingly, he feels no need to apologize for his commitment to self-preservation, pampering and perfection. Narcissus is pleased.

'Men's fashion is coming up in the world,' says model Malcolm Kelly, who appeared in a prestigious campaign for Armani. 'There's now much more emphasis on the whole culture of vanity for men.'[2] Sex and the modern male is on the agenda of the fall menswear season,' reported the *International Herald Tribune* in 1997. 'After a period of Plain John fashion – minimalist sportswear cut on straight lines – the peacock male is back. But designers who catch the spirit have a fresh take on sexuality, which is absorbed into the cut or the strokeable fabrics . . . ''It's buttoned-up sex – quite classical,'' said [Gucci designer] Tom Ford.' To help men achieve their desired look Under Wears, a New York store devoted solely to men's undergarments, sells a variety of shapewear. Customers can achieve faux firming through girdle-like briefs or augment their form with built-in 'bottoms' in the rear or 'endowment panels' in the front.

For new men, clothing is just part of the picture. At Joseph's, a London men's shop that opened in autumn 1997, proprietor Joseph Ettedgui promotes 'conceptual living'. The *Independent* reports that Joseph's clientele is urged to 'pick an attitude and a lifestyle and go for it'. For each segment of Joseph's broad target market – encompassing ad exec to yuppie, pop star to footballer – the store sells not only clothing, but also the requisite props: furniture, accessories, books and luggage. Expect a variety of style programming to speak to this rapt male audience via drivetime radio shows, Websites with fashion sense and twenty-four-hour direct TV channels.

Makeup, too, is bridging the gender gap. (Two famous examples: rocker David Bowie sporting eyeliner, and basketball star Dennis Rodman's eye shadow.) In the US, nail polish manufacturers are courting the male mass market with promotions and products. Urban Decay advertises its unisex colours in *Rolling Stone* and *Spin*; Hard Candy has launched Candy Man; and OPI features men in its ads for colourless Matte Nail Envy. As Urban Decay creative director Wende Zomnir explained to the *LA Times*, 'Guys these days are really breaking out into their own. You can see it with fashion and now you're seeing it with their grooming habits, which isn't just about getting a haircut.'

And where there's makeup, there's skin care. Men are hydrating, cleansing, exfoliating and self-tanning at record pace. Estée Lauder's Lab Series for Men, Clinique Skin Supplies for Men, and Technique Pour Homme from Chanel are but a few of the prestige lines of skin care products for men. Though typically less flashy than David or Dennis, the Average Joe is contributing to a decided boom in men's cosmetics and toiletries. Euromonitor estimated 1997's sales values for select men's markets as follows: US\$3.5bn; Japan, US\$1.9bn; Germany, US\$1.6bn; France, US\$1.5bn; UK, US\$1.1bn; Italy, US\$0.9bn; and Spain, US\$0.6bn.

In Japan, research by Shiseido indicates that 65 per cent of men under age thirty have bleached their hair, 38 per cent have had their eyebrows shaped and 32 per cent have applied a facial pack. When Shiseido introduced the market's first eyebrow-shaping kit for men (complete with eyebrow pencil) in 1996, the first-year sales target was surpassed in just six months!

For guys in need of a total overhaul, male beauty salons now deliver

head-to-toe treatment. Services offered by Marc Delacre in Paris, for
instance, range from the traditional manicure to the decidedly non-
traditional dyeing of chest hair. Initially intended as a sideline, beauty
treatments now account for 60 per cent of turnover. A salon in Madrid
offers five-hour courses on discreet makeup for men. Look for high-end
men's stores to provide facilities to manicure and beautify those who
aren't quite secure enough in their new-manhood to visit a beauty
parlour.

In recent years, men's interest in looking and feeling younger has
also accelerated. At the most basic level, this translates into maintaining
their personal health. (Monthly readership of *Men's Health*, a US magazine offering health and beauty tips, now approaches 500,000.) On a
superficial level, the cosmetic surgery industry is appealing not to male
boomers' vanity, but to their concerns about job performance. 'If you
are the head of a company, you are supposed to be on top of things,
and part of that, for better or for worse, is your appearance,' wrote
William J. Wolfenden, Jr. in *Forbes ASAP*. 'For men [plastic surgery] is
an investment that pays a pretty good dividend.' According to the
American Academy of Cosmetic Surgery, men accounted for about 21
per cent of aesthetic surgery patients in 1996, up from 14 per cent in
1992. Men's most common reasons for choosing cosmetic surgery are
1) to improve self-image, 2) to enhance career, 3) to keep up with
peers who have had cosmetic surgery, 4) because they recently have
become single, and 5) strong influence from spouse or significant other.[3]

## Next: Courting the Homosexual Consumer

One of the big sex-related stories this decade has, of course, been the
gay rights movement. As homosexuality makes its way out of the closet,
big business (particularly in Europe and North America) is responding
to what the British press has called 'the power of the pink pound'.
London, for instance, which some consider the gay capital of Europe,
now offers a vibrant social life, a cohesive gay community – and new-
found business and marketing opportunities. *Wall Street Journal Europe*
reports that the number of gay bars in London has grown to 107, from
just 38 in 1981. Bass Taverns, the retail unit of UK drinks-and-lodging
giant Bass PLC, has created an entire unit to spearhead efforts to reach
the gay market. Of the 2,800 pubs it owns nationwide, Bass now has 28
gay pubs, which it attempts to staff with gay managers and bartenders.

The travel industry has also zeroed in on gays and lesbians as a lucrative niche market. The International Gay Travel Association (IGTA), which has grown to include 1,200 members from just twenty-five in 1983, estimates that its member travel agents spend approximately US$1 billion a year. Fodor recently published *Gay Guide to the USA*. The publication follows research in the US that found that gays and lesbians spend more money on tourism than does any other consumer group. Fodor is also considering publishing gay guides to European cities.

Worldwide, images associated with gay men and lesbians have become increasingly prevalent in print advertisements for products ranging from Absolut vodka to American Express travellers checks, from Subaru automobiles to Gardenburger vegetable patties. Television spots feature same-sex couples, celebrities known to be homosexuals, drag queens and even a transsexual or two. Michael Wilke, reporter for *Advertising Age*, has collected close to 100 commercials from around the world that feature or evoke homosexual imagery. Some were spotlighted in the *New York Times*. Among them:

- An Australian commercial for Domestos, a spray cleaner sold by Unilever Plc, features a character who resembles the transsexual in the film *Priscilla, Queen of the Desert*. The spot ends with the character declaring a bathroom cleaned with Domestos as 'fit for a queen'. (Ad agency: Ammirati Puris Lintas; Sydney, Australia)
- A commercial for Diesel jeans focuses on a training class at a fictional Scout camp. As a handsome young man performs mouth-to-mouth resuscitation on his older, bearded Scoutmaster, images of a pretty young woman flash on screen. The spot ends, however, with the Scout and the Scoutmaster galloping off together on horses – and the older man winking at the camera. (Ad agency: Paradiset DDB; Stockholm)
- A spot for Imperial Car Hire, a South African auto-rental company, depicts two men driving along a highway. One exclaims: 'I love you. I need you. I have to have you.' The other man looks askance. Then these words appear on screen: 'Hands-free phones, soon in all our cars.' (Ad agency: Hunt Lascaris/TBWA; Sandton, South Africa)

## Next: Puritanical Backlash

As sexual images become more blatant and homosexuality more upfront, we've seen the expected resistance from those who prefer that sex – and sexuality – remain behind closed doors. We expect these forces to gather even more strength in the months and years ahead.

**Them vs Us – Battle Lines are Drawn** Although an increasing number of US employers (including IBM, ABC, Coors Brewing Company and Levi Strauss & Co.) are extending benefits to gay and lesbian live-ins, the US is apparently far from ready to embrace homosexuality. According to recently released results of the periodic National Health and Social Life Survey (regarded by many as the most extensive study of American sexuality), homosexuality is viewed as 'always wrong' by 67 per cent of American adults. Same-sex marriages – permitted in Denmark, Norway and Sweden – were banned by the US in 1996. The US Defense of Marriage Act defines marriage as a legal union between a man and a woman and allows states to refuse to honour same-sex marriages performed outside their boundaries. While states can legalize gay marriages, such unions will not be recognized by the US government for taxation or other purposes.

The battle is being waged on the consumer front as well. Delegates at the Southern Baptist Convention voted to boycott Walt Disney Co. because of its alleged 'anti-Christian and anti-family direction'. Complaints brought against Disney by the 15 million-member group include Disney's provision of health benefits to partners of its gay employees, its refusal to block gay/lesbian groups from holding events at Disney theme parks, and the fact that it allowed the title character of the TV sitcom *Ellen* to come out of the closet (ABC is owned by Disney). Southern Baptists are the largest Protestant religious denomination in the US.

**Naughty's not Nice** While upscale lingerie is entering a new era of desirability, advertisers must be careful that messages don't conflict with public conservatism. The tales of woe are many: when an advertising slogan for Gossard's underwear (UK) queried, 'Who said a woman can't get pleasure from something soft?' – critics termed the slogan 'lewd and inappropriate'. Deemed too sexy, US television networks banned lingerie ads featuring model Claudia Schiffer. Franchisees of the Holiday Inn hotel chain forced the parent company to cancel a commercial featuring a busty transsexual: the ad ran only once, during the 1997 Super Bowl. In Mexico, a billboard for Playtex Wonderbra found itself at the centre of a national controversy about public morality. The ad, which drew no criticism in Europe and the US, featured a blonde whose ample bosom is barely contained in a satin brassière. The caption: 'I like what you're thinking.' Citizen complaints led to an ad overhaul.

For many critics, it's a matter of morality. In 1996, Bruce Gyngell, one of Britain's most senior broadcasters and managing director of Yorkshire-Tyne Tees Television, told an audience of TV execs that they should not be afraid to censor. 'We broadcasters have that duty – to consider what we put out, to ensure that it does not undermine society as a whole,' said Gyngell, who has banned such programmes as *The Good Sex Guide* and *God's Gift*, a late-night dating game, from the Yorkshire region.

Even in 'private matters', people are increasingly expected to display a certain amount of reserve. Chicago psychiatrist Jennifer Knopf told *Newsweek* that she has observed a 'renewed commitment to conservatism and family values' among her patients, adding: 'I'm seeing less of the kind of affairs or flings that are wild and unpredictable . . . They're appearing to be more thoughtful. If there is such a thing.' And Silicon Valley family therapist Jean Hollands reported that for a man to be caught with a female colleague or hooker 'is not a sign of virility anymore, but a sign of stupidity'. A few years ago, writer Adam Gopnik noted in the *New Yorker*,' [The French] are in the midst of a nicely turned sex-and-power scandal . . . centering on Princess Stephanie of Monaco, who wants to divorce her husband because he was photographed in the nude embracing a *strip-teaseuse* . . . What troubles people, though, apparently including Stephanie, about this matter isn't the *strip-teaseuse* but the recklessness. "Didn't you think it was imprudent to make love at the edge of a swimming pool?" a tabloid reporter asked Fili.'

Those who successfully walk the line between desirability and conservatism can realize a significant upside. When Frederick's of Hollywood – once the purveyor of everything tawdry – threw out the see-through synthetics and peek-a-boo nighties, it opened the door to the mass market. 'Women in the US wanted sexy lingerie, but they were intimidated by Frederick's,' said spokesperson Ellen Appel. After dropping 'everything a basically conservative public might consider offensive', sales soared from US$49 million in '86 to US$150 million in 1996.

**Campaigning for Premarital Abstinence** A growing number of campaigns are spreading the word that it's OK (and perhaps even better) to preserve one's virginity. In 1993, conservative Christians responded to the rise in teenage pregnancy and promiscuity in North America with a major chastity drive called True Love Waits. Hundreds of thousands of young people in the US and Canada signed the organization's agreement, pledging to refrain from intercourse until marriage. The Canadian 'Challenge Team', an unrelated drive, uses trained university-age volunteers who spend about six weeks each year talking with Canadian teens about chastity. Funded by private donations, the team visits approximately 400 schools each year, and has had requests to appear in California, England and Ireland. The presentation asks teens to wait until marriage before they have sex, not because 'God says so,' but because it's what's best for relationships. And in 1997, the administration of US President Bill Clinton announced a US$250 million campaign aimed at telling Americans that sex before marriage is 'likely to have harmful psychological and physical effects'. The primary target is minority and low-income communities in which women are likely to have children before marriage.

The high-profile push for premarital abstinence may be paying off. Surveys reveal that sexual activity among American teens has declined for the first time since 1970. Two federal studies show that among girls aged 15–19, the number who had 'gone all the way' fell from 55 per cent in 1990 to 50 per cent five years later, and dropped from 60 to 55 per cent among boys. These studies were followed by a national survey of more than 200,000 teens for *USA Today* in which a majority said that a teenager should be eighteen years old before being sexually active. Thousands contended that sex should wait for marriage.

Ronan Keating, the twenty-year-old lead singer of Irish boy band Boyzone, has endeared himself to young, female fans by going on record as a virgin. 'I'm waiting for the right person,' he told the *Daily Telegraph*, 'and I would like to think that I would only sleep with the woman I marry.' Ronan is not the only virgin of celebrity status. In recent years, rocker Juliana Hatfield and MTV veejay Kennedy have come out as virgins, as has NBA star A. C. Green, founder of an athletes-for-abstinence campaign.

In Seattle, Washington, Laura Kate Van Hollebeke, a self-proclaimed former party girl, has started the Born-Again Virgins of America Movement (BAVAM), a non-religious support group for what she jokingly refers to as 'recovering sluts'. Any celibate person, even one who has had sex, can now declare herself a virgin – or, in keeping with the terminology of the movement, a 'recycled virgin'. Since making its public debut in 1996, BAVAM has received thousands of letters thanking Van Hollebeke for making abstinence cool.

Interestingly in this age of explicit sexual messages, abstinence, period, is more fashionable these days. In the UK, four out of ten single women aged 16–49 are not having sexual relations, according to a General Household Survey from the Office for National Statistics. 'The idea, 10 or 20 years ago, that you met someone in a pub and then hopped into bed is not so common now,' commented Michele Misgala, spokesperson for the UK's Family Planning Association, in the *Daily Telegraph*. 'There are safety considerations, not just because of sexually transmitted diseases. Women are saying, "Do I know this person well enough to want to take this further?"' Julie Cole, spokesperson for counselling organization Relate, added: 'There has been a great change in women's lives from the 1950s when the expectation was that you would marry and have children. In the 1990s when there is a great range of choice – careers, marriage, relationships, children, part-time work, in every permutation – there is a multiplicity of choice for women. Not having sex is one of those choices.'

A decrease in intercourse does not, however, necessarily spell the end of sexual relations. Oral sex – perceived by some as less intimate and less risky than intercourse – has become a commonplace initiation into sexual activity among American teens. Pregnancy is avoided, virginity is preserved, and many teens (incorrectly) believe that they needn't take any precautions against AIDS. One study among Los Angeles high school students found that 10 per cent of those who were still virgins had engaged in oral sex, and boys and girls were equally likely to be the receiving partner.

# [8]

# Family Styles

What constitutes a 'family'? A couple of decades ago, that might have seemed like a trick question. Everyone knew that a family was made up of a man, his lawfully wedded woman and one or more legitimate children. Today, that traditional nuclear family is becoming more and more uncommon. We're seeing a rise in single parenting and in 'blended' families, with 'his kids' and 'her kids' shuttling between two or more households. And these trends are felt throughout the developed world. Unwed motherhood is a bona fide option for today's woman. More than one in three French babies are now born out of wedlock, one of the highest rates in Europe and equal to that of the US. Outside traditionalist Catholic circles, illegitimacy no longer carries a stigma. In Scandinavia, in particular, we note an acceptance of unwed couples with children. It doesn't appear at all uncommon for couples to cohabit and to have and raise children together without bothering to marry. In the case of some couples, it would seem that marriage is greater cause for concern than parenthood.

In some ways, we're seeing a new flexibility in family life. Today, many people consider it perfectly acceptable for a lesbian to have a child via in-vitro fertilization or for a single man to adopt an infant. Surrogate parenting is becoming more common, and the upper limits to a woman's childbearing years appear to extend further with each passing year. We're also seeing some flexibility in sex roles, as reflected by the growing number of stay-at-home dads.

At the same time, today's families are facing new demands. In addition to the career and household pressures they feel, parents are raising children in a time when drugs and youth violence are common-place. With increased evidence that the youth of the world are in dire straits (or at least maturing at hyperspeed), politicians, sociologists and others point fingers of blame in any number of directions – violent TV programmes, sexual content on the Internet and explicit song lyrics, among others. But there is one segment of the population upon which the ultimate responsibility is placed most often: parents.

Why is it so difficult to raise children these days? Some criticize dual-career couples who entrust others to care for their children instead of taking on the responsibility themselves. In the US, for instance, about one-third of the estimated 10 million preschool children are in some type of organized daycare facility, up from a quarter of the preschool population just a few years ago. An additional one-fifth of kids are cared for either in the home of a non-relative or by a babysitter, and about half of US preschoolers are cared for by relatives other than the parents.

The issue of how we are raising our children will be a hot topic well into the next millennium. The remainder of this chapter outlines some of the other trends we're seeing among families today.

## Next: Women Divided

On the home front, women are facing potentially overwhelming pres-sure to succeed as wives and mothers *and* as wage earners. In the eighties, the media played up the idea that women had every chance of doing it all. They could run a corporation, be perfect mothers and keep their men begging for more (whether it be sex or their chicken and dumplings). In the nineties the game is up. For most women life is simply about juggling, about attempting to find some sort of balance they – and their families – can live with.

The think-tank Demos recently released findings from two national surveys of more than 3,000 British women in its report 'Tomorrow's Women'. The results point to one of the major consequences of the demands facing modern-day women – a widening gap, not between men and women, but between women of varying lifestyles. According to the report, conflicting needs and opinions will drive a wedge between women with children and those without, between single women and those who are married, between the highly educated and the lesser educated, and between the various generations of women.

Helen Wilkinson, co-author of the report, commented: 'If women's expectations are not met; if new opportunities are not matched by policies to enable women to balance careers and family; and if the barriers to less skilled women are not overcome ... then the gaps in pay and opportunities could widen once again; the frustration experienced by less-skilled women could explode; and a return of traditional values could push women back into the home.'

It's a dramatic scenario, but it represents just one of many possibilities that may alter the shape of families in the years to come. As women and men adjust to the new world order, they're establishing new parameters for relationships, families and parenting.

## Next: Childfree by Choice

The recognition that it may not be possible to 'have it all' is leading a growing number of women to opt for career over family. More than 25 per cent of American women aged 30–34 were childless in 1990, compared with only 16 per cent in 1976. And fully 22 per cent of women born between 1956 and 1972 will never have kids, a higher rate than at any other time in US history. Fighting the so-called 'tyranny of parentism' is the ChildFree Network, a nationwide support group of about 2,000 adults committed to the proposition that it's possible to have a perfectly fulfilling life even if one doesn't have children.

In Western Europe, decreased female fertility rates are already cause for concern, particularly in light of the fact that a shrinking population will exacerbate the economic burden caused by the rising proportion of elderly citizens. Demographer Jean-Claude Chesnais, in an article in *Population and Development Review*, suggests that raising the status of women in affected countries may be a precondition to increasing fertility rates. He notes that Italy, where benefits for children have been slashed in the past couple of decades and women continue to struggle to gain equality at work and at home, has seen its fertility rate fall from 2.4 children per woman in the early 1970s to 1.2 in the late nineties. In Sweden, where some 85 per cent of working-age women are employed and women account for 40 per cent of the seats in Parliament, fertility rates have held steadily at 2.0 children per woman, the highest rate in Western Europe. Social benefits in Sweden include childcare services and paid parental leave for both parents.

## Next: Building a Household 'Team'

One result of parents struggling to juggle responsibilities at work and home is increased dependence on outside helpers. Around the world, all manner of businesses are popping up to provide a vast array of family-oriented services. In the US, for instance, some daycare centres offer the convenience of dry-cleaning drop-off and dinners 'to go'. Ann reports that in Tampa, Florida, The Perfect Task offers house sitting, pet sitting, shopping, errands, gift wrapping, home organization, cheque writing, bill paying and computer work, among other services. Also in Tampa is a business called Rent-A-Husband, providing handyman services and household repairs.

A growing number of parents are taking to heart the African proverb 'It takes a village to raise one child.' In an era in which a decreasing proportion of families remains in one place from generation to generation, there can be far less reliance on 'parenting' assistance from grandparents, aunts and uncles, and other relatives. As a result, some parents are creating their own networks of helpers and nurturers. The following is an excerpt from an open letter than ran in the Dutch daily newspaper, *de Volkskrant*:

> We had children and they didn't. Such was destiny's decision and it was OK. Our friends, who lived around the corner, obviously enjoyed our children and cared for them as well. We shared the joys and the burdens, and soon enough they were our co-parents. Which we liked very much, considering the big responsibility with which one must cope – having children – from one day to the other, twenty-four hours a day. Whenever the children were at their place, our friends were the parents and we were visitors. The children were comfortable with it; on those occasions they did a whole lot of fun things, had their own rules, their own friends, toys and rituals.
>
> When we moved to Haarlem, our co-parents demanded arrangements concerning parental access – obviously. Now they lease our children one weekend a month, whether it does or doesn't suit us. The children are used to it and like it. For us it's lovely to have the weekend to ourselves. Except for the occasional weekend that coincides with such family things as Sinterklaas. We bite our lip, to be honest . . .

## Next: Corporate Co-operation:
## Flexitime and Other 'Family-Friendly' Policies

Parents haven't yet figured out how to add more hours to the day, but they are taking a proactive role in determining how their waking moments are divvied up – and more of them are expecting their employers to cooperate. Sus Røedgaard, account planning director. Y&R Copenhagen, notes: 'One of the most important changes we're seeing in the workplace in Denmark is a tendency towards more flexible hours. Telecommuting will be more normal ... According to a study by Andersen Consulting, there are already 10,000 telecommuters in Denmark, and the forecast is for 250,000 telecommuting jobs in the year 2000. The possibilities for flexible hours without fixed time will also grow. People want more flexible hours, and there is a tendency in the advertising business for the best people to go freelance, possibly not to work less, but to be able to work when and where they want.'

Røedgaard reports that retail businesses are also chipping in: 'In Denmark we have a very strict law for closing time in the stores. One of the large supermarkets is at the moment deliberately breaking the law in order to influence decision makers to change the law. I expect the law to be changed in the next few years, so people can shop whenever they like. One of the large supermarket chains has just launched Internet shopping, and it is already a success. People want to have more time with their families and friends and for personal interests, and therefore they welcome initiatives that can make time more flexible.'

In the States, companies are scrambling to be considered 'family friendly' – and the results are often as good for the business as they are for employees. The highest-rated 'family-friendly' company in a study conducted by *Business Week* in conjunction with the Center on Work & Family at Boston University, for example, was First Tennessee National Corp., which began treating family issues as strategic business questions a few years ago. The bank decreased its number of work rules, let employees schedule their own work hours, and instituted a number of family-oriented programmes. The result: supervisors rated by their subordinates as supportive of work–family balance retained employees twice as long as the bank average and attracted 7 per cent more retail customers. According to First Tennessee, these higher retention rates contributed to a 55 per cent profit gain over two years. Other 'family friendly' companies have reported increased employee loyalty and reductions in absenteeism and staff turnover.

Acknowledging the dearth of quality childcare available, the American Business Collaboration for Quality Dependent Care (ABC) – a consortium of twenty-one major corporations, including Kodak, Chevron, Johnson & Johnson and IBM – initiated a six-year, US$100 million investment in sixty-six communities around the US. The money is being used to build on-site childcare centres, train childcare workers and expand services for infant care and elder care. The initiative reflects a growing recognition among businesses that providing assistance with employees' family issues has a positive effect on the bottom line.

## Next: Rethinking Fatherhood

Debate over the role of fathers continues to be heated on both sides of the Atlantic. Recent studies blame absentee or 'disengaged' fathers for numerous problems experienced by children, including substance abuse, high dropout rates and criminal activity. 'Deadbeat Dads' (those not paying child support) are a hot topic in the US at present, although we're also seeing a countermovement among men who contend that child support and custody laws are biased in favour of mothers. One result of Americans' re-examination of the role and responsibilities of fathers has been the creation of the right-wing Christian organization Promise Keepers, which preaches that men must be the 'heads' of their households and assume the economic, spiritual and other responsibilities inherent in that role. Similarly, African-American leaders staged the Million Man March in Washington, DC two years ago to educate and energize potential male role models (fathers and others) within the African-American community.

A Whirlpool Foundation study by the Families and Work Institute with Louis Harris and Associates looked into what makes men and women feel successful at home. The results indicate that, despite the prevalence of women working outside the home, men continue to define their level of success in terms of how much money they bring home, while women look to healthy and well-adjusted children as a sign that they have been successful. Results of the study are as follows:[1]

| What Makes You Feel Successful | Women | Men |
| --- | --- | --- |
| Family/good relationships, spending time together | 26% | 27% |
| Children/good, well-adjusted, and healthy | 22% | 8% |
| Getting everything done/household management | 20% | 13% |
| Caring for family, spouse, children | 18% | 7% |
| Clean/orderly home | 15% | 2% |
| Receiving love/support from family | 9% | 5% |
| Being happy | 9% | 5% |
| Financial/being able to afford things | 5% | 20% |
| Time to do the things I want to do | 2% | 5% |
| Not feeling rushed/stressed | 1% | 1% |
| Having my own place | 1% | N/A |
| Other | 3% | 3% |
| Not sure | 7% | 6% |

Recent anecdotal evidence, however, points to a growing willingness on the part of some fathers to make sacrifices at work in order to devote more time to their families. US Labor Secretary Robert Reich, American Express President Jeffrey Stiefler and actor Mandy Patinkin (*Chicago Hope*) are just three of the high-profile men who have cited a desire to spend more time with their children as a primary reason for leaving prestige jobs.

## Next: Women 'Return' to the Home

We're also seeing increased calls for a return of mothers to the home full time. In the US, at least, women are listening. Recent surveys by the Bureau of Labor Statistics show that a smaller percentage of young mothers are working today than in 1987. A study by Donaldson, Lufkin and Jenrette found that between 1990 and 1995, the number of US families with only one wage earner grew at a rate of approximately 1.8 per cent a year, reversing the trend from the eighties when the number of dual-income families rose. Factors contributing to this trend include a stronger economy (meaning more job security for the working spouse and increased confidence that the non-working spouse can find a job once the children are older) and a desire on the part of younger women whose own mothers worked not to put their own children in daycare. A number of surveys show that young women today are more likely than those a decade ago to indicate an interest in staying home once their children are born. Being an at-home mother is beginning to carry the status of having chosen to place one's children before one's career. It's not necessarily that these couples are in a better position financially to keep one parent at home, but they're no longer willing to have their children pay the price for their economic success.

## Next: Parenting for the Millennium

In addition to coping with changing family structures, today's parents are faced with the unique pressures – and conveniences – of raising children in the Digital Age. Expectations are high. Resources are plentiful. Time (as always) is limited. And the race is on.

**Preparing Children for Life Next** In our increasingly competitive world, many parents worry that they are not providing the essentials their kids need to have an 'edge' in work and life. One result is that more and more parents are turning to products that promise to help their offspring reach their 'full potential' as quickly as possible. The Glenn Doman Baby's Reading Kit, from Love to Learn, Inc., promises to 'provide the vital stimulation essential to increase your baby's intellectual potential'. Parents are encouraged to buy the kit to help their babies 'learn to read as early and as naturally' as they learn to speak. Concerned your unborn child is already lagging behind his or her peers? Enrol your foetus in Prenatal University, a nonprofit organization founded in California in 1979. The course, which is based on the concept that interaction with the foetus 'stimulates brain development and fosters learning in infancy', has had more than 3,000 graduates.

The dedication to maximizing potential extends well into childhood. In the US sales of children's books soared from US$336 million in 1985 to US$1.36 billion in 1995. And in China, the first parent-financed school has opened in Beijing. In a country in which 260 million children face what child psychologist Feng Quihua terms 'killing competition' in school, parents are eager to give their children the sort of edge a private school can provide. To make up for perceived inadequacies in their children's education (China currently spends just 3 per cent of its GNP – approximately US$0.60 per child – on education), parents in that country spend, on average, 40 per cent of their income on educating their children, including cultural excursions.

Children's museums have become increasingly popular in the US and Europe. Based on the learning theories of twentieth-century child psychologist Jean Piaget – that children learn by interacting directly with their environment in developmentally appropriate ways – 200 dedicated museums for children already exist in the US and 100 more are in the works, according to *Business Week*. In Amsterdam, efforts to draw children to museums include quarterly 'free days' at participating museums, and the New Metropolis, a museum that includes a hands-on experience for children. Participatory activities in children's museums around the world include such things as simulated archaeological digs, climbing structures and exhibits set up to engage children's senses of sight, sound, smell, taste and touch.

Between academics, karate, piano lessons and the like, it's not at all unusual for today's youngsters to be scheduled for sixty hours a week. The result: Hurried Child Syndrome. Recently cited as a prime example was seven-year-old pilot Jessica Dubroff, who died while attempting to fly a light aircraft across the US. Concerned parents can now order a six-part audiocassette collection entitled *Helping Your Child Manage Stress, Pressure & Anxiety* (Bettie B. Youngs, PhD, Family First Network).

The desire to prepare one's child to succeed has also fuelled the tendency to label children academically and developmentally. In the US, programmes for the 'gifted' have multiplied rapidly, as have special classes and programmes for children diagnosed with such things as Attention Deficit Disorder (ADD) and Attention Deficit Hyperactivity Disorder (ADHD). There's also been what some people consider an alarming increase in the use of such drugs as Ritalin to help kids focus on schoolwork and behave more calmly. Parents (and educators) are also paying more attention to various learning styles, such as auditory, visual and kinesthetic.

**Raising Techies** One factor contributing to the premillennial pressures some parents feel is the perceived need to prepare their kids for an increasingly high-tech world. To make sure their children receive every educational advantage, more and more parents are purchasing 'edutainment' products that combine learning and fun. Often, such products are high-tech in nature. Shipments of electronic learning toys, for example, are growing at a rate of approximately 28 per cent a year in the US and reached nearly US$290 million in 1995, according to the Toy Manufacturers Association.

Nearly 40 per cent of families in the US with children under the age of eighteen now own a desktop PC, according to Find/SVP, and an estimated 8 million Americans under the age of fifteen have Internet access either at school or at home. Among PC owners, parents in 90 per cent of households report that their children actively use the PC – usually at the expense of watching TV. Though households in most other countries are not yet quite so high tech, manufacturers are taking steps to ensure that their products are becoming even more appealing to the global family market. Examples include low-priced colour inkjet printers (suitable for printing kids' digital artwork) and computers designed specifically for preschoolers. IBM and the Little Tikes division of Rubbermaid, for instance, have created Young Explorer (US$2,400), a computer housed in a tamper-proof, kid-sized desk with an attached bench. A three-year warranty and Edmark educational software are included. For now, the product is being offered only to preschools, daycare centres and libraries.

Educational software for kids is a booming business, with parents snapping up sophisticated graphics programmes, maths and spelling tutors, encyclopedias on CD-ROM, and many other types of edutainment software. Today, Microsoft's hottest growth area is entertainment and reference titles on CD-ROM. The company's goal, according to vice president Patty Stonesifer, is to provide 'hands-on experiences with engaging sights, sounds, and words [that] will inspire kids to discover their world and become lifelong learners'.

**The Virtual Parent** The very advances that once paved the way for the 'virtual executive' – pagers, fax machines, cellular phones, voicemail, and so on – are now helping to create the 'virtual parent'. 'By keeping you accessible to your family and loved ones,' in the words of a brochure from Motorola, 'pagers free you to go virtually anywhere without fear of being out of touch.' Analysts estimate that more than half of buyers use pagers primarily for personal, not business, use today. Also growing in popularity are personal 800 numbers (allowing kids to call home free) and 'follow-me, find-me' numbers that let family members track each other down no matter where they are.

In addition to communications related to daily household life, new technologies enable long-distance parents to stay in touch with their children, as well. A divorced father who keeps in touch with his son in another state via email, fax and phone even set up a Website (no longer available) in which families could share ideas about long-distance parenting.

Some child-development experts have expressed concern that new technologies are aiding and abetting parents with workaholic tendencies and allowing their employers to increase workloads while still considering themselves 'family friendly'. The experience of the authors of this book has been very different. When in the US, Ira works from his home office in Connecticut. This means he has an opportunity to breakfast with his younger children, drive them to school, and still be at his desk by 9 a.m. Ann and Christy, both parents of toddlers, also work at home. They are available to monitor their nannies' activities, help with crises that may arise during the day (especially during periods of teething!), and simply be a presence in the daily lives of their children despite holding down full-time jobs. Working at home gives them the added flexibility of being able to complete assignments in the evening after the boys are in bed or during naptime at weekends.

Instead of using high-tech tools to connect them to their families, employees can use these technologies to keep them connected with their co-workers, wherever they are. The result is a flexibility that makes overloaded schedules far more manageable and allows us to adjust our timetables to make room for our varied responsibilities.

## Next: Keeping Baby Safe

In an increasingly violent and insecure world, new parents are doing everything they can to protect their young ones from harm. And manufacturers are more than happy to provide the products that will help them do just that. In addition to car seats, baby monitors and cabinet locks, first-time parents are purchasing such things as antibacterial high chairs to ward off e-coli, salmonella and other germs; heat-sensitive bath mats that indicate when the water is too hot; cushion strips for the hard edges of fireplaces and coffee tables; carbon monoxide detectors; Plexiglas barricades for staircases; stove knob covers; and latches to prevent curious toddlers from opening ovens, toilets and clothes dryers. This heightened safety consciousness appears to be paying off. According to the National Safe Kids Campaign in Washington, DC, the number of children who die in the US each year from accidents in and around the home fell approximately 15 per cent (to 2,700) from 1987 to 1994, the last year for which statistics are available.

Today's new consumers in Europe and North America are also renewing their efforts to keep violence-oriented toys and games out of their homes. Toy guns and destruction-based video games are giving way to a growing market in socially acceptable 'edutainment' products. In the Netherlands, a controversy erupted a year or so ago over the introduction of a computer game called 'Carmageddon'. The goal of the game: for the 'car driver' to run over as many animals and people as possible. Outraged parents worked to outlaw the game, but the Minister of Justice ruled that the game, however distasteful, could not be prohibited under current Dutch law.

## Next: Permakids

In the end, parents may discover that their window of opportunity for having a direct influence on their offspring is somewhat wider than originally thought. According to the *Journal of Family Issues*, the majority of men aged 20–24 in southern Europe (Greece, Italy, Spain), western Europe (France, Germany, the UK) and the US live at home. The number of women living with their parents is lower because women tend to marry at a younger age.

In Greece, Italy and Spain, 91 per cent of men and 81 per cent of women aged 20–24 are living in their parents' homes; in France, Germany and the UK, those numbers drop to 61 per cent of men and 41 per cent of women. In the US, 52 per cent of men and 37 per cent of women aged 20–24 are living in their parents' homes.

## Next: Make Room for Fifi and Fido

They climb on to your dinner table, make confetti out of your furniture, take advantage of your hospitality, and leave little 'treats' on your favourite rug. And what do they have to say for themselves? Not a word. Of course not; they're pets, and they can't talk.

They don't *need* to talk. Pets enjoy one of the most privileged positions in human society. The world market for pet food is forecast to reach US$24.7 billion by the year 2000. There are reportedly 500 million pets worldwide, including 178 million fish, 98 million cats, 92 million dogs, 88 million birds and 28 million small mammals.

Why are we so devoted to pets? Everyone knows they're fun to play with (usually) and provide companionship and security, and that owning a pet can teach children responsibility. But the motivations for having a pet around may go much deeper, buried in 10,000 years of cohabitation and hundreds of thousands of years of sharing the Earth.

Many anthropologists and sociologists believe that our love and respect for animals is an integral part of the human psyche, the result of a shared heritage and sense of community that reaches far back into our ancestral past. St Francis of Assisi believed that this heritage was an essential source of life for humans. Perhaps Chief Sealth of Washington state's Duwamish tribe put it best, in 1855: 'What is man without animals? If all the animals were gone, men would die from great loneliness of spirit, for whatever happens to the beast also happens to man. All things are connected. Whatever befalls the earth befalls the sons of earth.'

This sense of connection may indeed be a remnant of *Homo sapiens'* survival instincts and evolutionary origins. Because the flight of an animal with more acute senses than ours is a sure signal of danger, the presence of an undisturbed, friendly animal purring in one's lap signals safety. Animals also have the ability to attract our attention outward, allowing us to shift from thinking or processing data to simply listening and looking. According to Dr Aaron Katcher, editor of *New Perspectives on Our Lives with Companion Animals*, the authoritative text on human–animal relations, the act of contemplating animals produces benefits similar to 'the descriptions of the healing effected when people go out alone into nature away from contact with people, away from the familiar round of social activities'.

Humans also enjoy the fact that their pets aren't constrained by human rules. That's one of the reasons they're so fun. Hedonism may come and go in human eras, but it's a constant among animals. Pet owners 'take secret delight in their pets' capacity to express greed, lust, gluttony, anger, jealousy, dependence, dominance and sexuality, which they, themselves, are forbidden', notes Katcher. Put another way, the pet represents the id or inner demon of the owner, allowing us to keep in touch with our 'human animality' which we learn to suppress as we grow into adulthood.

On the other hand, domesticated animals are pretty tame. Most have a strong commitment to predictable daily routines, and pursue the simple life with a vigour that has us bipeds wishing we could hang up our hats and run with the wind – or just curl up in a sunny spot. Pets help to maintain a sense of constancy by engaging their owners in repetitive cyclical activities. When a human is presented with significant and disruptive change, a pet can provide continuity between the past and the present. In today's high-tech, rapidly changing world, it's a comfort to know that Spot will still be scratching to get out of the front door at three in the morning because of a full bladder.

Can pets really be considered a part of the modern family? There's no question that most pet owners consider them just that. According to a 1997 survey of pet owners by the American Animal Hospital Association:

- 61 per cent of pet owners go on car trips and run errands with their pets
- 48 per cent take their pets to visit friends
- 35 per cent take their pets with them on vacation
- 76 per cent say they feel guilty about leaving their pets home alone
- 48 per cent say they frequently rearrange their plans, staying home for the sake of their pets
- 37 per cent think they share personality traits with their pets (though only 5 per cent believe they look like their pets)

**The Pampered Pet** Just as parents are increasingly willing to pamper their kids, so, too, are pet owners more inclined to pamper their pets. It's no wonder that boarding options for pets now extend beyond the standard cage, food and water to include luxurious 'pet resorts'. When Ira and his family enjoyed a ski week in St Moritz last year, their cocker spaniel, Shadow, enjoyed three walks a day and a gourmet dinner for US$40 a night. While Marian was living in Amsterdam, her golden retriever, Morgan, boarded at Yuppie Dog just outside the city whenever Marian was out of town for more than a few days. Among other amenities, Yuppie Dog offers door-to-door service via its own minibus. Marian also noted during her stay at Domaine du Royal Club Evian in France that the room-service menu contained an entire page devoted to pet cuisine. Amenities at pet resorts range from swimming pools and massages to mountain hikes and down-filled beds. In Los Angeles, one resort even plays videotapes of movies starring the dog's owner!

**Pet Gear** As owners increasingly regard their pets (particularly their dogs) as 'one of the family', niche marketers are providing products and services that allow pets to participate in family-oriented activities outside the home. For example, outdoor adventurers can now purchase life preservers, snowshoes, helmets and other equipment for their dogs. Dog owners in parts of North America and Europe can attend a human/canine 'summer camp', where owners and their pets spend a week or more together, swimming in a lake, hiking, playing Frisbee and enjoying a bit of fun in the company of other dogs and their owners.

Pet owners who refuse to leave their little ones at home have created a market for pet-carrying cases. These range from a basic nylon or denim model sold by Pet Pouch of Dallas to a très chic version from Fendi.

We can also expect to see continued growth in the overall gift market for pets, including mementoes, photographs, videotapes, edible treats, personalized bedding/clothing and the like. In the US, major greeting card companies are expanding their selection of pet cards, a trend that's not surprising given that 67 per cent of US pet owners sign cards and letters from their animals.[2] Hallmark's collection of approximately 100 pet-related cards include pet birthday and holiday cards, sympathy cards for bereaved pet owners and birth announcements for dog and cat litters.

**Canine Cuisine** Canines bored with their daily fare can now eat at one of the growing number of dining establishments catering exclusively to their kind: in 1995, Taipei saw the opening of Snowball, its first restaurant dedicated to doggy diners. The canine guests are fed in Plexiglas pens and receive rubber toys to occupy them between courses. Pet owners in New Orleans can take their dogs to Three Dog Bakery, an establishment in the French Quarter that handles dog parties, weddings and other chic canine affairs. A full-time pastry chef ensures that all of the low-fat goodies are up to snuff.

**Elderpet Care** It's not just the human population that's ageing. A million-dollar retirement home is being built on a 60-acre site in the upmarket Hamptons on Long Island, New York. It will feature round-the-clock medical care, sun rooms, recreation areas and on-site companions to care for the 100 residents. Why is this newsworthy? The residents will be dogs and cats. For a one-time fee of US$10,000, pet owners can reserve a place at the Bide-A-Wee retirement home for their pets, who will live in pampered comfort until they go to that great kennel in the sky. 'The home is for animals whose owners die,' said Julia Maucci, a spokesperson for the Bide-A-Wee Association, a charity that runs three animal rescue shelters in Manhattan and Long Island. 'Many people are worried about what will happen to their dogs and cats. Our home guarantees the cats and dogs will be cared for and loved for the rest of their lives.' According to the *Daily Telegraph*, the retirement home has already received more than 2,000 enquiries.

**The Healthy Pet** It's not at all unusual these days to hear of dogs and cats having open-heart surgery, kidney transplants – even orthodontic braces to correct overbites. And for the depressed pooch: Prozac, of course. In the US alone, consumers spend in excess of US$7 billion a year on medical care for cats and dogs. Pet medical specialists include dentists, cardiologists, neurologists and chiropractors. Not surprisingly, this increased care has opened up a new market for medical insurance. VPI Insurance Group, the leading pet health care insurer in the US, has sold half a million policies. The company is predicting revenues of nearly US$10 million per year by the end of the nineties. Another option for owners is healthcare credit cards for pets. These high-interest cards provide a line of credit and long-term payment options for owners faced with unmanageable veterinary bills.

As improved health care leads to a longer life expectancy for house-hold pets, we can expect to see an increased population of older dogs and cats. This, in turn, will lead to a growing market for specialized foods, medications and pet care services. The market for nutraceuticals, homeopathic and other 'alternative' healthcare products for pets is also likely to grow.

Pet owners concerned for their loved ones' health are taking prevent-ative measures to keep their cats and dogs fit. Whereas table scraps were once a mainstay of most pets' diets, consumers are now aware of the need to feed their pets food that is nutritionally sound. 'Health food' has been among the fastest growing sectors of the pet food market. Its popularity mirrors a similar trend in the human food market and is probably spurred on by the same concerns for health. Two areas to watch: low-sodium pet food with no preservatives and vegetation food marketed for pets that have either dietary restrictions or vegetarian owners opposed to living with a carnivore.

In fitness-crazed Los Angeles, pet owners have gone one step further. At Total Dog, corpulent canines can work out on specially designed treadmills, swim laps in the pool, or take a turn at the obstacle course with a full body massage at the end. It all costs owners as much as US$800 a year.

# What's Next?

**Postponing Motherhood** According to a study by the Guttmacher Institute, far fewer girls these days are becoming mothers before turning twenty. This is particularly true in Asia, North Africa, the Middle East and parts of Latin America. The report cited improved educational opportunities as one reason for this decline. (One notable exception is the US, where 14 per cent of American girls aged 15–19 gave birth last year. The US rate is double that of the UK, the country with the next highest rate of teenage motherhood.)

**Marriage-preservationists** Giving society's growing concerns over the erosion of family values, it's no surprise that a marriage-preservation movement is cropping up in many parts of the world. Countering the prevailing attitude of the seventies and eighties that divorce is often in the best interest of the children, current research indicates that divorce can have far-reaching and devastating consequences for the children involved. Increasingly common are schemes geared towards helping parents and children cope with divorce. In the US, programmes such as Kids' Turn and Sandcastles use art, role playing and other creative means to encourage kids to talk about their fears and other emotions. In some cases, these are mandated by law. Judges in Dade Country, Florida, for instance, will not grant a divorce involving children until the family has completed the Sandcastles programme.

**Active Parenting** After the 'me' decade of the seventies and the glitz and glamour of the eighties – in the US, particularly – many parents are seeking to return to a 'simplified' lifestyle that focuses on family values. The desire to be proactive in bringing up one's children can be seen in the growing popularity of parenting magazines (e.g.: *Child, Parent, Parenting, American Baby, Family PC, Family Fun*, in the States; *Ouders* in the Netherlands; *Parents* and *Enfants* in France; *Io e il mio bambino* and *Io e mio figlio* in Italy; *Forælde og børn* in Denmark; *Eltern* in Germany; and *Vi Foraldrar* in Sweden), and the high traffic experienced by such cybersites as Moms Online (http://www.momsonline.com) and ParentSoup (http://www.parentsoup.com).

We're also seeing a call for a return to disciplinarianism, a backlash against the 'permissive parenting' of the seventies and eighties. Among other books currently on the market: *Spoiled Rotten: Today's Children and How to Change Them* and *Raising a Responsible Child: How Parents Can Avoid Indulging Too Much and Rescuing Too Often*.

**Health 'Insurance'** Advances in science and technology are making it possible for parents to have their children 'screened' for potential illnesses and other physical problems. Children who are susceptible to depression, for example (including those whose parents suffer from the disorder), can now be identified through specially adapted brain-imaging techniques. Using MRI (magnetic resonance imaging) and PET (positron emission tomography) scans, researchers look for a distinctive pattern of metabolic activity in the section of the brain that registers strong emotions. Scientists have also developed a new vision-screening technology that can help ophthalmologists detect eye disorders in children as young as six months.

**Morality Markers** As societies continue to debate such 'hot button' issues as abortion, working women, gay rights and the like, brands will be called upon to declare their loyalties and leanings. And these companies will be tested again and again as consumers work to ensure there are no exceptions to where the brand sits on the left–right continuum. Some brands will discard images of traditional family life, as other embrace them. New messaging styles will be created to deliver fresh messages that reflect society's move away from traditional life and work patterns into a new multipart format that takes people through each decade of their adult lives.

**Pets by Prescription** Pets can do more than distract us from our everyday stresses; they can help us fight serious physical illness. Doctors have known for years that companion animals have the power to help us recover from illness or depression. This potential was demonstrated by numerous studies in the 1980s, including one that proved that the one-year survival rate of coronary care unit patients who owned pets was significantly greater than for those who did not. Expect doctors to prescribe pets, rather than pills, to patients who need to relax.

# 9

# @Home

The changing lifestyles and preferences of modern consumers are having an evolutionary effect on the home environment. Not long ago, builders and architects could comfortably make certain assumptions about family size (mother, father and 2.5 kids) and home function (a dwelling for sleeping, eating, and entertaining). But the nineties family is a testament to diversity, and such categorizations may no longer apply. The function of the modern home is expanding as well. In a wired world, it serves as both home and office. In an uncertain world, it has become a haven. On the macro level, an attempt to cultivate community has resulted in a unique blend of reaching out (new urbanism) and walling off (gated communities).

In 1923, Zelda Fitzgerald told the *Baltimore Sun*, 'The home is the place to do the things you want to do.' Today, home is also the place to do the things you have to do. In this chapter, we present an overview of trends currently affecting the home environment. If you're looking for a rundown of preferred colour schemes in modern kitchens, we respectfully refer you to the nearest magazine rack. We've opted to focus instead on trends that show promise of staying with us well into the coming millennium, not just the coming season.

## Next: New Approaches to Home Design
## and Community Development

**New Urbanism** In our work with clients, one of the dominant themes we've stressed in the last two years has been consumers' search for community. As we lose the sense of belonging that used to come with place-based communities, we are increasingly taking steps to create our own specialized communities, be they cultural, based on a special interest, or even developed in cyberspace. Some developers – known as new urbanists – are even trying to replicate the sense of community inherent in yesterday's small towns and villages, albeit with some nineties touches.

Addressing a New Urbanism conference in Austin, Texas, keynote speaker Neal Peirce, author of *Citistates*, observed, '[New urbanism] says to me that people do want some kind of association, and that they're not really happy with the disjointed nature of their lives and contacts. So, what does new urbanism have to do with it? It's permitting us for the first time in decades to think about community as geography – as a physical place. It's reminding us that for all our talk of communities, we've managed to let slip away what may be the most basic community of all: geographic, place-based community, where people have what matters to them most: personal contact made possible through friendlier streets and walkability and variety and personalism.'

Several core principles distinguish the village-style approach of new-urbanist planning: design for density versus sprawl by infilling urban cores or building compact developments; design for pedestrians versus cars, with planning that provides sidewalks and mixed-use development within 'walkable' proximity, supported by a network of narrow streets; design within borders, beyond which wilderness or agricultural uses are preserved; design for ritualized public space, such as pocket parks and town squares fronted by formalized public buildings (e.g., town halls, churches, post offices); design for an integrated mix of income types and land uses – such as low-income housing above retail stores – to diversify, densify and enrich the urban environment; and design to minimize energy waste from needless car travel, thereby reducing air pollution and time lost in transit and traffic jams.

**Green Building** In chapter 3 we cited the trends of pure consumerism and green buying. This desire to protect the planet (and, by extension, ourselves) is gaining momentum within the building industry as well.

Proponents of 'green building' also known as environmentally responsible or sustainable building, utilize such strategies as informed materials selection, energy planning and construction-waste management to ensure minimal negative impact on the environment. As explained in *Architectural Record*, green builders advocate a 'cradle to cradle' analysis of building components that considers the acquisition of raw materials; the processing and manufacturing process; the packaging and distribution impacts; installation, use and maintenance issues; and the potential for disposal, reuse or recycling. At the heart of the green builder movement is an understanding that the world's resources are limited and that utilizing available resources to their maximum efficiency is in society's best interest.

Energy conservation is one of the hallmarks of the movement. Although energy-efficient construction techniques can cost more than traditional alternatives up front, many have the advantage of saving money over the long run. A home that uses less energy and costs less to operate is appealing to most homeowners, regardless of their environmental stance. Techniques currently used to facilitate low-energy consumption include passive-solar design, which pays careful attention to building orientation, direct heat gain, daylighting, shading and well-insulated construction; high thermal mass construction, which retains heat in winter and remains cool in summer; high-efficiency windows, heating and cooling systems; low-energy light bulbs and sensors that switch off lights if no one is present; and the reduction of water waste through use of low-flow and water-conserving plumbing fixtures, xeriscaping (use of indigenous plants in landscaping to reduce watering needs), subsurface irrigation to reduce water loss from evaporation, rainwater-collection systems and cisterns and grey-water recycling (collects, stores and filters water from baths, sinks and showers before utilizing it for such purposes as flushing toilets or irrigation).

In addition to promoting techniques that result in lower electricity and gas bills, green builders also attempt to reduce 'embodied energy', which includes the power used to manufacture a building's components and to transport them to the building site. In Britain, for example, it's estimated that embodied energy may account for nearly a sixth of national energy consumption. Products and techniques that involve less manufacturing (e.g. reused roof tiles, demolition brick) or are locally available (e.g. earthen construction) require much less energy, so their use reduces the strain on the environment.

At present, green products typically cost more than their traditional counterparts. As demand increases, however, environmentally friendly alternatives are expected to become more affordable. Some building-materials retailers already specialize in used and/or environmentally sound products. In Boulder, Colorado, two green stores generate US$1 million per year: Planetary Solutions is a decor-oriented showroom for flooring, painting and wallcovering products; its sister company, Eco-Products, is a lumberyard.

As more of the earth's resources are depleted, the sustainable approach to building and development is viewed increasingly not only as possible, but necessary. Commitment to sustainable building is evident on many levels, from government agencies to nonprofit groups, from products manufacturers to architects.

- Earthen construction (buildings made from dirt) is being widely explored in both Europe and North America. An experimental village of thirty-five earthen houses, Domaine de la Terre, was recently built near Lyons, France. And in the Margaret River area of Western Australia, almost 20 per cent of the homes being built use stabilized-earth technology.
- To aid prospective buyers in the assessment of a 'green' home, Austin, Texas founded the United States' first city-funded green builder certification programme in 1992. Builders participate voluntarily. Last year the programme certified 471 of the 2,821 new homes in the city.
- In the UK, the Ecology Building Society in West Yorkshire has issued around 500 mortgages. Lending decisions are based on the perceived environmental impact of projects, with preference given to borrowers who intend to renovate older properties or build new homes that are energy efficient.
- In Temple Bar, the recently rejuvenated 28-acre area that comprises the heart of Dublin, one of the most sought-after addresses is the Green Building. The innovative residence sports roof-mounted solar panels and wind turbines that generate most of the energy the building and its residents require. Five artists contributed to the building's design, which includes a sculptured door that is a showcase of recycled objects such as old inner tubes.
- Machynlleth, Wales, home to the Centre for Alternative Technology, boasts phone booths powered by wind and sun,

urinals kept sweet-smelling by plant extracts, a railway with a regenerative braking system and energy-efficient homes.


**Flexible Housing** As noted by Andrea Saveri, director of the Institute for the Future in Menlo Park, California, 'A lot of [home] purchasing in the past has been based on an old paradigm of what constitutes a traditional household and traditional jobs. All of that is breaking down. If you get multiple people in the house doing different things, the reality of day-to-day life is very different than it was twenty years ago.' Perhaps stemming from a belated recognition that change (in needs, lifestyle and preferences) is the only constant, modern buyers seek flexible and adaptable home design that allows them to live in a given home as long as they like – without incurring costly renovations each time they go through a major (or minor) life change.

The demographics associated with home ownership are changing as the traditional nuclear family becomes less common. By the year 2000, the mother-father-two kids family will represent fewer than 25 per cent of total American households, reports John Schleimer, a market researcher from California. Housing expert Avi Friedman, a professor of architecture at McGill University, notes that '[In Canada] the number of what we call traditional families is now lower than 50 per cent. It's the first time in home buying that marginal groups combined form the majority.'

Tomorrow's homeowners promise to include greater numbers of single women, single parents, empty-nesters and couples with only one child who are looking for small, affordable homes. Conversely, multigenerational families will want larger homes that can be easily renovated to house family members and visiting friends or relatives.

There is also growing demand for homes that can be altered to meet the needs of the elderly. Not only are the realities of ageing catching up with the baby boomers, but, as we noted earlier, a distinct category of people known as the 'oldest old' (men and women aged over eighty) is now one of the fastest growing population segments worldwide. Design trends already common in planned retirement communities are becoming evident in mass-market residential construction, as well. Among them: shorter stair-risers, one-storey homes or two-storey homes with a master bedroom suite on the first floor, maximization of natural lighting (helpful to ageing eyes), use of levers in place of doorknobs and showers equipped with built-in seats. 'Hidden' accommodations also are being made. For example, negotiating stairwells and narrow doorways are just two of the challenges facing anyone with restricted mobility. To increase flexibility in current floor plans, some homes are being designed with 'bump out' floor plans (openings that easily can be enlarged to add more space) or with closets above one another in multistorey homes, making it possible to retrofit an elevator. Other provisions include shelving and counters that are adjustable to a variety of heights; reinforced interior walls which allow for later installation of handrails; prewiring for home automation of security, heating, lighting and electrical outlets; and designing a space that one day can be used by a live-in caregiver.

The advent of the home office has also drawn attention to the need for flexible design. Partitions that can be taken down and/or moved to suit homeowners' needs and preferences are one possibility. Also being considered in advance of construction are communications needs (existing and prospective). 'I think we will soon get panel floors in houses, as we do in offices,' Chris Westhead of Gordon Lindsay Design told *The Times* (London). 'Then we can bring out cables at any point, or change floor spaces whenever we want.' Westhead recently completed a house in London with a fibre-optic backbone running through its six floors, in anticipation of the wireless house.

Planning for the future, a team of professionals at Canada's McGill University has proposed the 'Next Home', and three-storey house in which people can choose to buy only the space they need and can afford. Once buyers decide how many storeys they want, they choose a design layout from a catalogue of choices. 'Homes can be sold the way cars are sold,' says McGill's Avi Friedman. 'In other words, there's no reason to require a single person who rarely eats at home to buy a large, expensive kitchen.' The Next Home is also designed to make moving walls and even plumbing a simple matter.

V. R. 'Pete' Halter, president of Atlanta, Georgia-based V. R. Halter & Associates, predicts that 'Builders who offer design flexibility will command a very strong competitive advantage. I'm talking about production customization, not true customization: taking the basic plan and allowing consumers some flexibility to adapt it to their lifestyles.'

## Next: The Wired Home

**Home Automation** From such humble beginnings as 'The Clapper', a device that allows one to turn lights on and off by simply clapping one's hands, home automation has transformed into a burgeoning industry. Installation of home-automation systems has grown exponentially in the US in the past few years, reports Washington, DC-based Home Automation Association. And smart homes are by no means just an American phenomenon. Puri Casablanca, a development of four condominium towers in South Jakarta, is equipped with an Australian-designed system that lets residents operate their lighting and electrical appliances via telephone. The passive infra-red sensory system turns lights on when movement is detected in a room.

In basic terms, home automation enables people to control monotonous, repetitive events by either time or situation. Consumers typically choose to automate their homes for one or more of four reasons: convenience, energy savings, security or comfort. A survey conducted among 750 affluent American households on behalf of the Consumer Electronics Manufacturers Association found that security was the primary interest of 38 per cent of participants, followed by convenience (23 per cent), energy-saving (22 per cent) and home entertainment (9 per cent).

As reported in *HFN*, the weekly newspaper of the Home Furnishings Network, modern consumers can expect to pay upwards of US$10,000 for home automation that ties together security, lighting, communications, home office, entertainment, environmental controls and appliance operations. Large systems are often electronically programmed with 'modes' or groups of functions. A professional dealer-installer does the programming, but homeowners can create or design their own modes. At the chosen time, for example, a typical 'good morning' mode might turn on designated lights, adjust the thermostat, activate the hot water heater, and start brewing coffee. Systems are accessed through the telephone, video remotes, home computers and/or keypads.

One of the more affordable dealer-installed home automation systems is Honeywell's TotalHome Control System, which integrates security, temperature, lighting, and appliance controls into one wall-mounted keypad for both new and existing homes. The basic system, which costs US$4,000, includes ten points of lighting, ten security points (doors, windows, or motion sensors), a smart thermostat, two touchpads and a voice module that allows users to control the system from any touch-tone phone.

As the vast majority of homeowners cannot afford to install a comprehensive home automation system all at once, manufacturers now offer simplified systems that perform only one or a few functions. This retail approach reduces the upfront cost-commitment required of consumers, who can then expand systems piecemeal, as finances allow and interest dictates. Already, do-it-yourselfers can purchase software and hardware systems that enable personal computers to program lighting, heating and cooling systems and appliances for daily, weekly or one-time events. While some systems are limited to on/off controls, others support macro capabilities which enable users to program in a series of events based on conditions (e.g. *If* no one is home *and* it's dark outside, *then* turn on the light in the den).

Broadening the home automation industry from custom installations to mainstream products could generate as much as US$2 billion a year for consumer-electronics retailers by the end of the decade. And while home automation is elective in the late nineties, it may well become a necessity in some parts of the world in the years ahead. As energy resources become less plentiful and more expensive, utility companies are experimenting with peak and off-peak usage plans that resemble the day/evening/night rates made popular by phone companies. When such plans are implemented, utility bills will reflect the advantage of running major appliances during off-peak hours (typically 10 p.m. to 6 a.m.). Home-automation technology supervises the turning on and off of appliances, enabling homeowners to sleep undisturbed. Trials of 'energy management systems' are already underway in the US.

**Plugging In**  For many of today's wired consumers, home automation is a nicety. Being connected to the Net is a near necessity. Already family members keep in touch with long-distance relatives via email and children utilize the Web to conduct research for school. Frank Feather, president of Ontario-based Glocal Marketing, reports that multimedia technology and information-highway compatibility is the predominant request in many new subdivisions. In south London, Thirlstone Homes has tapped this interest by wiring several new developments with computer systems. The developer provides multimedia equipment and half a day's computer training for each new resident. In the US, many consumers who custom-build their homes are also taking advantage of opportunities to design an integrated computer network for their new dwellings.

## Next: Home as Haven

Speaking at a design forum in the Philippines, Ilse Crawford of *Elle Decoration* offered the following insights into the modern consumer at home: 'Today's modernity is softer and more sensual; it is tolerant – mixing past with present, personal with practical, handmade with mass-produced. In short, the late nineties consumer wants easy modern living, a home that looks good, feels good and works . . . As an antidote to the stresses of working life, the home has become a place to recharge rather than show off. There is a greater interest in the things that make a home feel good physically, sensually and emotionally – from fantastic bed linen to feng shui, tactile flooring to aromatherapy.'

Increased space is a common goal in new dwellings. Jeremy Myerson, writing for *The Times* (London), recently observed that 'accommodation pressures at work, particularly new office arrangements which force employees into crowded open-plan setups, make the spacious oasis at home all the more alluring. Conversely, the generous proportions of so many new public environments – shopping malls, the giant scale of the new designer restaurants – remind people of what they are missing when they live in properties comprising a series of cubbyholes.' Myerson interviewed architect David Adjaye, who believes the trend towards openness is 'all about creating a breathing space in which people can be inspired'.

As the trend in home design moves to a more open plan – large living/kitchen spaces in lieu of distinct rooms – private spaces such as the bedroom and bathroom take on particular importance. 'While the kitchen is a place of gatherings, a social room; the bed and bath are an area of solitude, of escape,' observes Irene Wilson, divisional vice president and fashion director for catalogue retailer Spiegel. 'It is the place where you can be alone, to exercise, to eat, to watch TV, to read, to do office work, or just to enjoy beautiful bed linens and bath items and pamper yourself.' *Home Textiles Today* reports that in the US sales of sheets, comforters, decorative pillows and the like increased more than 13 per cent in 1997, to US$5.9 billion. Consumers also are buying larger mattresses, creating bigger beds in bigger bedrooms.

High-tech items, which initially contributed to the cocooning trend simply by allowing us to be home more often, now help to make 'home' a nicer place to be. From automatic breadmakers that deliver 'homemade' freshness on demand to online shopping that delivers practically everything else, consumers are becoming accustomed to the idea that high-tech can go a long way towards making a house feel like home. Barbara Caplan, of Connecticut-based Yankelovich Partners, predicts that 'lifestyle fit' will emerge as one of the leading drivers in consumers' new-home purchase decisions. 'Status is becoming more personal,' she notes. 'Instead of ROI (return on investment), people are looking for ROE: return on enjoyment.'

Consumers are increasingly certain that a high-maintenance home is NOT a haven. They want low-maintenance, easy-to-clean homes that utilize space efficiently. Functional items, including candle snuffers, pitchers, bookends and tray tables, have replaced curios as important decorative accents. And maintenance-free exteriors and interiors, achieved through use of materials that afford years of durability and require little or no upkeep, are growing in popularity. Home storage is also key; done well, it facilitates organization and enables people to 'stock up' on home and office supplies (thereby reducing the number of shopping trips). Smaller lawns, which require far less maintenance than expansive spreads, are a selling point among young, busy professionals and older homeowners.

A recent survey commissioned by America's National Association of Home Builders found that features formerly considered luxuries in new homes – high ceilings, pantries, great rooms with bars and media centres – are now regarded as desirables in homes built for average-income buyers. Current trends among the affluent that demonstrate trickle-down promise: old-world mouldings, home laundries with professional equipment such as pressing machines and kitchens equipped with stainless steel counters, a commercial range and an outsize freezer and refrigerator.

Finally: what is a haven, if not safe? Motion sensors, alarms and panic buttons. Hidden closets, bulletproof hideouts and disappearing barricades. The growing obsession with home security has led some to equate modern homes with 'armoured cocoons.' Commonplace in the US and Brazil, 'gated communities' have found a market in the UK as well. Many of these multifamily walled estates employ private security guards.

Until a few years ago, home-security systems carried price tags of US$1,500–$50,000 and were bought mainly by affluent households. Today, alarms start at US$99 or less. In the UK, the security industry has been growing between 8 and 15 per cent a year since 1990, Alex Volossevich, commercial manager for the National Approval Council of

Security Systems, told *The Times* (London). In the States, according to the *New York Times*, only 8 per cent of single-family homes had security systems five years ago; today, more than 20 per cent do (including one in three new homes).

Over-the-top security systems have even become something of a fashion statement. Los Angeles homes designed by Washington, DC architect Hugh Newell Jacobsen, for example, are intended to be as secure as nuclear-bomb shelters. He notes: 'The second an alarm goes off at the first sign of trouble, an entire family can get to a room protected by a steel door, rely on their own generator and water supply and use an unlisted number to call for help.'

## Next: Doing It Ourselves

The modern consumer, with more than a little encouragement from profiting parties, has come to believe that he or she can accomplish almost anything, regardless of experience or talent. Having visualized their ideal space, homeowners set out to create it – by buying it in bits and pieces, building it from the ground up, or growing it.

The pervasiveness of the DIY spirit is reflected in the volume and variety of books targeting do-it-yourselfers. British designer Sir Terence Conran, founder of the Habitat furniture chain, offers tips on how to achieve a cool, chic look in *The Essential House Book. Updating Your Home* recommends thirty ways to improve the way one's home looks and works, from changing a doorway into an arch to ensuring proper roof ventilation. Those with larger projects in mind can choose one of two spiral-bound step-by-step guides from Canadian residential designer and consultant David Caldwell: *Contracting Your Own Home* and *Renovating Your Own Home.*

Feng shui, the Taoist art and science of living in harmony with the environment that has guided the Chinese for centuries in the design of homes and cities, has been heralded as an up-and-coming trend in North American home design. Predictably, a number of books now provide step-by-step instruction on assessing, choosing and designing sites, buildings and interiors. *The Feng-Shui Kit*, by Man-ho Kwok, is one example. The kit includes a feng shui compass with ruler markings, pa kua mirror, a sheet of stickers printed with the names of ruler categories, and a 112-page book.

When it comes to interior design, DIY is so trendy that even those who don't 'do it themselves' want everyone else to think they did. As noted in the *Wall Street Journal,* hiring a decorator is still in among those who can afford such luxuries – but admitting to it is not. The solution? A 'ghost' decorator who designs interiors so subtle and casual that the client can claim credit. 'It's much more 'in' to seem to have done it yourself,' observed a real estate broker in the resort community of East Hampton, New York.

According to the American Express Retail Index, 31 per cent of American consumers were planning some sort of home improvement in 1998. Two-thirds of those planning improvements intended to do the work themselves, with projects ranging from interior decorating (31 per cent) to renovation and remodelling (33 per cent). With an average budget of US$2,660, cost appears to be the primary driver of the DIY trend: if money were no object, 55 per cent of home improvers indicated that they would hire an outside contractor to do the job, while only 35 per cent said they would still prefer to do the job themselves.

Although the implementation of DIY home improvements often remains decidedly low tech, the planning stage has entered the Digital Age. A range of software packages enable computerized DIYers to design their own homes and gardens. Titles include *3D Home & Office Design*, *3D Virtual Reality Room Planner* and *Garden Architect*. These enable users to make onscreen decisions about everything from furniture placement to knocking down walls, without having to actually go through the motions. Some programs enable a virtual 'walk through' of the home, while others estimate the cost of selected home improvements. Gardeners benefit from detailed information about caring for particular plants and also gain assistance in creating an overall landscape design.

Large building-supply and home-finishings retailers, who have the most to gain from the trend, are doing everything they can think of to inspire the DIYer lurking in every consumer. With its popular in-store, how-to seminars and knowledgeable sales staff, industry leader Home Depot has built its reputation on the belief that even the most unlikely of consumers can make such home improvements as building a deck, installing bifold doors and tiling a floor. Lowe's Companies, Inc. (http://www.lowes.com.), America's number-two home-improvement retailer, publishes an e-zine filled with step-by-step how-to guides for projects ranging from hanging a door and installing vinyl flooring to finishing wood. New projects are added each month, contributing to an extensive online archive.

As reported by *The Times* (London), some DIY stores (including Homebase, B&Q, Do It All and Fads) have conducted trials of in-store computer-visualization systems that enable shoppers to experiment with various finishes and design layouts prior to purchase. Among the systems tested was Crown Wallcovering's Wallpaper Wizard, a touch-screen computer system that allows consumers to visualize all types of wallcoverings, from textured wallpaper to paint, in a range of home settings. Interactive Colour Solutions is working with various manufacturers to produce a computer package that provides onscreen viewing of everything from doorknobs to paint in room settings.

Retail groups such as IKEA, John Lewis, Wickes and MFI use a photo-realism system called PlanIt, which was developed by ICADS and can be used to design kitchens, bedrooms, bathrooms, living rooms and conservatories. Within minutes, PlanIt can design a room using a given retailer's stocked range of units. Initial drawings are of draft quality, which allows the system to work fast. PlanIt will also add up the cost of the furniture and produce an itemized quote. Once shoppers are happy with the draft price and picture, the system redraws the image using photo-realism.

## What's Next?

**Green Thumbs** As gardening becomes an even greater preoccupation (more than 37 per cent of US households now have at least one serious gardener), expect to see increased efforts to prune the amount of time and energy it takes to pursue it. Product improvements and more options for online ordering will be available, as will a growing number of leasable, family-sized plots for flower and vegetable gardening in urban settings.

**Good Noise** Noise pollution is an undeniable source of modern-day angst. The opposite of 'bad noise' is good noise, pumped throughout one's haven to make dwellers happier, healthier and more productive. According to *Science News*, a growing body of 'acoustic ecologists' – individuals from such disparate fields as science, history, geography, technology and the arts – are beginning to focus attention on ways to preserve, encourage and multiply the sounds people enjoy. Acoustic ecologists study the effects of technology and human intervention on

the acoustic environment while devising ways to enhance aural awareness and create balanced sonic environments. Can an application of
this science to the home environment be far off?

**Spatial Sanctuaries** In an interview with *Builder* magazine, Watts
Wacker, resident futurist at S R I International, predicted that 'the ability
to find solitude' will be one of the leading factors driving consumers'
new-home purchase decisions in the years to come. In our view, designers will incorporate such peaceful elements as Zen gardens and meditation spaces into both residential and corporate sites.

**Culture Blending**  Mixed ethnicity is in. As they work to create a truly
personal space, we'll see consumers mix and match items from Africa,
Asia, Europe – anywhere and everywhere that catches their fancy.

# 10

# Gimme a Break

With all the talk about how new trends and technologies are changing the business world, it's easy to overlook the degree to which our personal lives have been affected as well. New technologies have reached into just about every aspect of personal entertainment, from the way we watch movies to how we buy our music CDs. They have also affected our expectations regarding entertainment fare and products. No longer are we satisfied with just a few sources of programming or entertainment information. Rather than wait for the Sunday-night airing of Mutual of Omaha's *Wild Kingdom* (as many of us did in the sixties), we turn to the 24-hour-a-day, seven-days-a-week Animal Planet expanded cable channel or pop a CD-ROM on animals into our multimedia PC. Children, who at one time were perfectly satisfied with a doll made of rags, now insist on animated playmates that can laugh, cry, yawn and even urinate on demand. Even such traditional board and card games as Monopoly, Scrabble and Solitaire have been computerized.

Our consumption of movies has undergone particularly significant change. Film fans aged thirty and above remember when we had two choices: we could go see a movie at our local cinema (typically a single-screen venue), or we could wait a couple of years for an edited version to appear on network TV. Today, we can choose to watch a movie at our local multiplex or wait just a few months to purchase it on Pay-Per-View, rent it from a video store, watch it on one of the premium cable channels, or purchase it on video, laser disc, or, most recently, DVD. Those of us who can't wait for a particular film to be released may also have the option of downloading clips from the Internet in advance of the film's opening night. In many cases, we can supplement our movie-watching experience by purchasing the film's soundtrack; buying related toys, clothing, book and other merchandise; and playing a game tied into the movie on our computer or video game system.

The Internet, satellite broadcasting, computer and video game technology and other facets of our Digital age are working together to change the very nature of entertainment around the world. Rather than sit back as passive witnesses, we are being invited into a world of interactivity. One result has been an escalating bid for the attention of members of the younger generations, who quickly grow bored in the absence of fast-paced action and stimulating visuals.

This chapter explores major entertainment and recreation trends that are developing in the late nineties.

## Next: Entertain Us!

They want us. They really, really want us. Retailers, movie studios, restaurants ... you name it. They want our patronage (a.k.a. our money), and they'll do what it takes to get it, whether it means providing play options for our kids or creating special effects that'll blow our minds.

**Eatertainment** American entrepreneurs Peter Morton and Isaac Tigrett couldn't possibly have known what they were unleashing in London in 1971 when they opened the world's first Hard Rock Café. As Morton tells it, he and Tigrett were simply trying to open a restaurant in which people could find a 'decent hamburger'. Just over twenty-five years later, theme restaurants are all the rage, with food very often being considered of lesser importance than the 'total dining experience'. The industry has exploded in the nineties, with the number of theme restaurants in the US rising from fewer than 40 in 1992 (most of them belonging to Hard Rock) to approximately 150 today (representing around twenty chains). In addition to food, the restaurants rake in big bucks by selling merchandise ranging from T-shirts to leather jackets and toys. The Hard Rock Café, for example, estimates that it has sold more than 34 million of its signature T-shirts. The National Restaurant Association (US) reports that more than a third of all table-service restaurants now sell merchandise, with customers spending well over US$5 billion a year on T-shirts alone.

Planet Hollywood (http://www.planethollywood.es/) opened its first film- and TV-inspired restaurant in 1991 and has attracted such high-profile celebrity investors/spokespeople as actors Arnold Schwarzenegger, Sylvester Stallone, Demi Moore and Bruce Willis. In addition to extensive displays of TV and movie memorabilia, the restaurants feature trailers of soon-to-be-released movies, custom-designed videos and a full line of Planet Hollywood products. More than fifty Planet Hollywoods have been opened around the world, in such cities as New York, San Francisco, Barcelona, Berlin, London, Paris, Tel Aviv, Jakarta, Seoul and Sydney. Expansion plans include sites in Africa and the Middle East. The company is in the process of testing Planet Hollywood SuperStores, which will not include restaurants: instead they will carry a broad range of merchandise, including goods designed by Demi Moore and other celebrity co-owners. Planet Hollywood has also entered into a joint venture with ITT Corp. and opened two theme casinos, in Atlantic City and Las Vegas. By all reports, Planet Hollywood Hotel and Casino in Las Vegas is thriving . . .

What's next for eatertainment? With Hard Rock Café and Planet Hollywood both growing passé, expect the next wave of eatertainment sites to be a tad more outré. Possibilities include futuristic restaurants featuring *Star Wars*-like laser battles (waiters vs the customers?) and 'playmate' cafés with aphrodisiac-laden menus.

**One-stop Family Entertainment Centres** As new consumers increasingly demand entertainment options that are fun, high tech and convenient, a growing number of companies and entrepreneurs are developing sprawling entertainment centres that accommodate everyone from young children and their parents to teens and Xers out on a hot date. 1997 saw the Seattle debut of high-tech arcade GameWorks (http://www.gameworks.com/), a joint venture of Steven Spielberg's DreamWorks studio, Universal Studios and Sega. The 30,000-square-foot complex is made up of a series of video arcades, virtual-reality rides, PCs linked to the Internet and performance arenas surrounded by walkways and restaurants on mezzanines. The standout feature of the complex is Vertical Reality, an interactive game designed by Spielberg, which revolves around three 25-foot-high video screens representing a skyscraper. Twelve players, arranged in a circle, are strapped into seats that move up – or down – a pole, depending on the players' success at shooting cyborgs with their cyberguns. The winner gets a shot at 'Mr Big' and a full freefall to the floor. More than 100 GameWorks are scheduled to be constructed worldwide by 2002; all of the sites will be linked via the Internet, so game players can compete against others around the world.

In a Los Angeles suburb, Walt Disney Co. has opened the first of a planned 100 Club Disney centres. Aimed at families with young children, they include multimedia PCs with Internet access, a playground, maze, film studio, arts and crafts centre, restaurant, retail shop and birthday party rooms. In San Francisco, Sony has created an entertainment centre that features a fifteen-screen movie theatre, 3-D Sony IMAX theatre, restaurant, live musical performances, Sony and Discovery Channel theme stores and interactive arcades and play areas designed by children's author Maurice Sendak (*Where the Wild Things Are*). Sony plans to expand the enterprise to cities around the world.

**High Stakes** For many people, nothing is more entertaining than the thrill of risking it all – whether on a sporting event, a hand of cards, or a horse race. Around the world, gambling is enjoying unprecedented popularity, both as an entertainment option and, increasingly, as an 'alternative' avenue to financial success. We see this trend as having its roots in a number of things, among them our increasing demand for 'instant gratification' (who wants to work hard at a dead-end job when a good day at the races could put us on Easy Street?) and the desire for thrill seeking that is a part of many people's reaction to the fears that come with the uncertainties of the impending millennium.

In Australia, 18.5 million people risk in excess of US$40 billion a year at race tracks and casinos, on lottery tickets, and in card machines at clubs and bars – an average of more than US$2,000 for every man, woman and child. With the Aussie government reaping as much as US$2 billion a year in gambling revenue, don't expect the trend to subside anytime soon. In a recent twelve-month period, gambling taxes provided more than 10 per cent of revenue for the government of New South Wales. In Victoria, Premier Jeff Kennett has encouraged the elderly to view gambling as a social activity, even though some are gambling away their life savings.

In the US, some form of legal, regulated gambling is available in forty-eight of the fifty states. Options include state-run lotteries, instant scratch-off games, casinos, horse and dog tracks, video terminals and riverboat gambling. In 1996, Americans spent more than US$550 billion on gambling, a figure, noted *Mother Jones*, that exceeds the revenue from movies, spectator sports, theme parks, cruise ships and recorded music – combined. *Annals of the American Academy of Political & Social Science* identified gambling as one of the fastest growing sectors of the economy in 1998, accounting for around 10 per cent of leisure expenditure.

As gambling takes off, a number of industries are trying to cash in on the trend. The travel industry, for instance, is taking advantage of travellers with cash in their pockets and time to kill, both at the airport and in flight. Two examples: Singapore Airlines uses an interactive video system to allow passengers to gamble while in fight. Stakes will remain small, the airline says, since its objective is to entertain passengers, not to allow them to win – or lose – large sums of money. Amsterdam's Schipol Airport draws passengers into its on-site casino, featuring seventy-five slot machines, a roulette wheel and cards.

Gamblers also are flocking to the Net, leading to expectations that Internet gambling – 'nambling' or 'Interbetting' – will be a US$10bn industry by 2000. Nearly 300 gambling-related Websites currently are in operation, ranging from virtual casinos to magazines and discussion forums. Approximately forty Websites allow gamblers to wager real money on games of chance such as blackjack and roulette, as well as on sports events. Typically, an electronic line of credit is established before bets are placed. Winners are paid via cheque or deposit to credit card accounts; losses show up on monthly credit card bills. Interest is worldwide: fans in the UK, Japan, the US and Russia placed bets with World Sports Exchange (http://www.worldsportsexchange.com) during the 1997 US college basketball championships, according to *Newsday*.

What's next? For a lot of people, treatment for addiction. According to the US-based Council on Compulsive Gambling, 5 per cent of gamblers become compulsive, 90 per cent of whom turn to crime to support their habit. Up to 80 per cent of compulsive gamblers contemplate suicide, and 14 per cent attempt it. A recently released study by Harvard University Medical School's Division on Addictions shows that 3.88 per cent of American teenagers are addicted to gambling, and another 9.45 per cent are problem gamblers. Reuters reports that, over the past three years, the number of people seeking treatment for gambling addiction has quintupled in New South Wales.

## Next: Great Escapes

Delighted as we are with our new and multiplying entertainment options, we can't help but note that our playtime, in general, is increasingly limited. While sitting in a seemingly endless meeting, waiting for a pubescent cashier to finish chatting with her friends, or picking up takeout for dinner (yet again), most of us experience a longing for something different. This discontent has its roots in everything from life/work imbalance and information overload to premillennial tension. Most of us don't have the option of 'getting away from it all' by taking a Grand Tour, renting a lakeside villa for a few months, or quitting our jobs and starting over in a new locale. Instead we make do with short-term fixes, brief respites from the stresses of our everyday lives that allow us to recharge and begin anew. While these 'escapes' often take the form of traditional entertainment – an engrossing movie or a day hike – they also incorporate a new breed of pursuits based on relaxation and rejuvenation.

**Going Retro**  For many young North Americans and Europeans, 'getting away from it all' now means turning the calendar back to what they perceive as a simpler time. Rather than adopt the electronic sound of 'techno' music and other high-tech trends, nostalgic youth are embracing entertainment options made popular in their parents' and grandparents' youth. 'Cocktail chic' is now all the rage in a number of cities, with twentysomethings heading to clubs to listen to Mancini and Vegas-style swing, sip martinis and soak up the lava-lamp-laden atmosphere.

Swing-noir – made famous in the thirties and forties – has also caught on big time. Young men and women are decking themselves out in the fashion of their grandparents (cocktail dresses, zoot suits, two-tone wingtips) and swinging the night away to big-band sounds in the growing number of clubs catering to this hip crowd. Lee Bennett Sobel, publisher of *Lo-Fi*, a 'zine about the American retro scene, explained the swing phenomenon to the *New York Times* this way: 'People are frightened by the coming millennium, and retro culture brings a measure of comfort.' Marc Campbell, owner of New York's Louisiana Bar and Grill, agrees. As he told the *Times*, 'Swing offers a joyous alternative to a generation that came of age during the AIDS crisis and a time when sexuality was hidden under grunge. This is a return to elegance, to touch dancing and wearing your sexuality on your sleeve. Swing is definitely the thing.'

Old pop and rock tunes also have been top-sellers of late. The nostalgia trend has sparked increased sales of boxed-set music CD anthologies, including such top-sellers as the three-volume 'Beatles Anthology' and the two-CD 'James Brown: 40th Anniversary Collection'. The retro trend is impacting on the instruments used in the music industry as well. Vintage guitars are in huge demand, and manufacturers are scrambling to reissue the designs used on old Gibsons, Martins and Fenders. Digital keyboards, all the rage a decade ago, are now being replaced by 'old-fashioned' analogue synthesizers. Yamaha is billing its AN1x keyboard as a 'virtual analog synthesizer, possessing the sound and feel of vintage instruments'.

The 1970s revival, under way for quite some time among trendsetters, has hit the mainstream. Today's retro fashion lineup includes polyester prints, flared denim jeans, navel-baring tops with zip fronts and v-necks, hip-huggers, platform shoes, super-short A-line skirts and floppy collars. In the past couple of years, hit songs of the seventies have been heard in a slew of US TV ads: 'Nacho Man' – based on the 1978 Village People tune 'Macho Man' – danced his way through an advertisement for Old El Paso products; a KC and the Sunshine Band hit from 1975, 'That's the Way (I Like It)', was among the seventies songs recently featured in Burger King ads; and seventies icon Barry White has been promoting Anheuser-Busch's Bud Light and Prodigy. The much-discussed Miller Lite 'Dick' campaign also pays homage to a decidedly seventies look.

On New York-based VH1 cable television network, reruns of *American Bandstand*, that originally aired from 1975 through 1985 have earned a place among the most-watched programmes. 'I've been trying to figure out why the seventies are so appealing,' said Joshua Katz, senior vice president for marketing at VH1. 'And, believe it or not, it's because, despite all the craziness – all the drug use, all the casual sex – people find it a more innocent time.'

In the US movie *The Wedding Singer*, Adam Sandler romances Drew Barrymore to a soundtrack of eighties hits and a backdrop of the decade's barely dead fashions. Is it too soon to wax nostalgic for the decade of designer jeans? In the age of pick'n'mix nostalgia, perhaps not. With the culture of an entire century on tap, trendleaders take inspiration from a vast palate of images and sounds. Consider Jennifur Brandt, twenty-two-year-old publisher of hip LA fanzine *Pesky Meddling Girls*. 'Every day is a different era with me,' Brandt told Associated Press, 'depending on what music I'm into at that time . . . Or if I saw a really good '60s movie the night before, I'll have an insatiable urge to wear hip-huggers or bell bottoms.' That might be followed by a week of forties fashions. Subscribers to Brandt's fanzine range from rocker Marilyn Manson and designer Anna Sui to Warner Bros.

For those with a somewhat more cultured bent, the revival of Jane Austen has provided just the right dose of nostalgic release. Millions tuned into the BBC's six-hour television adaptation of Jane Austen's *Pride and Prejudice* and to big-screen versions of *Persuasion*, *Sense and Sensibility* and *Emma*. What sustains this love affair with a writer whose prose isn't even of this century? 'The cult of Jane Austen, with its nostalgia for a more decorous and polite age, is one small sign [that people are growing sick of a modern-day culture that is coarser, more flagrant, more intrusive, more rude – more in your face],' reasoned *Newsweek* columnist Evan Thomas. 'The flaps over porn on the Internet, the demand for a computer chip that can screen out sex and violence on TV, the competition among politicians to espouse "family values" are all evidence of discontent with our age of incivility.'

**Vacations Redefined** Though escaping the maddening crowd via movies and music continues to be popular, physical escapes are still a draw. The difference these days is that pressures of work rarely allow for a 'proper' vacation. Instead, many of us are making do with quick trips – sometimes without even leaving our desks.

**Virtual Travel** Anyone's who's plugged in to new technologies knows how hard it can be to break away. In an interesting twist, a growing number of workers are using that very same technology to leave behind their business routines – even if only for a ten-minute, mind-cleansing virtual holiday. An Internet itinerary affords the convenience of continent-hopping without the threat of jet lag. From the rowdiness of the Munich Oktoberfest (http://www.oktoberfest-guides.com) to the adventure of an African safari (http://www.safaris.com/baobab), the limits of travel are dictated only by the speed of one's modem.

Those opting for more surreal virtual surroundings can try their hand at any number of fantasy computer games currently available. The undisputed leader at time of writing is Cyan Inc.'s Riven, the sequel to the record-breaking Myst; within two months of its release, more than half a million copies of the game had been sold. 'Riven, like Myst, is . . . an indefatigable argument for distraction,' wrote reviewer Tamara

I. Hladik on the Sci-Fi Channel's Website (http://www.scifi.com). The lush environments, high-resolution graphics, nonviolent puzzle-solving game play and stunning sound effects combine to immerse the player in an entirely new world. 'We don't like to call it a game,' explains Riven collaborator Richard Vander Wende, 'it's a world, and it's a very real place to us.' 'It's a vacation, an immersive diversion,' adds co-creator Rand Miller.

**Combining Business with Pleasure**  Business travellers frustrated by the amount of time they spend on the road are beginning to 'escape' by squeezing family vacations into out-of-town business itineraries. With a growing number of employers covering spousal travel, parents are able to maximize family time while minimizing expense. In 1995, more than 43 million (or over 15 per cent) of all business trips included a child, a 63 per cent increase from 1990, according to Travel Industry Association of America (TIAA). Catering to this market, fully 18 per cent of the American Hotel & Motel Association's 12,000 members now offer children's programmes. Camp Hyatt, for example, offers a range of special activities for children, including such educational offerings as language classes and nature hikes.

**Quick Trips**  Those of us who have a hard time taking even a long weekend are finding 'mini escapes' at local hotels and resorts. TIAA reports that the number of weekend jaunts has jumped 70 per cent in the last decade, and getaways of one to five days now account for about half of all US travel. To capitalize on this trend, France's struggling Club Méditerranée will revamp its operations by focusing on miniclubs, urban versions of its resort villages that one can visit for just a day – or even a few hours. The miniclubs will feature bistros, cafés, logo merchandise and fitness areas in which customers can rock climb or snorkel.

The *Independent on Sunday* reports that young urbanites in London are forgoing jaunts to Paris in favour of weekend trips up the M4 to Longleat Centre Parc, where an 'Executive' chalet, complete with maid service, costs just £88 per person. In the States, high-end hotels are luring customers not with images of romance, but with hard-core shopping, reports the *Wall Street Journal*. 'Only so much romance can occur over a weekend,' noted Richard Chambers of the New York Palace hotel. 'Shopping is something we can provide.' And provide they do.

Many hotels now offer discounts at local merchants, personal shoppers and gift wrapping and delivery. San Francisco's Maxwell Hotel is even less subtle: its lobby is adorned with a bronze statue of a female shopper. The hotel also provides free foot massages for weary shopaholics and, instead of mints, places US$25 gift certificates to neighbourhood stores on guests' pillows. In Chicago, the Ritz-Carlton, which sits atop a mall, sells three times as many shopping-spree packages as romantic weekends.

**Next Destinations** For those with time and money to invest in real-world travel, the *New York Times* has identified the following next destinations: Lhasa, Tibet (for peace and quiet); Tasmania (nature adventures); the Hindu Kush, Afghanistan (skiing); and Cambodia (beaches on the Gulf of Thailand).

Costa Rica-based Temptress Adventure Cruises is pioneering the concept of 'soft adventure' cruises in Central America. These tours are for people who want to visit exotic destinations without the hassle and hurry of plane travel, but who also want to do more than just shop when they get there. 'Our itineraries include cruises to remote, natural habitats where passengers can participate in guided tours through native village encampments, hike through primary and secondary forests and enjoy various water sports in the Pacific Ocean and Caribbean Sea,' says Sandra Jofre, vice president of sales and marketing for Temptress.

**Luxurious Indulgence** Luxurious indulgences are back. And our renewed focus on finery is not limited to the privileged few. Even 'off-the-rack' consumers are treating themselves to the relatively inexpensive props of a more luxurious age: cigars, martinis, pocket watches, forties fashion and the like. What better way to escape the hustle and bustle of our everyday lives?

Luxury needn't involve conspicuous consumption, however. Today's trendsetters are happy to indulge in life's luxuries in the privacy of their own homes. The appeal of a product now has more to do with quality and authenticity than with overt opulence. One example of a company that has successfully mined consumers' twin desires for luxurious indulgences and nostalgic reminders of a simpler time is Lush, a UK 'cosmetics grocer'. Lush sells fresh, handmade lotions and potions in retail outlets designed to resemble organic-food emporiums. Soaps, which are cut from huge cheeselike rounds and sold by the kilo (wrapped in white paper), are made primarily from fruit and vegetable extracts combined with essential oils. The indulgent products (including Skinny Dip, a violet-scented shower gel with cocoa butter chips and white Belgian chocolate) are kept in chilled cabinets to maintain freshness.

**Aromatherapy** Sometimes the best means of escape can be found right under your nose. How many scents can you detect right now? Gannett News Service reports that the average person can differentiate approximately 10,000 scents, and research shows that many of these scents do more than just smell good. 'The sense of smell is located near an area of the brain that's associated with basic urges,' explains Lucinda Patterson, a licensed massage therapist who uses aromatherapy in her Atlanta practice. 'It's a very direct way to affect the memory and emotions.'

Aromatherapy is a subspeciality of herbal medicine and a product of 4,000 years of perfume making. It's practised widely in Europe and Japan, where some medical schools teach students to prescribe essential oils for ailments ranging from depression to premenstrual syndrome, anxiety and rheumatism. Essential oils currently in use to combat stress and anxiety include basil, bergamot, cedarwood, chamomile (Roman), cypress, geranium, jasmine, juniper, lavender, marjoram (French), neroli, petitgrain, rose and ylang ylang. The scent of apricot is used to calm anxious dieters at Duke University's weight-loss clinic. And in some Tokyo office buildings, citrus scents are pumped into ventilation systems to improve alertness and reduce mistakes. The travel industry has been quick to latch on to the aromatherapy trend, as well. First- and business-class passengers on Air New Zealand receive kits containing such aromatherapy products as nasal gel (to combat dry cabin air) and 'switch on' gel, a weapon against jet lag. The kit also contains an eye compress and facial spray mist.

Among the best-known manufacturers of aromatherapy products is Aveda. 'People use scents to create balance in their life,' Aveda massage therapist Carol Venclik told the *Atlanta Journal and Constitution*. 'Peppermint on the temples will wake you up if you're sluggish. And bergamot and tangerine, mixed together, are very uplifting.'

# What's Next?

**Culture Prescriptions?** Researchers in Sweden have concluded that cultural activity may add years to one's life, notes *Forbes FYI*. A team supervised by Lars Olov Bygren surveyed more than 12,000 people about their lifestyles in 1982, 1983 and 1991 and discovered that those who regularly attended movies, concerts, plays, and other artistic events – or rooted for their local sports teams – were half as likely to be among the 850 or so subjects who died during the period of the study. Such activities, Bygren speculates, influence longevity more than do education, income, physical activity or smoking, because they generate strong emotions, which stimulate the immune system. As more and more physicians accept the benefits of 'alternative' methods of healing, expect 'take in two operas/ballgames/plays and call me in the morning' to become a standard prescription.

**On the Fringe** Fringe festivals – thespian fairs made up of small performing companies doing everything from avant-garde performance art to juggling – offer a hefty dose of culture. Because of the relatively low cost involved in producing a fringe show, performers are free to do whatever they wish without requiring approval from funding agencies or boards of directors. According to *Utne Reader*, the movement was born in Edinburgh fifty years ago, when local performers angry about being left out of their city's international arts festival created a counterfestival to showcase their own work. Now the *Guinness Book of World Records* lists the Edinburgh Fringe (which draws more than half a million visitors each year) as the biggest arts festival in the world, and fringe festivals are popping up everywhere from Australia to South Africa and Hong Kong. New York City hosted its first fringe festival in August 1997, and festivals are set to debut in Boston and New Orleans this year.

**Beyond Karaoke** Japan's list of cultural exports is growing: martial arts, bonsai, sushi, cartoons, sentimental songs, tamagotchi. Without a doubt, though, the country's biggest cultural export of recent decades is karaoke. No bar for Asian business folk can hope to do good business without a karaoke system. For self-effacing Asians, karaoke has proved the perfect way to show off with an individualistic fantasy while remaining part of the group. So what's next? Be on the lookout for systems that take the fantasy a step further – not only putting the singer's voice into the mix, but also integrating his/her face into the accompanying video.

**Mood Foods** With all the conflicting information we receive each month on what we are – and are not – supposed to eat, it should come as no surprise that a growing number of people are rejecting health specialists' advice in favour of comfort foods. Although comfort foods vary from country to country, they are almost always connected to one's childhood, to a time when one felt coddled and safe. And now there's scientific evidence that some comfort foods actually can affect us not just spiritually but also physically. 'What you eat can affect your mood – whether you feel up or down,' wrote Jean Carper in *Food: Your Miracle Medicine*. 'There's evidence that people often make unconscious food choices that change brain chemistry and put them in a better mood.' So, while the French may turn to creamy garlic soup (garlic can have a mood-elevating effect), the Chinese may opt instead for chicken soup flavoured with ginger (in addition to having an antidepressant effect, ginger aids circulation and warms the body). Giving new meaning to the term comfort food, tomorrow's 'mood food' will be enhanced with such mood-altering substances as aromatherapy scents and mild stimulants, depressants or hormones.

**Make-believe Consumption** Where overflowing closets and bulging waistlines are the norm, the time may be right for the ultimate in 'less is more' marketing: make-believe consumption. The Associated Press reports that 'conceptual dining' is being piloted in Tel Aviv, Israel, where Café Ke'ilu (loosely translated from Hebrew as 'Café Make Believe') is serving up fat-free, sugar-free, cholesterol-free, substance-free food. *Substance-free*, as in *thin air*. Owned by top-rated Swiss chef Philippe Kaufman, the café charges US$3–$6 for would-be orders of eel mousse, salad of pomegranates (in season), or ram's brain in lemon-lime sauce. It's about the ritual of eating, not the reality. If successful, a franchise will open in New York.

**In-home Theatres** While in-home screening rooms were once the exclusive province of Hollywood stars and producers, they're now becoming a common feature in large homes around the US, regardless of the owner's occupation. These 'entertainment rooms' typically feature a sophisticated stereo and large-screen home theatre system with an overhead projector and multiple speakers. Some of these rooms feature theatre-style draperies that operate electronically, lounge seating for as many as thirty people and a full-scale bar. Other touches may include an old-fashioned popcorn or hot dog cart. Those movie buffs lacking the space for a full-size home theatre can turn to Noise Cancellation Technologies for flat-screen speaker technology. In addition to offering high-quality audio, these speakers come in a lightweight frame featuring a special acoustically permeable material on to which a variety of prints and textures can be digitally imprinted. The speakers are less than two-inches thick.

**Virtual Beings** A modern rule of thumb in the digital revolution seems to be that if something looks and acts real, it's as good as real. At a minimum, it's entertainment. From Sony's Toki Memorial virtual dating game (which has been snapped up by half a million Japanese teens) to the cult status of computer-generated heroine Lara Croft and the album sales of virtual icon Kyoko Date, the parallel universe of cyberspace is creating life forms of its own.

**Patawhereia?** These days, the ends of the earth is literally the only place where the rich and famous can 'get away from it all'. That reality no doubt has contributed to the celebrity influx in the remote wilderness of Patagonia, a region spanning a half million square miles of lakes, woodland and mountains in southern Argentina and Chile. Fans of outlaw history might recall Patagonia as the place where Butch Cassidy and the Sundance Kid tried to evade the long arm of the law. Now, celebrities such as George Soros, Sylvester Stallone, Ted Turner and the Benetton brothers are buying huge plots of land in hope of escaping the long lenses of the paparazzi. According to the *Electronic Telegraph*, the land rush is not popular among locals, who find themselves shut out from much-loved nature spots by newcomers' security measures. At present, nearly a sixth of Patagonia is owned by just 350 foreigners.

**New Music Meccas** The connection between music and youth has long been established, and Anglo-American music in recent decades has had a tremendous impact on the development of youth culture around the world. These days, however, that influence is waning, as young people in Asia, Continental Europe and elsewhere begin to take a more active role in the global music scene. Though the US continues to account for more than a quarter of worldwide music sales, its days of domination appear numbered. And despite the recent upswing in Britain's music industry (thanks in no small part to Oasis and the Spice Girls), its influence, too, is on the decline. In 1985, artists from the US and UK accounted for 65 per cent of music sales in Europe; by 1995, that percentage had dropped to 45. In life next, expect to hear more from local acts in Asia, Latin America, Africa and Eastern Europe. We'll also see a rise in 'world music', populated by the likes of Bulgaria's Folk Scat, Tibet's Yungchen Lhamo and Tanzania's Hukwe Zawose. The world's cross-cultural pollination continues!

# 11

# Sports of all Sorts

Whether you are talking about football in Milan, hockey in Toronto, baseball or basketball in New York, bullfighting in Madrid or sumo wrestling in Tokyo, one thing is certain: big-league sports are no longer just about the game and its fans – they're about big money. Go to any major stadium in the world, and you're likely to see business deals being conducted before, after and during the game. Corporations are buying up luxury suites at stadiums in which to entertain clients and prospects. Championship tickets are thrown in to 'sweeten' a deal. At New York's Madison Square Garden it's not at all unusual these days to see business people plunk down in their seats, open their briefcases and laptop computers, and not emerge again until the end of the game.

Until recently, professional sports hadn't been a huge money maker in Europe, but that's all changing. Now major-league sports – and the concomitant advertising revenues, athlete endorsements and merchandising opportunities – are beginning to hit the big time everywhere from Amsterdam to Zaragoza. The past few years have seen the birth of dozens of digital TV sports channels and pay-per-view events, escalating players' salaries, and huge increases in bids for broadcast rights. The 1998 World Cup in France had nearly 40 million viewers for the sixty-four matches, which is more than twice the number who watched the Olympic games in Atlanta two years earlier.

In the US, there are fewer and fewer professional sports venues that are not aligned with a corporate identity. All of the college football bowl games – a key component of many Americans' New Year's Day activities – now carry a corporate logo. In contrast, while working on a sponsorship deal in the early days of the Madison Square Garden cable network, Ira remembers being unable to negotiate 'dasher board' signage: hockey officials and Garden executives deemed the approach 'too commercial' for sports. Now, even television time-outs have live sponsors for the in-person audiences.

Around the globe, sports are turning profits for everyone from fashion designers, software manufacturers, publishers and equipment makers to the athletes themselves. And this doesn't just apply to the top sports. The current Japanese fishing craze is expected to double the market for fly and lure fishing to nearly US$1 billion by 1999, according to Nomura Research Institute. And the market for snowboarding, popular throughout Europe, the US and Japan, is now valued at US$700 million. According to the National Sporting Goods Association, a trade group, Americans currently spend US$37.6 billion a year on sporting goods.

Nike Inc. has been particularly successful in tapping the desire of today's consumer to 'Just Do It', a campaign that now is being augmented with the somewhat gentler tagline 'I Can'. The Oregon-based company commanded an impressive 47 per cent of the US athletic shoe market in 1997, and has managed to achieve a ranking as one of the world's top ten brands, alongside the likes of Coca-Cola and McDonald's. The self-imposed challenge before the company today is to capture a greater share of the international sneaker and sports apparel markets. To do so, according to Nike CEO Philip Knight, will require one thing: establishing a greater presence in the world's largest sport, European football. Nike's efforts to unseat Germany's dominant Adidas AG have included Knight's US$200 million purchase of the Brazilian national team. More recently, the company launched a global events marketing division to showcase its athletes around the world. But the road ahead will not be easy. When Nike and Adidas competed for sponsorship of the All Blacks (currently the best rugby team in the world), the New Zealand Rugby Football Union chose Adidas – an indication of the edge that globally oriented companies will have over their more nationalistic counterparts in culture next.

Intensified competition among sporting goods retailers and manufacturers is far from the only major story in sports today. Around the globe, technologies are redefining how and where games are played –

and watched. The following highlights some of the primary trends taking place in sports.

## Next: Athlete of the Millennium: Swifter, Higher, Stronger

In recent history, the breaking of sports records has seemed as dependent upon advances in equipment as upon improved physical conditioning. In the pole vault, for instance, the world record edged up a mere 2 inches between 1942 and 1960, hovering around 16 feet. But with the replacement of rigid poles by aluminium, fibreglass, and graphite composites in 1963, the record increased by 2 feet in a period of three years, and now stands at 20 feet, 1.75 inches. The latest technological advance to hold similar promise is the Superbike II, an ultrathin bicycle with a solid (not spoked) rear wheel that could shave several seconds off racing times. Every little advantage helps: in the 1996 Atlanta Olympics, the US swimming team wore synthetic suits that promised a lower drag even than smooth skin. Tiny striations reduced the turbulence produced during forward movement, much as the winglets on an aeroplane convert air turbulence into smooth flow.

Modern sports scientists are mapping the human body's limits in an attempt to understand where improvement is still possible. At the US Olympic Training Centre, the swim team reaps the full benefit of these efforts: swimmers are towed through the pool so they can determine where the drag on their body is greatest and then modify their technique to reduce that drag. The transparent bottom and sides of 'The Flume' – a water treadmill that pumps 60,000 gallons of water through a specially designed pool – make it possible for cameras to record a swimmer's every stroke. Data are then fed into a computer that calculates fluid force equations, with the result being a stick figure of the swimmer with vectors representing lift and drag. An added bonus: the Flume is housed in a hyperbaric chamber, thereby enabling swimmers to train at any 'altitude'.

And don't think the mental aspect of athletics is being ignored. The zone. Flow. Harmony. The Zen moment. Whatever one calls that optimal meld between mind and matter, it's no longer being left to chance among athletes. In countries around the world, almost every sport now consults psychologists to help athletes integrate mental focus with physical ability. Visualization, self-hypnosis, even tapes of simulated competitions with the voices of Olympic announcers all hone the mind–body link.

Sadly, the lengths to which athletes are willing to go to improve upon their natural abilities are perhaps best illustrated by the continued wide-spread abuse of expensive and/or dangerous performance-enhancing drugs. To detect abuse of steroids and other banned drugs, the International Olympic Committee designed a US$3 million-plus testing programme for the Atlanta Games, complete with the most sensitive mass spectrometer ever used in competition. Despite this effort, certain drugs may continue to defy detection. Two examples, as reported by *Newsweek*, are human growth hormone (hGH) and 'EPO' (a synthetic version of the hormone erythropietin). HGH is a natural substance that fosters growth and muscle development in childhood and adolescence and is produced through genetic engineering. Despite astronomical costs (US$20,000 for a one-year supply) and no evidence that the hormone improves athletic performance in adults, the black market for hGH is said to be booming. An international effort is under way to develop an effective screen in advance of the Sydney 2000 Games. Administered just prior to an event, EPO speeds the body's production of red blood cells to five to ten times the normal rate. More red blood cells in circulation let the body carry and burn more oxygen, resulting in a quick burst of energy. EPO is known to be cancer-causing, but this hasn't seemed to deter some people from using it to hype their athletic performance.

## Next: It's a Woman Thing

On and off the playing field, girls and women in the late nineties are leading more active and sporting lifestyles, and manufacturers and retailers are scrambling to secure their share of the market. (According to Women's Sports Marketing Group in Massachusetts, one in three American women plays some kind of sport today, up from one in twenty-seven in the 1970s. Women also buy more than half of all merchandise sold at many sporting goods chains, including purchases for family members and others.)

For the past five years, the Oshman's Sporting Goods chain in the US has held an annual Women & Sports promotion. The five-day event includes clinics with female Olympic athletes; Grants for Girls (supporting girls' sports programmes); and distribution of the *Girls' Sports Book*, a colouring book featuring scenes of girls participating in various sports. The names of such sponsors as Spalding and Reebok are included in the sketches. Nike's push into the women's market includes its highly touted 'If you let me play' campaign and charter sponsorship of the Women's National Basketball Association. In addition, Nike was sole sponsor of the first two editions of a special girls' insert in *Sports Illustrated for Kids*. The sixteen-page editorial inserts, titled 'Girls and Sports Extra', featured supplemental coverage of women's sports and female athletes.

Sporing goods manufacturers are responding to this market surge by designing equipment specifically for the female figure. Women, for instance, have a lower centre of gravity than do men, less upper-body and hand strength, smaller hands and feet and calves that extend farther down the leg than do men's. Spalding has brought out a line of fast-pitch softball gloves featuring narrower hand openings and fingers. The company also produces shorter-than-standard golf clubs with smaller grips, as well as smaller and lighter golf balls. Rawling has developed a helmet for softball players with a hole to pull a ponytail through. Louisville Slugger has developed lightweight bats for women. Rifle manufacturer Browning has come out with a 12-gauge shotgun that weighs several ounces less than the men's version and has a stock that configures better to a woman's figure and hand. And Eddie Bauer, REI and others are selling sleeping bags for women that are shorter than men's.

On the fly-fishing front, Robert Redford's 1992 film, *A River Runs Through It*, has been credited with spurring women's interest in the sport. Orvis, the oldest mail-order catalogue in the States, has introduced 'Orvis for Women by Women', a line of waders, vests and hats designed by leading female fly-fishers.

## Next: New Sporting Alternatives

Snowboarding is one of the strongest trends in today's sporting goods industry, having captured youth across Europe, North America and Japan. Worldwide, participation in snowboarding is growing at a rate of more than 30 per cent annually, with snowboards and gear generating estimated wholesale revenues of more than US$700 million.

According to a report in *Business Week*, the snowboarding craze is pitting small US companies against such old-line European ski manufacturers as Salomon and Volkl, both of which are experiencing flat or declining sales. In an effort to compete, a number of European ski manufacturers are producing flashy snowboards under other names. Finland's Amer Group, for instance, has been producing snowboards under the Oxygen label, while Volkl manufactures snowboards for the US brands Sims and Santa Cruz. A key factor that differentiates snowboarding from the ski industry is that approximately a third of snowboarding sales come from accessories such as grungewear and funky goggles. Snowboard company Ride even markets a line of condoms called Safe Ride.

Other 'extreme' sports – including rock climbing, paragliding, bungee jumping and heliskiing – also continue to grow in popularity among teens and young adults worldwide. In the States, an entire cable TV channel, ESPN2, is devoted to such sports. Outdoor activities such as hiking and water rafting are also growing in appeal. Hiking, for instance, is now the most popular sport in France, and wilderness adventures are becoming increasingly common in Spain.

## Next: Still Going . . .
The world's baby boomers may be ageing, but don't expect them to settle into rockers anytime soon. The only concession many seniors are making to age is a move to less vigorous sports. Among the trends to expect in coming years, according to *American Demographics*:

- Safer sports: catering to people whose mindsets are somewhat younger than their bodies, savvy businesses are creating safer alternatives to the most dangerous sports. For example, in a new twist on climbing walls, an organization in Colorado recently opened the world's first ice-climbing park. It allows climbers of all ages to participate in this wintertime version of rock-climbing, but without such dangers as unstable ice.
- Grand experiences: Kathie Davis, executive director of IDEA, an organization for fitness professionals, reports a surge in sports-specific training as middle-aged boomers bring their goal-oriented sensibilities to outdoor recreation. As boomers grow older, we can expect increased demand for activities that ultimately lead to a 'grand experience', whether it be completion of an Ironman competition or the spotting of a bald eagle during a bird-watching hike.
- Spa sports: as ageing bodies begin to lose their physical prowess, feeling good will become an increasingly important goal. From massages and steam baths to yoga and t'ai chi, we'll see a rise in the 'softer side' of recreation.
- Companionship clubs: by 2010, when the oldest boomers are aged sixty-four, almost half of elderly householders in the US will live alone, according to projections. One result may be increased membership in recreational clubs.

## Next: Just Wear It

For many consumers, looking like an athlete is almost as good as being one. Companies are raking in money from casual clothing (at both ends of the price spectrum) that let even the most devoted couch potatoes feel that they're somehow 'sporty' and 'active'. In Europe, the US and Japan, customers favour high-end technical sports apparel. Top sales prospects in France, for instance, include polar fleece clothing and products that combine polar fleece and Gore-Tex. Also considered fashionable are technical details such as zippers. Eddie Bauer has enjoyed great success with its EBTEK system of outerwear, which is made up of seven interlocking pieces that can be mixed and matched in 160 ways. The items are made of Gore-Tex, Polartec and goose down.

The popularity of American basketball players in Europe and parts of Africa has spurred adoption of the sport among teenagers there, while also creating demand for T-shirts, caps and other products with American sports team logos. In the US, logos of minor league and expansion teams have been all the rage in recent years.

Designer gear is happening the world over, too. Upscale designers hoping to get a piece of the growing sports market are coming out with their own lines of athletic wear. Among them are Ralph Lauren's Polo Sport, Tommy Hilfiger and Donna Karan. As reported in *Advertising Age*, Salomon Bros. predicts that the top six designer brands will account for 7 per cent of a US$8.5 billion industry by the year 2000.

As in other industries, catalogue sales are a growing category in the sporting goods market. Niche catalogues that have sprung up in the past few years include Soccer Madness and Title 9 Sports, a catalogue specializing in women's athletic apparel. In addition, a growing number of sporting goods catalogues are offering such things as branded seminars and travel adventures. L. L. Bean, for instance, offers Outdoor Discovery Schools, which feature family-oriented skiing, canoeing and kayaking trips. Eddie Bauer offers guided trips to exotic locations around the world.

## Next: Playing It Safe(r)

No matter where in the world you live, chances are you're aware of a current sports scandal. Recent scandals involving such figures as US boxer Mike Tyson, Dutch soccer player Patrick Kluivert, and football star Paul Gascoigne (not to mention ex-American football legend O. J. Simpson) have made it increasingly risky for companies to tie their fortunes (and reputations) to celebrity athlete spokespersons/endorsers.

Though top-of-the-line athletes such as US basketball star Michael Jordan and golfing sensation Tiger Woods will continue to rake in endorsement dollars, companies already appear more cautious about the process. Kodak, for example, purportedly conducted extensive consumer research before signing the famously flamboyant basketball star Dennis Rodman to its roster of endorsers. The company went on to regret its decision in late 1996, when it found itself fielding calls from irate consumers offended by Rodman's outburst of profanity during a live postgame TV interview. Nonetheless, US advertisers continue to value the 'renegade' images projected by such stars as Rodman, Dallas Cowboy Deion Sanders and tennis ace Andre Agassi. Rodman, for instance, currently earns approximately US$10 million a year in endorsement contracts.

Outside the US, athletes are more likely to be admired for their athletic prowess and good works than for their on- and off-court 'bad boy' antics. Going forwards – in what we believe is an extension of our communal search for security – we'll see more and more marketers linking up with bona fide heroes, people who are using their celebrity for the common good. In Brazil, for instance, the most admired celebrities these days aren't flashy movie stars or singers, but athletes who have risen from poverty to fame and fortune, and who are using their money and prestige to help those at the bottom of the economic ladder. Two examples are soccer star Zico, who has built a soccer school for destitute children, and basketball standout Oscar Schmidt, who organizes Olympic Games for the physically challenged.

## What's Next?

**Sport/Entertainment Tie-ins** With sports continuing to be extremely lucrative, we'll see all sorts of industries negotiating to get a piece of the action in the years ahead. One certainty is increased cross-licensing between sports leagues and entertainment companies. Warner Bros (which has trademarked the phrase 'Sports is entertainment') licensed its Looney Tunes characters with the US National Football League in 1993, a move that has since been imitated in other sports by such entertainment companies as Disney and Marvel Entertainment. Disney's venture into the world of sports has been most dramatic. In addition to producing such items as Mickey Mouse basketballs and

Donald Duck golf balls, the company now owns two teams (the Anaheim Angels and Mighty Ducks), Walt Disney World Sports Complex and sports channel ESPN.

**Virtual Spectators** Fans unable to get to major games increasingly will have an opportunity to attend virtually, via Websites that feature live camera feeds, commentary, continually updated statistics and discussion forums. The recent Olympic Games in Nagano, though generally panned as a TV event, were well covered by IBM's official Olympic Website, as well as by 'subdomains' created by and for US broadcaster CBS. When Japan took the gold in ski jumping, IBM's site registered 98,226 hits a minute; the hit rate for the entire Atlanta games was surpassed in a day. To track Sydney's virtual progress, visit http://www.sydney.olympic.org.

**Move Over, Snowboarding** As snowboarding becomes established, widespread, and perhaps even demodé, a couple of newcomers are vying for honours as alternative winter sports: skiboards are short, bi-directional skis that have points at both ends, thereby allowing skiers to jump forward and backward, and perform some impressive stunts; snowskating, a derivative of in-line skating, is being promoted by Kent Rodriquez, inventor and sole manufacturer of snowskates, and chairman and CEO of Sled Dogs Co. 'We appeal directly to the in-line skater,' he says. 'We have the potential to reach 22 million in-line skaters who don't have a winter sport, yet.'

**Electric Bikes** Entrepreneurs are exploring the market potential of electric bikes, which can be pedalled like normal bikes or powered by unobtrusive, battery-driven motors. Although the bikes must be recharged every 15 to 20 miles, they plug into normal electrical sockets. Prices typically range from US$900 to US$1,500. Two prospective markets: middle-aged and elderly cyclists, who generally love the exercise but loathe the hills and urban commuters. Americans have purchased 5,000 electric bikes since the US product debut in 1993, but sales are much higher abroad. The bikes are particularly popular in Japan, where parking spots are scarce.

**Tomorrow's Workout** Already, new technologies are changing the face of health and fitness clubs around the world. One example: in an effort to keep their customers coming back for more, some gyms and health clubs have turned to FitLinxx, a company that uses technology to customize workout routines. The FitLinxx Training Partner records individuals' routines on a number of types of exercise equipment; users enter a Personal Identification Number (PIN code) at each workstation, which then provides a record of such workout details as number of repetitions, seat settings and weight amounts. At each visit, users are also prompted to input information regarding lifestyle changes and indicate whether they are bored with their current routine; FitLinxx adapts workouts based on those responses. The results have been promising, with FitLinxx customers reporting dramatically increased membership-retention rates.

**Boomer Bruises** Increased participation in sports, particularly among ageing baby boomers, is proving to be a boon for the sports medicine industry, with sales of such products as athletic tape and supports, bandages and hot and cold wraps up across the board. Expect a large number of product innovations in this area over the course of the next few years. One such product, introduced recently, is BIOflex, a neoprene biomagnetic support designed to speed recovery of muscle-and joint-related pain and injury. The product uses magnets to widen blood vessels, thereby allowing more blood to flow to the damaged area.

**Walking, Talking Billboards** Expect to see more high-profile sports figures, including coaches, accept sponsorships from fashion designers. Former New York Knicks coach and walking fashion faux pas, Don Nelson, for instance, was taken under the wing of designer Tommy Hilfiger, who became the coach's official outfitter, clothing him for all public appearances on and off the basketball court. The resultant look was sufficiently impressive to earn Nelson a spread in *GQ* magazine. Basketball coaches in the NBA and on college campuses in the US are also becoming increasingly visible in advertising. A recent TV ad campaign for Taco Bell, for example, featured three college b-ball coaches.

**Football Sells** While America's NBA still rates in the US, and while growth in basketball interest is meaningful in other parts of the world, it's football which sells – and which will sell more in the future. Sales of colour TVs have more than doubled in Beijing, Shanghai, Tianjin and Guangzhou since the World Cup began on 10 June 1998. Sales of VCRs also boomed. Analysts estimated that 57 per cent of Beijing's residents watched the World Cup playoffs, despite the fact that China's team didn't qualify for the finals. Jean Dumas, European market development chief at electronics firm Thomson, reported a similar scenario in Europe, with sales of new and top-of-the-range TV sets having increased sharply in Germany, France and Italy prior to the World Cup.

To mark the occasion of France 98 there were in excess of 400 officially licensed World Cup products to buy. Among them: mini soccer balls made by Paris-based luxury leather goods manufacturer Louis Vuitton and watches engraved with the World Cup trophy. French clothing manufacturer Sun Island was one of a number of companies offering consumers prizes for correctly predicting match results. And Germany's best-selling newspaper, *Bild*, used a stripper to raise readership during the World Cup. A blonde model dressed in the German national team uniform offered to remove an article of clothing for each game won by the German team.

Around Europe, a growing number of soccer clubs (20 in Britain alone) are being listed on financial exchanges. South Africa's Kaizer Chiefs may soon be joining the trend by being listed on the Johannesburg Stock Exchange. In addition to providing capital for the club, this move is expected to provide many South African soccer fans with their first foray into the financial markets.

**Globalizing Games and Gear** America's National Football League (NFL) has created an international division to market its brand of football outside the US. NFL International is conducting research in Canada, Europe, Japan and Mexico in order to determine how best to educate consumers worldwide about US-style football. Current plans for Europe include producing television packages of game highlights that contain brief, entertaining segments about the game and its rules, and creating 'football festivals' that combine music, interactive games and football.

**Sports2watch** Analysts predict that the most popular sports among US kids in 2006 will be basketball (including girls' basketball – spurred on by the recent debut of two US women's professional basketball leagues), ice hockey, figure skating and golf (currently one golf course is being opened every day in the US, and companies are producing merchandise for junior golfers).

# How We Work:
# Next Livelihood

## [12]

# The Future of Offices

'What leaders must learn to do is develop a social architecture that encourages incredibly bright people, most of whom have big egos, to work together successfully and to deploy their own creativity,' wrote Warren Bennis in 'Becoming a Leader of Leaders', published in *Rethinking the Future*. The authors of this book have had the great luxury of working in office environments that encourage just such creativity.

Though we've embarked upon new adventures within the advertising industry, we have our roots within Chiat/Day, a virtual office environment – the first and (thus far) the only. Our virtuality began as an extreme experiment, one that bordered on revolutionary change and that would enable each of us to reinvent ourselves and our careers. As you read our story, we caution you that any change of this magnitude evokes a broad variety of personal reactions and consequences. It is necessary to reassess continually one's goals and progress, and to work to eliminate the bugs that are an inevitable side-effect.

Has our experiment with virtuality paid off? Yes. The simple truth is, when we were the Department of the Future, it simply would not have been possible for seven people to have provided a comparable level of service to our parent company on a daily basis if it were not for our virtual workstyle. The fact that the seven of us lived in three time zones meant that for an average of twenty hours a day, at least one member of our unit was reading, thinking, processing information and generating strategies that were then passed along to colleagues in the next time zone.

The person we have to thank for introducing us to virtuality is Jay Chiat. Central to Jay's philosophy was the creation of a culture of change. These changes sometimes altered the agency's core business practice – at other times, they were simply ideas and modifications intended to shake the agency out of its complacency – the characteristic that, after lack of intellectual curiosity and moral character, disturbed Jay most.

As president of Chiat/Day New York, Jay Chiat's home base, Ira had an opportunity in 1994 to be a part of another important milestone in the history of Chiat/Day: He was charged with ensuring the agency's smooth transition to a 'virtual' office. In his words:

As I write this from a cottage in Bellagio, Italy, and transmit it to Marian in Geneva and to Ann in Tampa, Florida, I can't help but be aware of the extent to which our work environment has changed in a few short years. In late 1993, Jay Chiat outlined for me a vision he said had come to him, fully formed, as he skied down Telluride Mountain in Colorado. The essence of his vision was of an organization in which members were not constrained by physical or hierarchical restrictions, where each person would have access to the tools needed to create the environment in which he or she could work best.

Having enjoyed the unique advantage of being a Macintosh beta site, where the computers were tested and tweaked before launch, the idea of using computers as a core business and communications tool was not new to us. Nor was the idea that walls and doors were barriers to the free flow of ideas. Jay had removed these barriers years ago, creating open spaces in which each employee maintained his or her own 'workspace', complete with desk, Macintosh computer, file cabinet, etc. Approximately 70 per cent of our physical plant was taken up by these personal workstations; the remaining 30 per cent was collaborative (mainly conference rooms).

In conducting an audit of space utilization, we found that at any given time some 50 per cent of employees' private spaces were empty, while meeting spaces were always 100 per cent occupied, often with queues for access. Some staff members would be on vacation or sick; others would be in meetings, at clients' offices, in production studios and so on – at no time was everyone at their desks.

Our next step was to conduct a 'storage audit' – figuring out what was in those endless rows of filing cabinets and other storage units. Some of the 'stuff' we found was legitimate 'intelligence' – data related to client business. In many cases, though, we found that this information existed in multiple hard copies and – even more distressing – was not always shared with relevant staffers. We also found such items as last year's bad bottle of wine (proffered as a Christmas gift by a media supplier), scores of old newspapers, remains of meals long past their prime and so on.

In sum, even with an advantageous rental rate in our downtown location (vs Madison Avenue – the traditional, pricey home of the advertising industry in the States), we were funding some very expensive closets!

Jay's vision was to restructure the office in a single step change. Our space was to be physically organized the same way we were – by client team. Fifty per cent of the office would be converted into a 'project room' – a permanent facility in which current client activity and core team interactions would take place. An additional 20 per cent of our space would be devoted to 'temporary' project rooms, places in which to mount new business pitches, work on campaigns and hold private conversations. These temporary rooms could be booked electronically (for anything from ten minutes to ten weeks or more), so they would be available to function as private offices as needed.

Critical to this concept was the reorganization of information storage and retrieval. All paper documents were transferred to electronic files and stored on a central file server. Once there, they would be password accessible for every staffer, either through the in-office network or via modem-facilitated remote access. Beyond liberating 'file space', this system ensured universal access to the agency's collective intelligence, allowing staffers to be productive anywhere, anytime.

What we had, then, was a fair exchange. Our staff members were asked to give up their private space in exchange for the freedom to work where they liked. As most of the staffers were young (median age twenty-four), we found the best model was a university. Groups came together for collaboration (in the manner of a lecture or seminar) and left with an assignment and a due date. No one told them how to do the work, nor how to schedule, nor where the resources were. Their responsibility was to deliver their best effort, on time. If you did well, you succeeded; if not, you failed. And that applied at all levels of the agency.

We even borrowed the idea of the 'student union', creating a place in which staffers could meet, greet and interact. This is also where each staffer's personal locker is located. It was interesting to watch the weekly paper dump, as people came to trust the virtual system and progressively gave up the security of the paper they had smuggled from the uptown office.

Our last step was to deal with all those phones that used to ring off the hook in unoccupied workstations. We simply cut the cords. Rolm provided a cordless PBX phone system that allowed portable telephony throughout the 30,000-square-foot physical plant.

The result? In addition to cutting back our space requirements by nearly two-thirds, the transition to virtual infused the agency with a powerful rush of energy as employees became more adept at using technological tools to make their working hours more productive. It's for this reason that Marian and I have practically become 'virtual evangelists'. When we were with the Department of the Future, we worked hard to show our European counterparts all of the benefits that could be gained from cutting the cords of physicality. We had embraced virtuality to such an extent, in fact, that it was initially difficult for Marian to adjust to the working style of her Amsterdam base. She kept feeling that she was expected to remain at the office during business hours 'just to be polite', despite the fact that her most productive hours were those spent working at home. Slowly but surely, our European co-workers adjusted to Marian's virtual work habits, just as they came to terms with the fact that they were in constant collaboration with two colleagues whom they were unlikely ever to meet.

In the past couple of years, we've watched as others in our business and other industries have begun to adapt and adopt some of the fundamentals of Jay Chiat's vision. In that time, we've grown increasingly confident that virtuality will permanently alter the workplaces – and working styles – of the future.

## A New Way To Work

Think of the enormous changes that have taken place in the workplace in the past fifteen years. In the early eighties, the use of fax machines was just becoming widespread, slowly replacing telex machines. Those businesses that relied on computers had them connected to an enormous mainframe, carefully guarded in a climate-controlled room. Secretaries and other assistants typed letters on IBM Selectrics, and important documents were hand-delivered by messenger.

Fifteen years later, even home offices in the States are equipped with computers and fax machines. Typewriters are relics of the past. Business documents are zapped near instantaneously from office to office, country to country via modem. Personal couriers have largely been replaced by FedEx, DHL and other courier companies that 'absolutely, positively' guarantee delivery overnight. And how many of us can't seem to make it across town these days without making a business call or two on our cellular phone?

To what extent will virtuality be embraced by other offices and industries in the years to come? We don't see a time – at least in the next few decades – when face2face contact will be entirely eliminated. After all, most of us still place some credence in the value of a handshake – and in building relationships over lunch or dinner, as well as in a conference room. We do expect, however, to see a dramatic increase in the amount of business communication conducted virtually, whether in intranet conference rooms or online chatrooms or via videophone.

The move towards virtuality is the most dramatic example of changes in the workspace, but there are plenty of other, more subtle shifts.

### Next: Intranet Explosion

Across North America and Europe, more and more companies are creating 'intranets', internal company networks based on the same technology as the global Internet. Cordoned off from the public Internet via software programs known as 'fire walls', intranets allow employee access while blocking (in theory at least) unauthorized users. Sample uses include data retrieval from networked computers, company services inquiries and interoffice email. Some analysts anticipate that the next 'big leap' will be the creation of virtual corporations, enabling companies to reduce both physical plant and paper transactions.

Hundreds of companies, including AT&T, Levi Strauss and 3M, are making use of intranets: Pharmaceutical giant Eli Lilly & Co., for instance, has created an intranet that links approximately 16,000 workers – almost two-thirds of the company's worldwide staff. At Ford Motor Co., an intranet that links design centres in Asia, Europe and the US helped engineers craft the latest Taurus. Fully 85 per cent of US corporations that responded to a study by Cognitive Communications are implementing, piloting or planning an intranet; survey respondents included 162 Fortune 500 companies, together with some privately held corporations.

In 1997, the intranet market swelled to US$8 billion. In Europe, the market is growing 25 per cent faster than is use of commercial Internet services. Zona Research, Inc., in California, predicts that in 1999, spending on host computers and software for intranets will exceed Internet spending by 6:1, and that the overall market for Internet/intranet products and services (which it calls the Adjusted Gross Internet Product (AGIP)) will top US$100 billion by the year 2000. The cost outlay may well be worth it: META Group, Inc. recently announced the results of a study analysing the return on investment (ROI) of intranet applications. Sponsored by IBM, Novell and Microsoft, the study found that 80 per cent of the 55 companies surveyed generated a positive ROI, with an average annualized return of 38 per cent.

A Novell research study (based on 1,200 telephone interviews with board directors, IT managers and employees in seven European countries) found that one-third of companies surveyed – and nearly half of the UK companies – had no plans to implement an intranet. But this will change, the researchers contend. 'Intranets help solve problems which currently bedevil companies and place a cost upon the whole economy. It has been well documented that Europe is falling behind in the adoption of computing technology, compared to North America. We cannot afford to fall behind with intranet technology,' commented Andrew Sadler-Smith, deputy managing director, Novell UK and Ireland.

## Next: Alternative Workstyles

Though many corporations would deny a trend towards virtuality, the reality is that they're already heading in that direction.

**Telecommuting** Sometimes called teleworking or homeworking, telecommuting is common in the US already and is being adopted by a number of European nations as well. According to the '1997 Olsten Forum on Managing Workplace Technology' (http://www.olsten.com), a majority (51 per cent) of North American companies now permit employees to telecommute through pilot and ongoing schemes, with 74 per cent expecting their use of telecommuting to increase. Telecommuters may work for a local company (perhaps splitting their time between the office and home), as freelancers or consultants, or even as employees of a company on the other side of the globe. According to market researcher Link Resources, 37 million American households – 38 per cent of the total – contain at least one person doing income-generating work at home. The fastest-growing segment of the telecommuting population (currently standing at 8.4 million) is individuals employed by corporations who work at home full or part time. Telecommunications giant AT&T, for example, has turned 50,000 US employees into telecommuters, resulting in annual savings of US$80 million in overhead costs.

In Europe, there are currently 1.25 million telecommuters, a number that is expected to increase dramatically as the Continent becomes more wired and the telecommunications infrastructure is improved. Most common in Sweden and the UK, telecommuting is also establishing a presence in Germany and France. It is far less common in the south of Europe.

**Hot Desking and Hotelling** 'Hot desking' (having fewer desks than workers) is also becoming increasingly common in parts of Europe. Offices that have given up permanent, individualized workspaces include Digital Equipment's headquarters in Stockholm and the British Gas Research Centre in Loughborough, England. In a variation of hot-desking, some companies have adopted the practice of 'hotelling'. At each office, a concierge assigns desks on an as-needed basis. For most workdays, though, an employee's 'workspace' consists of a state-of-the-art computer equipped with voicemail, remote access, etc.

Accounting firm Ernst & Young has implemented hotelling in its New

York and Chicago offices, thereby cutting its physical plant by 25 per cent. The offices now maintain one desk per every three workers. According to *Fortune* magazine, Ernst & Young expects to save US$40 million annually once all of its offices are similarly reconfigured. Andersen Consulting in Paris has taken desks away from 900 analysts. Employees in need of a workspace my reserve a desk by email the day before. Project teams are formed and dissolved as consultants move from floor to floor, carrying portable computers that link them to Andersen's databases, applications and worldwide systems. Smart cards located within these computers allow management to track employees' movements inside and outside the building. The result, thus far, has been annual savings of US$4 million and a physical plant that has been reduced by half.

**Flexible Workdays** Among other signs of increased flexibility in the workplace is the growth of employee flexitime, job sharing and 'alternative' schedules (forty-hour, four-day workweeks, for example). According to the US Department of Labor, approximately 22 per cent of professionals, managers and administrative employees in the US currently have the option of varying their hours. And more companies are giving employees a set number of paid days off each year that they may schedule as they see fit (rather than the company dictating which holidays they'll have off). There's also a movement under way to make 'comp time' (or earned time off) an alternative to overtime pay.

## Next: Office of the Future Takes Shape

Expect to see significant changes in office design as the 'office of the future' continues to take shape. Physical-plant changes are expected to encourage teamwork at the expense of privacy, with such facilities as centralized technology units, kitchens/lounges and service centres featuring such amenities as dry-cleaning drop-off/pick-up, takeout food (for meals at the office or at home) and daycare centres. Industry experts at the International Association of Corporate Real Estate Executives symposium in Tampa, Florida agreed that the office of the future will have reduced space per employee (with workspaces made more efficient by technology) and will also be designed with more attention to the workers' day-to-day environment. Skylights, windows that open and improved ventilation systems are some of the features expected to be incorporated in the next decade.

Also undergoing change will be office furniture, which will become both more mobile and more flexible. One example: Steelcase Inc.'s Personal Harbors. Costing US$7,000 apiece, Personal Harbors are small, cylindrical booths with a door that can be closed. The interior space is large enough to hold a flat work surface, computer set-up, phones, a file drawer and other standard desk items. There's also a whiteboard and built-in CD player. Unlike the ubiquitous cubicles of today, Personal Harbors offer both total privacy and the ability to communicate with co-workers: The harbours are grouped around a large puzzle-like table that can be broken into several pieces. When harbour doors are open, employees can move in and out of the group space to talk to colleagues, participate in meetings or just listen in.

According to SIGCHI (Special Interest Group on Computer–Human Interaction), an estimated 80 per cent of all salaried workers will work at video display terminals by the year 2000. 'Cognitive ergonomics' will be the next big thing in office design. Based on the theory that there's a direct relationship between where one works and how one thinks, office space will be designed to maximize communication, creativity and interaction.

**Advent of the Paperless Office?** Will we soon see widespread growth of paperless offices? That's unlikely, according to a study the authors conducted among 200 early adopters of new technology. While the majority of respondents anticipated a decrease in the use of paper, 82 per cent believe that paper will remain a staple for both business and personal use. Sample responses:

- 'Paper is a hard record . . . Computer records can be trashed or lost if you don't back up. I like to have both.'
- 'You can read paper documents in bed.'
- 'You can take a hard-copy document anywhere and find it quickly in a crunch.'
- 'I usually print information to remind me to follow up in a different medium (by snail mail, phone, etc.) or to give to people who might not have ready access to email. Also, some pieces I print to keep on display for a few days at home or at work (e.g., humorous collections).'
- 'I can highlight hard-copy documents and make comments/notes on them.'

- 'I may want to use a paper document for presentations, for teaching children, to add to journals, to read when I don't have access to a computer.'
- 'I can pull a sheet of paper out of my briefcase much more quickly than I can turn on a computer and access the file on disk.'
- 'I like to print out long documents that are cumbersome to scroll (e.g., FAQ, instructions, detailed technical information, long text that I'd like to read from a hard copy and not from a computer screen).'
- 'I don't think we'll ever forgo the desire to see some things in writing. It helps me to pull thoughts together if I can see the written page. If I've requested help on a programming problem, for example, and the answer is fairly complex, it is easier to me to print it out and use the hard copy as I work on the program than it is for me to switch windows to read the information. I find reading text on the screen to be a negative thing – I read it much easier in hard copy.'

## Next: Working Anywhere, Anytime

One of the great advantages (and disadvantages) of new technologies is that they have made the office portable. No longer tied to his or her desk, today's executive can conduct business at a client's office, in a hotel, on a plane – anywhere his or her laptop computer and modem can travel. This 'office-in-a-bag' spells increased convenience for many business people, while at the same time making it even more difficult to prevent business from intruding on one's personal life.

One result is a growing population of 'road warriors', the label bestowed by the travel industry upon the growing number of business travellers who spend more time on the road than in the office – 70, 90, even 100 plus days per year. This new class of super-frequent traveller represents the top 1 per cent of people who travel for business each year. Still talked about at Hilton Hotels is the management consultant who stayed at the chain for 330 nights in 1993 – a record. (Hilton estimates that the 10,000 customers who represent the top 1 per cent of their frequent-customer programme account for approximately 15 per cent of all revenue from these customers, or approximately US$60 million (1994 figures).) Perks accorded these road warriors by airlines and hotels include upgrades, admission to private lounges and housing on exclusive floors with around-the-clock snacks and special attendants.

The very best customers have even been awarded such bonuses as new cars, golf trips to Scotland and tickets to the US Grammy and Academy Awards shows.

In contrast to the home-oriented telecommuter, the road warrior takes advantage of new technologies to meet business obligations in other cities, other countries and in the airspace between. The technological gadgetry that made the home office a reality (and that was supposed to eliminate business travel) – fax, phone, email, video teleconferencing, et al. – has had a freeing effect on personnel who were all but chained to their desks and corporate campuses a decade ago. They now have the flexibility to go where business requires, packing the office in their bags much as they would that reliable blue suit.

Rather than considering face2face contact an old-fashioned formality, many futurists see increased travel as a sign that such contact is becoming more important. '[Road warriors] are the leading indicators of what's in store for the rest of us,' says Paul Saffo, a director of the Institute for the Future, a California-based research foundation.

## Next: Never Out of Touch

Perhaps more than any other industry, telecommunications is in the midst of sweeping change. Telephony products are becoming both more personal and more pervasive, as consumers come to expect twenty-four-hour access to anyone, anywhere.

Whereas just a few years ago we relied almost solely on the telephone and mail service to keep in touch with colleagues and family, today we expect instantaneous communication and data exchange via cell phones, pagers and the Internet. Companies are scrambling to meet the demand for faster, more convenient and more global methods of communication: Britain's GSM, for example, has introduced roaming capabilities for its pagers that enable users to be paged while visiting France, Germany, Switzerland, Italy and the Netherlands. Microsoft's Bill Gates is formulating a plan to launch 288 low-Earth-orbit satellites that would provide Internet access to any location on Earth by 2002. The satellites would send data at 64 megabits/second downstream and 2 megabits/second upstream. A service from Germany's Bertelsmann AG will enable users to make phone calls, hold videoconferences, do online banking and exchange email via the Net. Customers who don't own a PC and modem will be able to use a specially designed telephone with a video screen and keyboard.

Our growing reliance on the Internet – for both business and personal use – has created a growth category for businesses that can provide Net access in non-traditional locations. For instance, 4th Network, a Microsoft Solution provider, through a strategic alliance with Thorn Business Communications and M.A.I.D. plc, plans to have its Internet-on-TV service running in nearly 50,000 hotel rooms by the end of 1998. AT&T is also targeting the business traveller, having signed a deal with Hilton Hotels to provide free WorldNet Internet access software to Hilton guests in Chicago, New York, Los Angeles and Washington, DC.

To provide Net access for people on the go, Ohio's Diebold Inc. is working on an ATM that will allow bank customers to access the Net for both banking and non-banking information. Australia's WebPoint plans to have 5,000 Internet kiosks worldwide by the year 2000; 20,000 users currently take advantage of the kiosks, which cost US$1.34 per ten minutes. And a real estate company in the United Arab Emirates is building a wired mall, the first of its kind in the Middle East. The complex will 'bring buyers and sellers together with facilities like demonstration centres, where buyers can actually run real-life applications and modern video conferencing to allow multimedia presentation, grouping buyers and sellers in different continents', according to project chair Mohammad Ali Alabbar.

## Next: Internet Telephony

Without much fanfare, the Internet has begun to demonstrate its potential as a medium for carrying vocal data. Internet Protocol (IP) promises to cut significantly into the revenues of traditional phone companies in the next decade. The International Telecommunications Union believes that IP telephony could eliminate the profits of US long-distance carriers by taking just 6 per cent of telephone traffic. By 2002, the Internet could account for 11 per cent of US and international long-distance traffic, up from 0.2 per cent in 1997, according to IDC. Action Information Services predicts the Net will take close to US$1 billion in revenues from telephone service providers in 1998 and US$3.5 billion by 2001.

As reported by *USA Today*, rates for IP are projected to be between 5 and 7.5 cents a minute. IP phone calls are cheaper, in part, because they are exempt from fees long-distance carriers must pay for access to the local networks, where all long-distance calls begin and end. Among the major telecom companies that have announced plans to enter the

IP fray are AT&T, Deutsche Telekom, MCI and Bell Atlantic. Companies can expect to cut their phone bills by 35 per cent through IP technology, according to 3Com CEO Eric Benhamou.

## Next: New Security Needs

Increased reliance on portable – or 'laptop' – computers has led to a sharp increase in computer thefts over the past couple of years. In the US, in excess of 200,000 portable computers were stolen in 1995, according to computer insurance company Safeware. Some companies have begun to warn employees to be increasingly vigilant while travelling (airports are a prime target) and to back up files and activate passwords to protect sensitive materials lest they fall into the wrong hands.

The UK's National Criminal Intelligence Service (NCIS) has requested added powers to face the growing incidence of fraud, theft and terrorism expected to be conducted via the Internet in the coming century. NCIS has also called for legislation on the theft of electronic information, calling Internet crime 'the policing challenge of the next millennium'. The software industry and advocates of free speech on the Net are expected to oppose efforts of the NCIS to regulate cyberspace.

Network security is one of the fastest growing markets in the US according to research firm Frost & Sullivan. The market attained more than half a billion dollars in revenue in 1996, representing a growth rate of 217 per cent over 1995. Rapid growth is expected to continue as the number of Internet and intranet commerce users expands. Net-based e-commerce transactions and business use of the Internet and intranets are forecast to be the major drivers of the network security market.

# What's Next?

**Data Dominance**  Whereas today 90 per cent of the world's telecommunications are 'voice', digital transmission of data in the form of email, fax, computer telephony and electronic commerce will grow to the point of overwhelming dominance. As noted by *Newsweek*, industry reports show that voice phone calls will account for less than 10 per cent of all telecom traffic by 2002.

**Number Crunch** Toll-free numbers are growing at such a rapid rate in the US that the new 888 prefix faces depletion after only two years. The volume of toll-free calls has grown from 7 million in 1967 to nearly 20 billion in 1997.

**USPS Email** The US Postal Service plans to offer official time and date postmarks so users can send certified and registered letters via email.

**Certified Online Transmissions** UPS (http://www.ups.com), the world's largest package distribution company, will soon offer online document delivery via UPS Document Exchange. For critical or confidential documents, UPS OnLine Dossier utilizes encryption, digital certificates (to verify identity of sender and recipient) and third-party validation; it offers insurance for up to US$100.000 in business losses. UPS OnLine Courier, for less sensitive documents, utilizes passwords and encryption. Both services offer tracking and confirmation of receipt.

**General Electric Call Home** Home appliances will be equipped with microchips capable of accessing the Internet and downloading software to fix operational problems on their own.

**Mobile Wallets** Logica is teaming up with mobile phone operators Cellnet and Motorola to develop a 'mobile wallet', a phone that can send and receive cash electronically. Customers can use the phone to pay for theatre tickets, a pizza or to transfer money between accounts, pay bills and view bank statements – perfect for today's busy road warriors.

**Virtual Dating** Videophone capabilities will offer a safe virtual meeting place for those who never liked kissing on the first date anyway.

**Online Utility Monitoring** Utility companies will tap into businesses' electricity usage over the Web and send an instant online monthly bill. Cost-conscious customers can adjust their habits after periodically logging in to check the status of their bill.

**Corporate Campus** Blending of work and home will spur more corporations to create 'campuses' complete with on-site child and elder care, health facilities (dentist, chiropractor, certified nurse practitioner), personal services (dry cleaning, takeout meals), etc.

**Return of the 'Company Town'** High-tech companies will lure workers to subsidized apartments, homes and condos wired to the workplace.

# 13

# You Call This Work?

As we usher in an era of global markets, automated production and virtuality, we're not just seeing changes in the workplace, we're also seeing changes in the worker. The fact is, our transition from a nation-based Industrial Age to a global Digital Age will require new job parameters, new skills and new approaches to how we conduct our day-to-day business – and plan our careers.

In an increasingly competitive world, companies no longer have the luxury of keeping on more employees than they need or workers who are not contributing fully to the bottom line – whether as a fault of their own or simply because their skills or areas of knowledge are no longer aligned with the needs of the company. As a result, more and more companies are beginning to pay close attention to extending the value of their existing 'human resources', recognizing that it is often far more expensive to recruit and train new workers than it is to maximize the value of the workers they already have. One of the buzzwords we've been hearing in the past couple of years is 'headlighting', which refers to companies taking a close look at where they want to be in the medium to long term, and determining what changes need to be made to ensure they get there. Texas Instruments in the US has been doing some headlighting by listing, as much as a year in advance, which jobs are in jeopardy and asking those employees, 'What do we need to do to broaden you to assume a new job inside or outside this company?' Workers and companies alike have come to find that if they don't spend time now preparing for the future, they may well find they have no role to play once they get there.

Today's university graduates, by and large, recognize that they cannot expect to stay with a single company for their entire career – and many have no desire to do so. Mergers, downsizing and other broad business trends have created a work world that is far more fluid than it was for previous generations, as workers move from job to job, company to company and even industry to industry throughout their careers. The perceived decrease in company loyalty has resulted in employees who are far more inclined to take responsibility for their own success rather than pin their hopes on the achievements of any one organization. Those workers best positioned to succeed in the coming decades will be those who recognize that they must continually upgrade their skills and work to maintain or extend their competitive edge, for there is no guarantee that the organization they work for today will continue to need their current skill set tomorrow.

What is the attitude of young people about to enter into today's business world? Overall, they appear optimistic, and they are evincing a strong desire to attain a balanced lifestyle and personal growth, as opposed to being willing to sacrifice all for a top salary or prestigious position. Last year, Coopers & Lybrand released the results of a survey conducted among more than 1,200 business students from thirty of the world's leading universities in ten countries: Australia, Canada, France, Germany, Japan, South Africa, South Korea, the Netherlands, the UK and the US. The study found that 'achieving a balanced lifestyle [and] having a rewarding life outside work' is among the top three career goals of 45 per cent of respondents. This goal was followed by 'building a sound financial base' (cited by 33 per cent of respondents) and 'having a position where I can work and travel internationally' (28 per cent).

Nicholas G. Moore, chairman of Coopers & Lybrand, commented: 'Apart from some minor cultural and geographical differences, we found that students all over the world share many common views on most aspects of life and careers. Students today have grown up in a world of international television, cinema, magazines, music and literature. Many have travelled throughout the world. The [Coopers & Lybrand International Student Survey] findings indicate that 23 per cent of the students responding have international work experience. This is truly the world's first global generation.'

When asked what is the most important factor they consider when looking for a first employer, 37 per cent of respondents chose 'ability to lead a balanced lifestyle'. This was followed by 'opportunities to reach management level' (31 per cent) and 'competitive salary' (30 per cent). Students ranked their own personal growth and development as more important to them than building a career, spending time with close friends and relatives and building a family. Seventy-four per cent of respondents believe national borders will lose economic importance in the future. Sixty-six per cent said business will have a greater influence than will politics on the future of the world. Seventy-three per cent think 'the global economy will strengthen and flourish in my lifetime'.

The remainder of this chapter covers a number of trends we're seeing as workers – and organizations – reinvent themselves to meet the challenges of a changing world.

## Next: An End to the Permanent, Full-Time Employee?

Though economists have been predicting the demise of Europe's cradle-to-grave welfare state for years, changes have been slow in coming. True, Sweden has made significant cuts in its social safety net and Germany has placed some provisions of its postwar social contract on the bargaining table, but if labour protests in France two years ago serve as any indication, the foundation of the welfare state is likely to stand strong in the near term. One clear result has been high unemployment rates, fuelled in part by employers' unwillingness to pay the high cost that comes with hiring permanent workers. In Spain, for instance, where unemployment has reached in excess of 20 per cent, companies hesitate to hire permanent workers for fear of having to continue to support them in the event of layoffs. Spanish law dictates that laid-off workers are entitled to forty-five days' pay for every year they've worked. According to *Business Week*, when Gillette Co. closed its Seville plant, the average employee took home three years' pay – and started collecting unemployment benefits that equalled as much as 90 per cent of his or her old wages for four years.

Rather than shoulder the financial burden of permanent, full-time employees, many companies are turning to part-time and temporary workers. A survey of 5,000 medium and large firms in Europe revealed a strong increase in part-time and temporary work. Conducted by Cranfield University's European Network for Human Resource Management (Cranet-E), the survey pointed to increased flexibility among employers as evidenced by their hiring of contract workers, allowing employees to telecommute and work flexible hours, and limiting overtime work.

In North America, temporary services firm Olsten Corp. has found that more than a third of firms employ temps in managerial or professional positions. Among firms using temps, 53 per cent utilize accountants, 32 per cent retain information systems specialists, 28 per cent utilize human-resource professionals and 27 per cent use administrative professionals. Forty-five per cent of firms surveyed by Olsten plan to increase their use of temporary employees during the next five years, and 51 per cent intend to maintain current levels. Increased demand for temporary workers worldwide has created a boom for temp agencies. For instance, Adecco – the result of the merger of Adia SA in Switzerland and Ecco SA of France – has more than 2,400 offices in forty countries. The company notes that today's temporary worker tends to be older (median age 27.5) and to work longer at each assignment (median assignment length is now six weeks).

As unions work to save jobs, limited workweeks are expected to become increasingly common in Europe. In the Netherlands, for instance, the four-day, thirty-six hour week is catching on, despite the objections of many business leaders. Among companies that have already implemented this policy are Dutch retailer Koninklijke Bijenkorf Beheer (KBB) and banks Internationale Nederlanden Group and ABN AMRO. In France, the Socialist government is enforcing a legislated thirty-nine-hour limit on workweeks with renewed vigour. Thousands of citations have been issued to companies that have employees working overtime without compensation; penalties can include fines as high as US$1 million and jail terms of up to two years. Among companies cited have been Electronics giant Thomson-CSF, home furnishings manufacturer and retailer IKEA and retailer Auchan, all of which have been forced to introduce time clocks for managers. The law is intended to divvy up jobs among a larger proportion of the population.

In *Job Shift: How to Prosper in a Workplace Without Jobs*, transition consultant Dr William Bridges mapped out a vision of a work world in which just about all employees are temporary or contract workers. He believes that in coming years people will no longer *have* jobs, they'll simply *do* jobs. In essence, workers will build and run their own companies, packaging and selling their expertise for certain tasks. Ideally, Bridges says, these workers will be paid by the task and get a slice of the profits. Among other benefits, 'dejobbing', as Bridges terms it, will help companies to avoid the increasing burden of healthcare and other benefits.

## Next: Humans Replaced by Computers

Analysts predict that in the coming century, employment as we know it is likely to be phased out in most of the industrialized nations of the world. For the first time in history, human labour is being systematically eliminated from the economic process. A new generation of sophisticated information and communication technologies, together with new forms of business reorganization and management, is wiping out full-time employment for millions of blue- and white-collar workers.

Jeremy Rifkin (*San Jose Mercury News*) wrote: 'The hard reality that economists and politicians are reluctant to acknowledge is that manufacturing and much of the service sector are undergoing a transformation as profound as the one experienced by the agricultural sector at the beginning of the century, when machines boosted production, displacing millions of farmers. We are in the early stages of a long-term shift from "mass labor" to highly skilled "elite labor," accompanied by increasing automation in the production of goods and delivery of services. Workerless factories and virtual companies loom on the horizon. While unemployment [in the US] is still relatively low, it can be expected to climb steadily over the next four decades as the global economy makes the transition to the Information Age.'

Just as manufacturing jobs were taken over by robots in the 1970s and accounting/finance jobs were taken over by batch-processing computers in the eighties, middle-management jobs are under siege in the nineties. According to a report in *Time* magazine, some analysts predict that by 2001, only one manager in fifty will be promoted in the US, compared with one in twenty in 1987. A key reason is advances in technology that have moved information out of the possession of management and into the general population. Most easily replaced by computers are those middle managers charged with assembling and analysing large quantities of statistical data.

Andersen Consulting estimates that in just one US service industry – commercial banking and thrift institutions – technological and management changes will have eliminated 30 to 40 per cent of jobs by the end of the nineties. That's nearly 700,000 jobs. The number of banks in the US is likely to decline 25 per cent by the year 2000. Technological innovations – including automatic teller machines and financial transactions conducted over the Internet, the use of electronic bar codes and scanners in retail outlets and the promise of home shopping via TV – are significantly reducing the number of humans required to get the job done. The industries spawning these technological innovations are unlikely to generate additional employment, because – unlike the invention of the automobile, which rendered the horse and buggy obsolete but created millions of jobs along the way – the products and services created in the Information Age require fewer workers to produce and operate than did the products and services they replaced.

In a more general survey of senior executives, Olsten Corp. found that 42 per cent of North American corporations report that the changing workplace has caused them to downsize their secretarial and administrative staffs over the last five years. Among firms that have reduced support staff, 78 per cent cite cost cutting as a reason, while 74 per cent attribute reductions to increased automation, including email, voicemail and the rise of computer literacy among managers.

## Next: Growth of SOHOs

As workers begin to rely less on corporate loyalty and more on their own skills, while also taking advantage of the opportunities new technologies afford, more and more of them are setting up shop on their own. Eurostat reports that approximately half of small to midsize businesses in Europe are one-person companies. European nations with the highest concentration of small businesses are Mediterranean countries: Spain, Portugal, Italy and Greece.[1]

Germany hosts the largest number of home-office workers in Europe – about 3.6 million people in the western part of the country alone. Growth in the German SOHO (small office/home office) market is driven primarily by entrepreneurs who have decided to establish their own SOHO, usually in a particular professional field (e.g., real estate, accounting, information services) or to work as self-employed subcontractors for organizations or companies. Spearheading a trend among large companies to alleviate fixed costs through the promotion of home office work, IBM in Germany has an estimated 25 per cent of its staff working out of home offices.

In the US, 30 million households have home offices, one-third more than in 1992, according to IDC/Link. Men and women work from home in approximately equal proportions, according to the US Department of Labor, but women are more likely to work exclusively from the home. Sales of online information services to the SOHO market are expected to reach US$2.5 billion by 2000, according to SOHO Market Analysis & Forecast, a report from Cowles/Simba Information. The study found that online marketing information and lead-generation services will be the largest SOHO sales segment.

## Next: Searching for the *Equal* in Equal Opportunity

Internet and other new technologies will come to serve as a powerful ally for women in any number of fields, for these technologies provide new channels of communication, easier access to information and an increased ability to network with other women – and men – in their industries. Women *have* come a long way, but, as the following statistics demonstrate, the battle for equality around the world is far from over:

- 'Office girls' may be the stylesetters in Japan, but even the most powerful Japanese businesswomen account for no more than 7.9 per cent of Japan's administrative and managerial workers, many fewer than hold the traditional secretary/stenographer/coffee-server positions. Despite the passage of equal-opportunity legislation nine years ago, Japanese employers frequently specify gender preference when advertising jobs. In a bid for greater opportunities, many Japanese women are working abroad. We found it very interesting that while researching a book about Japanese who are employed in Hong Kong, Sumiko Iwao, psychology professor at Keio University, found that whereas all of the Japanese men he interviewed had been transferred to Hong Kong by their employers, all of the women had come of their own accord.
- In Europe, where women constitute 41 per cent of the workforce, they earn up to 40 per cent less than their male counterparts in manufacturing jobs and up to 35 per cent less in service jobs. In the private sector, fewer than 2 per cent of senior management jobs are held by women. 'Family-friendly' benefits such as flexible hours and job-sharing arrangements are rarely accommodated.
- In Britain, five years of campaigns by pressure groups have yielded moderate success: 41 per cent of the 100 largest British companies today have a female board member, as do 12.8 per cent of British companies overall. Women now claim about 2 per cent of senior management jobs in Europe, ranging from Britain's 5.8 per cent to Germany's 1 per cent and Italy's 0.5 per cent. In the US women account for half of the workforce and hold 10 per cent of board seats and 5 per cent of senior management jobs.

Though still significantly behind the US with regard to opportunities for women, the tide in Europe may be turning: A well-established British programme, Opportunity 2000, has convinced 300 member companies to set voluntary numerical goals for promoting women. Among member organizations, fully 32 per cent of management spots are filled by women. One of the bases on which change is promoted is by showing companies the financial benefits of women-friendly policies. According to *Business Week*, Opportunity 2000 convinced entertainment and leisure company Rank Group PLC to let new mothers phase in their return to work as a way of cutting recruitment and training costs. The result after five years: Rank saved US$1.5 million by increasing its retention rate for skilled women from 20 per cent to 80 per cent. French women are also gaining ground in a number of business areas, having assumed positions of power in the medical and legal professions, the military and government. By 2000, women will make up 75 per cent of new workers in Europe, according to the European Commission, and will hold 50 per cent of the slots in European business schools. One result: companies may no longer have any choice but to hire women as managers.

**Making their own Breaks**  In the US, women-owned businesses represent a third of all domestic companies and 40 per cent of all service and retail companies. They generate more than US$1.6 trillion annually and employ more workers than Fortune 500 companies employ worldwide. Women-owned businesses are experiencing greatest growth in the construction, wholesale trade, transportation and manufacturing sectors. The number of such companies in the construction sector, for instance, grew 94.8 per cent between 1987 and 1992 (that compares with a growth rate of only 10.8 per cent in the construction sector generally).

Businesses owned by minority women (black, Asian American, Hispanic and Native American), which today account for more than US$184 billion in sales, are growing at three times the overall rate in the US, according to a report by the National Foundation for Women Business Owners. Between 1987 and 1996 the number of such firms grew 153 per cent, to 1.1 million. This compares with growth rates of 78 per cent for all businesses owned by women and 47 per cent for businesses overall. The areas of greatest growth among businesses owned by minority women were in non-traditional fields, including construction, wholesale trade, transportation and public utilities.

In Germany, one-third of all start-ups are now woman-owned, up from 10 per cent in 1975. Altogether, economists estimate, the 150,000 new female-run companies in Eastern Germany alone have created approximately 1 million new jobs and contribute about US$15 billion to Germany's annual gross domestic product. Researchers who study new business growth in Germany say that companies run by women develop more slowly than those managed by men. One reason is that the profit motive isn't as strong among women entrepreneurs. According to government surveys, women cite earning profits as a fourth or fifth reason for setting up their own companies, after their desire to be self-sufficient and develop their own ideas. Male entrepreneurs cite profits as the number one motive.

**Technofemmes**  Fifteen years ago in the US, 70 per cent of all personal computers were bought by men; today, men and women are buying in equal numbers. A survey by CommerceNet and Nielsen Media Research found that the Internet's 'gender gap' has narrowed significantly. By mid-1997, women accounted for 42 per cent of active online users in the United States and Canada. (In fall 1995 women accounted for just 34 per cent of Net users.) Companies targeting women in cyberspace include cosmetics manufacturer Clinique, which handed out 100,000 free Internet packets at its counters in the US so as to give women the chance to explore the Clinique Website (http://www.clinique.com). Through a partnership with Netcom, Clinique customers received three days of free Internet access.

Women's involvement in technical careers is also growing. In response to studies citing the many obstacles girls face when attempting to pursue studies in maths and science, a number of projects have been developed in the US to encourage and support girls in technical fields. Among them is Camp T-Equity (pronounced tek-witty), based in West Springfield, Virginia, which helps young girls gain entrance into traditionally male professions by opening doors of opportunity related to science, mathematics and technology literacy. Such efforts are beginning to pay off, as women by the thousands are achieving advanced degrees in technical subjects. For example: in the last fifteen years, American women have earned more than 15,000 PhDs in technical fields. Graduate schools in medicine and dentistry are routinely 50 per cent female, and more than 30 per cent of graduate students in astronomy are women.

Once they've established a foothold in a male-dominated field, many women are doing their part to ensure that the climb is a bit easier for the women who follow in their footsteps. For instance, Gillian Marcelle, an economist and lecturer at the University of East London, England, urges her fellow female technocrats to use their positions to help guarantee access, control and diffusion of technology to women worldwide through such means as designing bureau systems and supporting library access to the Internet. Women in Technology International (http://www.witi.org) is one of a number of Websites that furthers such efforts by facilitating and encouraging networking among technocratic women.

## Next: Finding a Job on the Net

New technologies aren't just changing the way we do our jobs – they're changing how we find them. According to a survey released at the 49th Annual Society for Human Resource Management Conference and Exposition in California, approximately two-thirds of the 600 human resource executives surveyed indicated that they currently use the Internet for recruitment purposes. The majority began using the medium within the past year.

Whether one is looking for work or trying to fill a position, the Internet has become a valuable resource. CareerMosaic (http://www. careermosaic.com/), for instance, provides employment information in industries ranging from technology to healthcare, finance and the military. The Monster Board (http://www.monster.com) is also a valuable site. As reported by Newsbytes News Network, a recent survey found that fully 25 per cent of job seekers at The Monster Board site get at least one job offer, and those receiving offers get an average of three. Sue Zaney, the site's VP of product development and marketing, attributes the job board's high success rate to two factors: the growing diversity of job seekers on the site and the fact that 44 per cent of site users are 'passive job seekers . . . people who already have jobs, but are willing to look for something better'. Launched in 1994, The Monster Board was receiving in excess of 2 million visits a month as of January 1998.

## Next: Hot Jobs for the Millennium

As US companies compete to attract and retain talented workers in a tight job market, an increasing number of employers are reshaping their work structures to be not only more flexible, but also more fun. The purpose is to improve employee morale, reduce stress, help manage conflict, motivate workers to be more productive and simply make the workplace a more enjoyable place to be. Companies uncertain of how to inject fun into their business equation can hire such organizations as Playfair Inc., in Berkeley, California, to give their managers tips on how to see their employees as complete human beings with outside interests and concerns. Playfair's approach emphasizes humour as an essential team-building technique. In Boston, Grand Circle Travel has appointed one of its employees 'director of fun'.

Which occupations will thrive in the next millennium? The following are likely to be on the upswing:

**Personal Services**  In an era in which time is an increasingly valuable commodity, we can expect all sorts of people to vie to meet our needs. Sample occupations include the following:

- Online moms: entrepreneurs who do everything from sending email reminders for anniversaries, birthdays, etc. to scheduling dental appointments and providing healthcare pointers.
- Online researchers: don't have time to search the Web for that critical piece of information? Hire someone to do it for you, perhaps keeping him or her on a retainer basis.
- Educational consultants: in addition to providing advice on which schools one's children should attend, these consultants can create individualized education plans, complete with tutoring sessions, educational software selections, edutainment options and so on.
- Babyproofers: specialists who come into the home and make it safe for babies and active toddlers. Also expect a rise in in-home babysaver (infant CPR, etc.), massage and nutrition classes.
- Security: Home security specialists who make sure one's home is as protected as possible from crime.
- Neighbourhood childcare: increasingly common will be neighbourhood 'drop in' centres for children. These might be located in a home or in a variation of a daycare centre.
- Home cooks: expect to see a rise in businesses that deliver frozen home-cooked meals to families on the run. One advantage over takeout meals is that these can be prepared according to individual needs (diets, allergies, etc.).

**Business Services** The rise in contract workers, SOHOs, and temps will create a number of business opportunities. Examples:

- On-site repair services: Under many maintenance agreements, if a recently purchased computer has broken down, the manufacturer sends a technician within days to repair it. Expect such services to be available for all types of electronic equipment.
- Equipment lessors and business sites: rather than invest in expensive equipment right away, savvy entrepreneurs will lease the needed equipment or rent a cubicle (or meeting space, as needed) from a business supersite. Also certain to grow are videoconference centres and technology consultants, who will advise small-business owners with regard to technological purchases.
- Skills trainers: the rapid pace of technological change, combined with the growth of contract workers, will create an increasing need for people who can train not only current employees of a company, but also freelance workers.
- Executive coaches: one of the latest twists on businesses devoted to helping busy people cope is the field of 'executive coaches'. At a cost of as much as US$500 per month, coaches make weekly phone calls to clients in an effort to help them prioritize their goals and better manage their businesses – and their lives. At the centre of the field is Coach University, founded in Salt Lake City, Utah in 1992. The training facility is entirely virtual, attended by 500 students who participate in classes via teleconferences and download data from the university's Website (http://www. coachu.com). The thirty-six course curriculum costs US$2,495 and graduates professional advisers who are part consultant, part therapist and part friend.

And, of course, the Digital Age will clearly spawn new job opportunities for all sorts of high-tech specialists, including multimedia software designers and intranet coordinators.

# What's Next?

**Escalating Competition** Worldwide demand for senior executives is soaring as a result of such factors as increasing economic confidence in Europe and North America, expansion of the financial services sector and growth of both consumer product and high-tech companies. Most in demand in Europe, according to a study by Korn/Ferry International, a global leader in executive search: marketing, sales, advertising and public relations professionals, a sign that the fight for global market share is heating up among European companies.

We'll also see increased competition for highly skilled technical workers, who are being lured already from one company to another by million-dollar signing bonuses and the like. International Technology Association reported 190,000 vacant jobs at large and midsized companies in the US in 1997. Aggravating the demand for technical workers is the fact that the number of college students graduating with degrees in computer science fell 43 per cent between 1986 and 1994, from 42,195 to 24,200. This IT skills shortage is also being felt in Europe, where Logica's CEO announced that his company was unable to recruit sufficient staff last year, placing a number of lucrative contracts in jeopardy.

**Sabbatical Respites** Now that employers and companies are no longer wed for life, we can expect to see more widespread embrace of 'sabbaticals' between career segments. Workers may choose to take a break from work for a number of reasons – to raise a family, go back to school, start a home-based business or another entrepreneurial endeavour or simply to step back and take the time to consider in which direction they next want to go. We suspect that spiritual replenishment will be the focus of a growing number of voluntary sabbaticals, whether the time is used to give back to the community (by spending a year or two teaching in an inner-city school, for example), to travel on a religious pilgrimage or to achieve a life-affirming goal, such as climbing Mount Everest or bicycling across Europe.

As adjuncts to this trend, expect to see the growth of counselling sessions that help individuals plan for their financial security while they enjoy these occasional down years of rebirth and replenishment; extended working years, as individuals opt to put off their eventual retirement in order to take some time-outs earlier in life; and the emergence of partially paid sabbaticals as a corporate benefit in high-stress fields.

**Nix the Tie**  Office dress codes will continue to be relaxed, as boomers taking the corporate reins extend 'casual Fridays' to the rest of the week. Look for men's designers and clothing retailers to increase their lines of 'dressy casuals'.

**Electronic Classrooms**  Top-notch business training and development will be but a click away. We'll also see increased sharing of face2face training sessions as companies see the benefits of dividing the cost of such sessions among corporate neighbours.

**Telecommuting Hubs**  Telecommuters will form place-based workplaces that revolve around workers' philosophies and lifestyles rather than chosen profession.

**Removable Hard Drives**  Compact, portable drives will allow computer users to carry the 'brains' of their computers with them (from work to home to temporary office site to airport lounge), insert them into available hardware, and get right to work.

**Camp Iworkformyself**  Intensive entrepreneur camps will teach teenagers the skills they need to succeed in the next century.

**Harassment Insurance**  As allegations of sexual harassment in the workplace continue to make headline news in North America, insurance policies guarding against such claims will become increasingly common. Today, as reported by Associated Press, more than seventy US companies offer employment practices liability coverage. One company, Hartford Financial Services Group, has sold approximately 1,000 such policies since it began offering them in 1996. The average company buying the policy has approximately forty workers and pays an annual premium of US$3,000.

**Career Partnerships**  Flexible working styles will inspire a growing number of formal and informal 'partnerships' between employees. As workers move from one job and one career to another, this steady partnership with a co-worker will provide stability and increased flexibility, allowing both parties greater leeway than either might have if working alone in a corporate setting. Such partnerships also benefit the employer, ensuring a constant work flow even when one person is absent due to vacation, maternity/paternity leave, or simply an extended business tip.

**Gender-blurred Talking Styles** Gender differences in communication styles are decreasing, according to a study by telecommunications company MCI. The MCI One Monitor study found that men and women are abandoning such stereotypical behaviours as the 'strong, silent' male and the 'emotional' female. The survey found, for example, that men and women today are equally likely to pay attention to body language when communicating in person, report similar tendencies to talk about their personal lives at work and prefer to give bad news in person (something men were thought to avoid). Watts Wacker, the pollster who conducted the study, commented: 'As topics, forms, and styles [of communication] continue to merge, gender communication myths will increasingly be broken. This trend will only be accelerated as gender-irrelevant communication styles develop for modern technologies – further disintegrating the communications barriers between men and women.'

**Fit for Work** As job pressures increase levels of stress, illness and absenteeism, a growing number of companies are investing in initiatives designed to encourage employees to be fit and healthy. In addition to providing corporate gymnasiums or reduced rates at nearby fitness clubs, corporate managers are creating 'lifestyle centres' that incorporate such things as health screening and counselling, behaviour modification classes and healthful cooking courses.

**No-work Weekends** In what is certain to be emulated by other companies, accounting firm Ernst & Young has instituted a telecommunications ban on weekends. Employees have been instructed to resist the temptation to check email and voicemail messages between Friday evening and Monday morning. The new policy stems from concerns over employee stress and the firm's difficulty in retaining female hires.

# 14

# Business Next

When one looks at the primary causes of business failure over the last decade, resistance to change routinely emerges as a culprit. This bodes ill for entrenched traditionalists, for change is one of the few constants businesses will find in the global marketplace in the year 2000, according to an Economist Intelligence Unit (EIU) survey of 10,000 business executives in North America, Europe and Asia. In marketing, we're experiencing that much-overused term – a 'paradigm shift' – as we work to reinvent our industry in an effort to keep pace with rapid changes in communication and consumerism. One result of increased globalization and developments in new media is a push to prepare ourselves for the future by evolving and taking advantage of emerging technologies and cross-border marketing opportunities. By getting in on the early stages of these developments, we're in a good position to foresee – and profit from – emerging forces among consumers and markets and in the ways in which information is imparted and absorbed.

Taking advantage of emerging trends ahead of the competition is a goal of any business, whether selling shoes or building communications networks. Now that so many of us are working in a global market, we face the added challenge of attempting to discern whether a trend spotted locally has implications on a broader scale. Some trends, such as snowboarding and hip-hop, spread relatively quickly among youth populations from one continent to the next. Other trends never make it beyond a particular city or region or continent. Kinders, for instance, the popular children's egg toys made by Ferrero in Italy, are all the rage in parts of Europe, but a similar product failed miserably in the States. Japan's tamagotchi 'virtual pets' have been a phenomenon in Asia and were subsequently introduced in North America and Europe with real success. It remains to be seen whether the American Beanie Baby craze will soon be giving Kinders a run for its money elsewhere in the world.

In Amsterdam, we were particularly keen on watching trends take shape with regard to new technologies. We noted, for instance, the lines of women that very often formed in front of the Internet access pole outside the Van Gogh Museum. (This innovation allows users to surf the Web and send email from a public terminal.) We considered that of particular interest, given some analysts' prognostications that the online gender gap would exist for some time to come in Europe and that business usage, rather than at-home users, would drive the industry. In our view, Net usage in Europe eventually will be driven as much, if not more, by home users than by business usage – paralleling its pattern of growth in North America. It will be interesting to see whether women play a similar role with regard to the adoption of in-home PCs.

A second trend in Amsterdam, which may well be adopted in other multicultural cities, is the use of signage and outdoor advertising in which symbols and graphics have replaced copy (which is increasingly scant) as the conveyor of the essence of messages. As more brands become global, we can expect to see greater emphasis on logos and other symbols that provide a clear voice for a brand without regard to language or culture.

## What's in Store for Business

Business trends, by their very nature, tend to travel more slowly than consumer and marketing trends. Many more organizations talk about fundamental change – throwing around such buzzwords as 'change agents', 'value migration', and 'business ecosystems' – than actually succeed in effecting genuine transformations. To be effective, plans to bring about basal corporate change must fulfil two key requirements: they must be linked directly to performance objectives, and they must be created and managed by people who have an understanding of both the current and preferred business structure.

In much of the developed world today, companies are coming to terms with the notion that the business environment isn't changing, it *is* change. As we discussed in earlier chapters on the emergence of the virtual office and the new worker, technological developments of the last two decades are in no small way driving organizations to re-evaluate how they do business. One clear sign that the business world is focusing on future shifts and opportunities rather than dwelling on past results is the increasing number of companies eliminating the 'review of operations' sections of their annual reports in favour of essays on growth potential and strategies for taking advantage of changes in their businesses and industries. As Les Segal, president of Addison Corporate Annual Reports told the *New York Times*, 'The whole business world is changing so fast that investors don't want to look backward; they want to look forward.'

In the EIU survey mentioned above, 67 per cent of European respondents stated that their companies' organizational structures will undergo great change by the year 2000; 62 per cent expect a similar shift in their corporate cultures. 'It is very hard to win in a status quo environment,' commented respondent Rob Cawthorn, CEO of French pharmaceutical firm Rhone-Poulenc Rorer. To keep his organization in a 'desirable state of flux', Cawthorn (now retired) took steps to prepare his executives for a company in which 'authority is pushed down the line and an entrepreneurial approach is encouraged throughout the company'.

As we move forward in an era of increasing entrepreneurialism, we can expect heightened efforts to close the gap between top executives and their employees, both psychological in nature (executives dressing more casually, for instance) and structural (executives working in the same room as their underlings rather than being ensconced in private corner offices).

This chapter details some of the other broad-based trends we're seeing in the business world today that promise to have an impact on both companies and consumers in the coming years. Business trends specific to advertising and marketing are covered in chapter 18.

## Next: Keep It Simple, Stupid! (The KISS Principle)

A growing awareness that consumers are overwhelmed by the product choices they face has spurred companies in a wide variety of industries to simplify their product lines. According to consulting firm Kurt Salmon Associates, almost a quarter of the products in a typical US supermarket sell fewer than one unit per month. In contrast, 7.6 per cent of all personal-care and household products account for 84.5 per cent of sales, according to Paine Webber, Inc. Responding to the overkill of duplicate brands and unmanageable product lines, Procter & Gamble has slashed its product roster by a third since 1990. Nabisco Inc. has cut its new-product launches by 20 per cent and is taking approximately 15 per cent of its existing products off the market. Toyota has simplified its car design by stripping vehicles of unnecessary parts.

Though almost 24,000 new products were introduced into the US marketplace in 1996 (up from 20,080 in 1995), only 7 per cent of those products were truly new or different from existing products, according to Marketing Intelligence Ltd, a product-tracking service. That represents a big decrease from just ten years earlier, when more than 18 per cent of products introduced were truly innovative. Today, most 'new' products are simply copycat versions of old products or line extensions that bring no meaningful new features or benefits to consumers. In general, though copycat products may eventually carve out a small piece of the market, it's the innovative products that are the big 'home run' winners when it comes to generating sales.

## Next: the Urge to Merge

Until the last few years, Europe historically has avoided mergers, preferring instead to concentrate on local markets, even at the expense of profits. The globalized economy is making that practice ever more unrealistic, however, and European companies are joining the mania associated with blending, merging and acquiring. Among other factors driving the merger movement is fear that the US and Asia will muscle European companies out of entire markets, global pressures for industrial efficiency and the increasing number of European companies falling into foreign hands. Industries deemed most likely to consolidate in Europe include automotive, airline, banking and pharmaceuticals.

One of the most important factors driving mergers around the world is the desire (and need) for global expansion. In a 1997 Watson Wyatt Worldwide survey of top executives in twenty-three countries, nearly half (46 per cent) of the respondents cited global expansion as their company's primary business strategy over the next five years. The survey, 'Competing in a Global Economy', included responses from executives at 2,143 companies. Of executives responding, 40 per cent were CEOs; more than seventy-five participants were members of the Global Fortune 500.

On average, global executives estimate that 30 per cent of their customer base is international today. As the focus of global expansion intensifies over the next five years, they expect that percentage to increase to 38.

*Percentage of Customer Base Expected to Be 'International' in 5 Years*

| | |
|---|---|
| Sweden: | 55% |
| Canada: | 50% |
| Germany: | 50% |
| United Kingdom: | 43% |
| Mexico: | 41% |
| Hong Kong: | 38% |
| United States: | 29% |
| Japan: | 22% |

'The recent economic woes in Asia have only heightened interest among leading executives in serving global markets,' commented George Bailey, global director of the human capital group at Watson Wyatt. 'Currency devaluations and falling stock markets seem to have made companies more determined to expand internationally, not less.'

## Next: This Does Not Compute – Information Overload in the Nineties

According to 'Dying for Information?' a survey of 1,300 managers in Australia, Hong Kong, Singapore, the UK and US (conducted by Benchmark Research for Reuters Business Information):

- 31 per cent of managers receive enormous amounts of unsolicited information.
- 49 per cent feel they are unable to handle the volumes of information received.
- 38 per cent waste substantial time trying to locate the right information.
- 47 per cent say collection of information distracts them from their primary job responsibilities.
- 50 per cent take work home or stay late as a result of having to deal with too much info.
- 61 per cent report that their personal relationships have suffered as a result of info overload.

What are the key factors contributing to information overload? They include the Internet (48 per cent of respondents to the above study believed that the Internet would be the prime cause of info overload in the next two years); telephone/fax; pagers; PDAs (personal digital assistants); the cable-sparked explosion in TV news; the rise in special-interest news; and the expansion of network news offerings.

According to the Reuters study, Information Fatigue Syndrome may harm businesses by creating in their workers high levels of stress, illness, decreased efficiency, paralysis of analytical capacity, inability to make decisions, increased anxiety and self-doubt, and a tendency to blame others. Other results include a lost sense of proportion, inability to determine the relative importance of one piece of information over another, loss of confidence in news sources (73 per cent of respondents to a *Time*/CNN poll in the US reported being 'sceptical about the accuracy' of the news they're getting), and increased need for branded content (information businesses and consumers can trust) and information filters. This spells opportunity for marketers and purveyors of certain products and services, but the overall warning is quite disturbing. If we can't successfully combat information overload in these early stages of the Digital Age, what might the state of our businesses be five or ten years down the road?

## Next: Strategic Planning Back on the Front Lines

After more than a decade of downsizing to raise productivity and efficiency, companies are returning to strategic planning in a bid to increase profits. Business strategy is now the single most important management issue and will remain so for the next five years, according to a survey by the Association of Management Consulting Firms.

'The increased focus on shareholder values that developed in the late 1980s and became acute in the early 1990s has had a profound effect on the way business is conducted – on the motives behind the actions and the impact on the consumer,' says Laurence Bernstein, an account planner at Y&R Toronto. 'As the focus of business and marketers shifted from sales improvement to share price improvement, product development, marketing planning, personnel development, etc. all became more short-term focused. Rightsizing (or downsizing), the fundamental expression of corporate re-engineering, resulted in fewer mid- and long-term programmes – those managers and employees left were (and still are) hard pressed to accomplish their immediate functional tasks, leaving little opportunity for strategic planning and development.'

Bernstein continues, 'Marketing was especially hard hit, as new-product development, market-share investment, etc. fell by the wayside. As a result, traditional industry leaders allowed smaller, less accomplished companies to introduce leading-edge products, grow their market niches and so on. Large corporations are now scrambling to become more current (they seem to have missed a technological wave); and many seem to be floundering. There will probably be a flurry of small and medium company buyouts in the next few years as companies realize that their focus on 'core competencies' in a climate of intense technological change was fundamentally flawed.'

Today's breed of strategic planning is different from the eighties version in that the process is no longer confined to the senior elite. The trend towards 'democratized' planning calls for input from all levels of the company, and also from customers and suppliers. Finland's Nokia Group, for instance, involved 250 employees in a strategic review in early 1995, according to *Business Week*, and the company's top executive team now holds monthly strategic meetings. One result: creation of a 'smart car' unit in Germany to develop products for the auto industry. In the US J. M. Smucker Co. enlisted 140 employees (7 per cent of its workforce) to devote nearly 50 per cent of their time to a major strategy exercise for more than six months. Additional input was solicited from all 2,000 employees. At the conclusion of the project, the company anticipated that resultant initiatives would double its US$635 million in revenues over the next five years.

## Next: Quest for Competitive Intelligence

Long accepted in Europe, competitive 'snooping' is now taking hold in the US, reports *Business Week*. The number of large US corporations with CI units has tripled since 1988, to about 10 per cent, according to the Futures Group, Inc. And, of course, snooping has become far easier in this world of computers and modems – and hackers for hire. A survey conducted by *USA Today* in co-operation with a US congressional committee suggests that more than half of major US corporations have been victimized by computer break-ins – more than one-fifth of which were believed to be the work of competitors. Fifty-eight per cent of participating companies reported a break-in during the past twelve months, with nearly 18 per cent of those reporting losses of more than US$1 million. President Clinton signed legislation in October 1996 making industrial espionage a federal crime in the US, carrying penalties of up to fifteen years in jail and US$10 million in fines.

Reasons for the growth in industrial espionage are manifold: economic globalization requires better intelligence to anticipate threats from abroad and to penetrate overseas markets; the quickening pace of technological change and deregulation make it easier than ever to be blindsided by a competitor, who can take the lead with a single innovation; and digging up information on rivals' products and strategies is facilitated by the Net and CD-ROM databases, which contain information it once would have taken days or weeks to ferret out. Assisting in such searches are such companies as Real World Intelligence Inc., which offers customized software developed for the US Central Intelligence Agency.

## Next: Renewed Focus on Developing Customer Loyalty
With more women in the workforce and the increased need for men and women to juggle the responsibilities of work and home, many consumers are growing increasingly frustrated by the retail shopping experience. Key complaints: inadequate selection, high prices, poor service, and inconvenient hours and locations.

**Innovative Retail Techniques**  To attract and retain today's difficult-to-please consumers, retailers are turning to innovative strategies. Hyperefficient operators (e.g., Wal-Mart, Home Depot), based on the French hypermarket concept, are expanding their offerings while shrinking prices. Specialist stores (e.g., Sunglass Hut, PetsMart, Baby Superstore, Tie Rack) are seeking to dominate narrow categories via deep selection and low prices. Large companies are staking a claim to convenience by bringing the mountain to Mohammed. Examples: in-mall McDonald's; bank branches in supermarkets; and travel offices and post offices in department stores.

Retailers are also attempting to reinject 'fun' into the shopping equation. Borders book superstores, for example, come complete with CD listening stations, a kids' reading area (regularly featuring puppet shows, storytelling, and other events), in-store cafés and live entertainment. IKEA attracts busy shoppers with in-store dining and play areas for children.

It's interesting to note the potential of Internet retailers to take advantage of each of these retail strategies. Consumers in search of the bargain

prices they associate with hypermarkets and other discounters can scan
the Net for the lowest prices on a variety of products via such services
as Whats4Sale (http://www.whats4sale.com/), CompareNet (http://
www.compare.net/), PriceHunter (http://www.pricehunter.com/), and
KillerApp Computer Channel (http://www.killerapp.com/). And there
can be no better place than the Web to locate speciality products. Among
other highly specific sales sites already online are Lens Express (contact
lenses) at http://www.lensexpress.com; Any Watch U Want (wristwatches) at http:/www.anywatch.com; The Hat Shack (http://www.
hatshack.com); The Pepper Plant (http://www.pepperplant.com); and
Cheese Cake City (http://www.cheesecakecity.com).

**Corporate Concierges** In an effort to strengthen customer loyalty, a
growing number of companies is offering concierge services to valued
clients. As reported in the *INSIDE 1to1* e-letter (http://www.1to1.com/),
these services may range from scoring tickets to sold-out events to
finding a hard-to-locate product or getting a car serviced. Many of these
companies outsource the service, relying on such organizations as San
Francisco-based LesConcierges (http://www.lesconcierges.com) and
Washington, DC–based Capitol Concierge (http://www.capitolcon-
cierge.com), which maintain the high-tech databases and call-centre
infrastructures necessary to handle consumer requests around the clock.

While the corporate concierge business has traditionally been local
or regional, it is now going national and, for some clients, global.
According to *INSIDE 1to1*, American Express, Visa, MasterCard, Diner's
Club and General Motors are just some of the big names that have
adopted concierge services as a value-added amenity. Companies in an
array of other industries – including telecommunications, airlines and
insurance – are considering such services as well.

**New Ways to Reach Youth** As superstores continue to edge smaller
operations out of the market, manufacturers are under increased pressure to produce a greater variety of products more quickly. This is
particularly evident in the toy category. Today, just four retailers –
Toys 'R' Us, Wal-Mart, Target and Kmart – account for approximately
two-thirds of US toy sales.

With limited retail shelf space a growing problem for some manufacturers, alternative distribution routes are evolving. For example, Bright
Ideas (now owned by Addison Wesley) uses consultants to demonstrate

and sell educational software in consumers' homes – it's the Tupperware party of the nineties. The company recently added another distribution channel by launching Bright Schools, a hands-on workshop that shows teachers how to integrate software into their classrooms.

Increased retail competition in the children's market is also spurring the formation of all manner of creative production and marketing part-nerships. Preschool-toy giant Fisher-Price and computer manufacturer Compaq, for example, are collaborating on a line of compu-toys geared to families with kids under age seven. Kraft Foods Inc. and cable net-work Nickelodeon have entered into a deal whereby Kraft will spend US$10 million on advertising on the cable network, while also offering coupons on twenty-five Kraft 'kids' food' brands for Nickelodeon toys.

In coming years, we can expect to see familiar toys being sold on shelves right next to related software packages, offering a variety of choices and different learning styles that appeal to children.

**Join the Club** A broad variety of companies have begun to encourage multiple sales and brand loyalty by inviting kids and parents to join special clubs. In the US the Book-of-the-Month Club has begun a divi-sion for children aged six months to ten years. The Books of My Very Own Club features a low-cost introductory book package and monthly mailings of books geared to the child's age group. There's also a club featuring books by Dr Seuss (The Beginning Readers' Programme, by Grolier Books). In the sports apparel category, Kids Foot Locker and Nike teamed up to offer the Future All-Stars Club. Kids who signed up received a free Michael Jordan or Gail Devers poster along with a 'letter of encouragement'. The Lego Builders Club, offering discount coupons and a Lego magazine, is one club that builds loyalty while also soliciting consumer feedback from kids.

An increasing number of companies don't even wait for the child to be born before targeting parents with club memberships: Carnation, for example, offers expectant mothers a Disney Babies Mom-to-Be planner, information on childcare and discount coupons for Carnation products. Supermarkets have also been targeting expectant parents, mailing dis-count coupons, product samples and other incentives to parents who sign up for their 'baby club'.

**Service with a Smile** In Europe, consumer dissatisfaction with the retail process very often has as much to do with poor service as with long lines or lack of parking. The European attitude to service has often baffled visitors from North America and Asia. The key to understanding the surliness, sloppiness and general unhelpfulness of many European service workers is the mindset that the job exists for the benefit of the person doing the serving, not for the benefit of the person being served. A logical consequence of this has been the tendency of shops and offices to close, to suit the staff, at just the times when customers need them.

As Edward Appleton, managing director of Y&R GmbH Frankfurt, commented, Germans find the idea of service demeaning. They are far from alone in Europe (with the honourable exception of professional waiters and bar staff in France and Italy). But the demise of many older industries and the rise of service-based industries is forcing Europeans to rethink their attitudes towards service. Customers may have accepted grudging service in the past, but as competition increases, their preference is likely to go to businesses that provide service that is both competent and friendly.

Y&R offices in Spain, Italy, Germany and Sweden anticipate greater emphasis on the quality and variety of services in their countries.

## What's Next?

**Going Dutch** Look for the Netherlands to emerge as a centre of European business. According to the Holland International Distribution Council, the Netherlands is already home to a growing number of European distribution centres, including 57 per cent of centres established in Europe by US companies, 71 per cent of Taiwanese, 60 per cent of Korean and 52 per cent of Japanese centres. In the past, when overseas companies set up businesses in Europe, their distribution centres were scattered around the Continent. As more companies move towards centralized distribution, the Netherlands has emerged as the site of choice because of its multilingual population, stable government and economy, and lower start-up costs compared with those in neighbouring countries.

**Ethical Consumption** Europeans with a social conscience used to vote socialist and regard the idea of 'consumers' and 'consumption' with distaste, but socialism lost and Europeans are all consumers now.

In the future, these urges will express themselves as ethical consumption, with a warm glow as part of the added value.

In past years, German consumers have been particularly militant, refusing, for instance, to buy drinks in plastic bottles (glass good, plastic bad) and boycotting Shell in protest over its proposed sinking of an oil platform in the North Sea. 'Fair trade' and 'sustainable production' products are widely available, and not only at Body Shop outlets. In Denmark, consumers can buy eggs produced in cages at 1,00 Kroner each or happy eggs at 2,83 Kr. These eggs are produced in *voilières* and on the pack are the farmer's name, a picture of the farmer, and a description of how happy the chickens are.

As Sus Røedgaard of Y&R Copenhagen points out, companies will have to be increasingly careful about the ethical implications of their actions, which will open up opportunities for agents to help them source ethically impeccable products.

**Corporate Philosophers** There's still hope for liberal arts majors! As reported in *Slate* (http://www.slate.com/): 'The job market for academic philosophers is as desperate as ever, but deep thinkers now have a range of alternative careers. A French outfit, Philocit, offers pricey "philosophical consulting" to companies looking to add Heideggerian heft to their marketing strategies. (Clients can subscribe to Philocit's telephone consultation service for US$2,600 per year.)'

**Land of the Rising Sun Looks West** In a sign that Japan's multi-national corporations have become more sensitive to global standards of accountability (particularly towards shareholders), Matsushita Electric Industrial Co., one of Japan's most conservatively run corporations, has committed to a number of Western-style management changes, reports the *New York Times*. Matsushita, maker of Panasonic electronic appliances, announced it would repurchase shares, introduce a stock option plan for senior executives and directors, link managers' salaries to the performance of its stock and streamline its board room.

'Steps like this are hopefully marking a beginning of change from the Japanese style of capitalism to one that's more Western- and shareholder-oriented,' said Clifford Shaw, president of Mercury Asset Management Japan Ltd, a subsidiary of Merrill Lynch & Co. 'It's a straw in the wind, but it's a promising one.'

**Blurring Borders** In a trend that has enormous implications for business next, the Population Reference Bureau (US) reports that migration is at an all-time high around the world and is likely to increase. Today, approximately 125 million people live outside their birth country – roughly equal to the entire population of Japan or 2 per cent of the world population.

**Wired CEOS** If you want to catch the attention of business executives ten years from now, don't rely on traditional news channels. Ninety-one per cent of US executives surveyed by Deloitte & Touche (http://www.us.deloitte.com) expect the Internet to be an important business news source for them in 2005, while only 50 per cent expect to get their news from daily newspapers. Following the Internet, the next most important sources of news, according to executives, will be the corporate intranet (80 per cent) and email (74 per cent).

# How Commerce and Media Work Us: Next Persuasion

## [15]

## Cyberbiz

'The Internet promises to revolutionize the dynamics of international commerce and, like the telephone and fax machine, may be a major force in the democratization of capitalism. Small companies will be able to compete more easily in the global marketplace, and consumers in emerging markets, in particular, will benefit from the expanded range of products, services and information to which the Internet will give them access,' wrote John A. Quelch and Lisa R. Klein in 'The Internet and International Marketing', an article published in the prestigious *Sloan Management Review*. Their 1996 prediction has already become a reality.

In the mid-1990s, Jay Chiat often said that the only people making money on the Internet were those who were holding conferences about it. We shared the point of view that new-media strategies and opportunities should be embraced enthusiastically – but conservatively. The newness of the field spelled enormous opportunity for companies that could exploit these new technologies ahead of the competition, but there was no sense in devoting a level of resources that was entirely out of scale with the expected returns. Why pay for a product that was still in the 'testing' phase?

In those days, we worked hard to divine the value of the Internet as an advertising medium and connectivity tool, for we all recognized that the goals of any interactive initiative must emanate directly from our client's business goals. For example, if a client company has a direct-sales organization, a goal of any of its communications – interactive included – must be the generation of leads. In turn, the cost-effectiveness of that interactive lead-generation effort must be compared with all other methods of generating leads in terms of specific return on investment.

If an agency's interactive work is compelling and effective, it is because its approach is no different for new-media work than it is for any other type of communications. It is still built on the discipline of combining keen consumer insight with the development of distinctive creative output. Part of that insight has come from understanding and utilizing the 'coin of the realm' of new media: information, interactivity, promotion of user participation and information exchange and entertainment.

With all the hype one hears about the Internet, many people who expected early miracles have become cynical, discounting the progress that actually has been made. And while it's true that some early estimates of business usage were inflated, it's equally true that – to one extent or another – companies in most, if not all, industries have begun to take advantage of the services the Internet offers. Business being conducted on the Net today ranges from direct sales to advertising and promotion, from 1:1 marketing to bulk emailing. And more and more businesses are reaching the conclusion that 'if they build it [a Website], the customer will come'.

Of course, the degree to which the Internet has been interwoven into our business and personal worlds varies radically from continent to continent, country to country and even person to person. Yet even in countries that are only just beginning to embrace the Net (much less e-commerce), there is a sense that big developments are just around the corner.

## North America Leads the Way

Just a couple of years ago, when the Internet was often presented as a mysterious entity clouded with hype and hope, cautious marketers could reasonably ask, 'Fine, but who's on it?' quickly followed by 'OK, so who's making money from it?' Today, the answer to both questions is 'many people'. User numbers are building fast, and numerous smart retailers, both established and brand new, have shown that it's possible to do big business online.

Nearly one-third of US consumers with online access have purchased products or services on the Internet, according to consulting firm Ernst &

Young. The firm also notes that 53 per cent of Internet users in a recent survey cited convenience as the main reason for its appeal; 45 per cent said cost savings were also a factor. A report from the US Department of Commerce (http://www.e-commerce.gov/retail.htm) forecasts that Internet retailing will reach US$7 billion by the year 2000. If mail-order sales can be used to determine the potential for Web retail sales, as some suggest, that figure could reach US$115 billion in five to eight years.

Among other factors spurring Net sales are increasing demands on consumers' leisure time and the improvement of overnight and second-day delivery services. These factors, which spurred the growth of catalogue shopping in the 1980s and 1990s, are now leading people to shop over the Internet. By the end of 1997, 10 million consumers in the US and Canada had purchased something over the Web, up from 7.4 million six months earlier.

Consider the following stats:

- 1-800-FLOWERS sold US$30 million online in 1997. While Internet sales represent only 10 per cent of the company's total revenues, their profit contribution to the overall business is nearly equal to that of its store-based business, which is twice as large.
- In 1996, online bookstore Amazon.com recorded sales of less than US$16 million. In 1997, its sales reached US$148 million.
- Sixteen per cent of all new car and truck buyers used the Internet as part of their shopping process in 1997, up from 10 per cent in 1996. By 2000, the Internet will probably be used in at least 21 per cent of all new car and truck purchases.
- *Inter@ctive Week* reports that online travel services are favoured to be the top money-making category for electronic commerce over the next five years. According to the Travel Industry Association of America, nearly 14 million people (9 per cent of US travellers) used the Net to plan trips or make reservations in 1997. This figure was expected to reach 75 million (38 per cent of the US adult population) by the end of 1998. One such site, Microsoft's Expedia travel service (http://expedia.msn.com/daily/homedefault.hts), logged more than US$100 million in sales during 1997 and draws about 1 million unique visitors per month.
- Andersen Consulting predicts that online grocery shopping will grow to US$60 billion and account for nearly 12 per cent of the consumer packaged-goods business over the next ten years.

- In the clothing sector, The Gap's Website is close to being one of the chain's biggest stores in terms of sales volume.
- The *New York Times* reports that between June 1997 and March 1998, the percentage of people who purchased online stocks and mutual funds doubled from 14 per cent to 28 per cent.

## Nexts Contributing to the Marketspace Opportunity

### Next: Online Window Shopping as a Precursor to True E-commerce

With many 'newbies' initially hesitant to make purchases online, Internet window shopping has become an important process of introducing consumers to the world of e-commerce. Comparing products, models and prices is much easier online, even if the buyer intends eventually to buy over the counter.

Research figures indicate that Internet users are getting wise to the window shopping potential of the Net:

- According to IntelliQuest Information Group (February 1998), although just 17 per cent of Internet users currently make purchases online, nearly 60 per cent of them shop online. Finding information about a product's price or features, checking on product selection, and determining where to purchase a product are the most popular shopping activities.
- An American Internet User Survey found that fully 75 per cent of adults who use the Web sought online product and investment information in the last quarter of 1997, up from 54 per cent in the second quarter.

### Next: Barriers to E-commerce Will Continue to Fall

The potential for today's online window shoppers to become tomorrow's e-shoppers is great. Research has found that as users become more comfortable with the Internet, many of their concerns regarding the security of e-shopping are ameliorated. 1-800-FLOWERS, for instance, recently reported that fewer than one-third of its customers worry about credit card security, compared with almost 75 per cent in 1996. Word of mouth, combined with new technologies and standards for safeguarding sensitive information, will help to alleviate consumer concerns even further.

Around the world, companies eager to transact business in cyberspace are taking steps to remove obstacles to consumer e-shopping. Examples:

**Obstacle** Fear of Credit Card Fraud

In the 'real world', walking around stores with a wallet and credit cards is a security risk – loss and theft are not unusual, and there are numerous scams to perpetrate credit card fraud. Despite this, consumers appear to be far more concerned about using credit cards online. Online transactions are much less familiar, and newcomers are reluctant to send credit card details to a computer that may be thousands of miles away. Even more worrying to some is the risk of one's financial details being intercepted by a third party.

**Solution** A Mix of Experience and New Safety Mechanisms

Conducting transactions online seems to be the best way to ease such concerns. Ernst & Young reported in January 1998 that 70 per cent of Internet users said they are uncomfortable sending their credit card number over the Web. This sense of insecurity lessens with experience: the majority (52 per cent) of people who make purchases via the Web claim to be happy with Internet security.

New safety mechanisms also are easing fears:

- ISP Prodigy is offering a '100% Safe Shopping Guarantee'. This protects the consumer from any liability resulting from unauthorized use of their credit cards.
- Wave Systems will incorporate a chip that acts like a credit card into IBM computers. The chip – which, according to Wave Systems, provides a more secure method of online payment – will hold consumers' account balances, transaction logs and software execution licences. The company believes it will also change the way people purchase online, offering the ability to rent, pay-per-use, or rent to own.
- eCHARGE Corporation has launched an electronic payment system that charges online purchases to the customer's telephone bill. The system will automatically identify a customer's computer and bill accordingly.

■ ■ ■

**Obstacle** The Need to Return Goods
What happens when a buyer finds that a product ordered online is
faulty or not as expected? Returning a product to a catalogue company
is one thing, but what about a merchant that only provides a cyber-
address or is located on another continent?

**Solution** PackageNet Returns Made Easy!
Microsoft Network is partnering with United Parcel Service to offer a
returns service called PackageNet Returns Made Easy! for online merchandise that doesn't meet the customer's needs.

■ ■ ■

**Obstacle** Fear of Big Brother
Cybersites like to gather as much data as possible about their visitors –
the more they know about users' Web-surfing habits, purchase patterns
and personal details, the better they can target promotions and/or sell
information to interested parties. So when a buyer connects with a
merchant's computer, who knows what information the computer can
ferret out?

**Solution** Privacy Safeguards
In an effort to assuage consumers' concerns about providing personal
information to Website operators, industry leaders, including the Electronic Freedom Foundation and CommerceNet, have championed
eTRUST, a program aimed at protecting personal privacy rights on the
Net and building consumer confidence in e-commerce. The backers
believe that informing consumers of how their information will be used
by Website operators is an important first step towards gaining their
trust – and patronage. The Boston Consulting Group, authors of the
'eTRUST Internet Privacy Study', estimate that if 10 per cent of online
retail sites were to adopt eTRUST, the resultant increase in transactions
could add a quarter of a billion dollars to electronic commerce in the
following year.
    Concerned about the potential loss of personal privacy online, the
international WWW Consortium (W3C), which oversees use of the
Web, is developing a Platform for Privacy Preference (P3P) to enable
Web users to dictate how much, if any, information is collected by

Internet providers about site visits, purchases, and other Web habits.

Technology has broken through the brick wall. Now it is up to executives to determine which way they want to go. Just a few months ago, skeptics were calling the Internet the 'World Wide Wait' due to congestion, long response times and busy signals. Today, the network backbone has been enhanced and service providers have caught up with demand.

When mail order catalogs first came out, consumers did not want to give their credit card number over the telephone. Convenience won out and many consumers now regularly phone in their orders. The Internet can fulfill the ultimate promise of convenience. No need to even wait for the catalog.

Stuart Lipoff and Dr Janice Huxley Jens, Arthur D. Little[1]

## Next: Front-Running E-Shopping Products Are 'Knowns' and 'Understoods'

In time, virtually all goods and services will be available online. In the Internet's nascent stages, however, consumers are tending to purchase items that don't require 'looking' or 'touching'. According to Ernst & Young's 'Internet Shopping' study (January 1998), the best-selling products in cyberspace today are computers, software, books, travel, music and magazine subscriptions. Apparel is emerging as a popular choice as well, particularly among women.

E-shopping is proving especially ideal in categories that traditionally have faced limited shelf space, including music, books and videos. Unencumbered by the cost of real estate or the need to tie up capital in stock, cybersites are able to offer a far more diverse selection than can their offline counterparts. Amazon.com, for instance, offers a selection of 2 million book titles to Internet customers. In comparison, traditional book superstores carry approximately 150,000 titles. Similarly, Reel.com, the world's largest movie store, maintains a selection of more than 85,000 film titles online. This breadth of selection is particularly appealing to those in search of hard-to-find titles. As a result, the top-selling movies on the Net today aren't classics or blockbusters, but a mix of cult classics and offbeat films. According to Reel.com, the top ten movies sold in 1997 were *In the Realm of the Senses*, *Better Off Dead*, *A Clockwork Orange*, *Blade Runner*, *Clerks*, *Beyond the Valley of the Dolls*, *The Manchurian Candidate*, *Poison Ivy 2: Lily*, *Pink Flamingos* and *Brazil*.

## Next: E-commerce's Entrepreneurial Edge

Joining the e-commerce revolution doesn't automatically mean strato-spheric increases in sales, as many established companies have dis-covered. E-shopping requires a different way of thinking – and one that may not come naturally to larger companies. In 1998, Internet-only startups have the advantage of being totally focused on their online business and having structured their operations accordingly. As noted in a recent report from the US Department of Commerce, 'These new Internet-only businesses had a head start of one to two years during which they invested heavily to build a brand image and gain market share before super retailers like Wal-Mart, Barnes and Noble, the Gap, and JC Penney equipped their Websites with a sales capability.'

It's interesting to note that only 15 to 20 per cent of the impressive sales figures rung up in cyberspace thus far have gone to online sites of conventional retailers, according to investment company Piper Jaffray. Most were rung up in the travel and financial services industries and in business-to-business sales, noted the *New York Times*. The merchants finding the most success at selling online tend to be ones that exist only online (e.g., Amazon.com).

Established companies have every reason to hone an entrepreneurial edge in order to compete in cyberspace, though. Traditional retail already is finding that competition from online retail is making life tougher. The US retail sector fired 55,393 workers in 1997 (up 32 per cent from 1996), in part to cope with increased competition from online shopping business, according to a survey by outplacement firm Chal-lenger, Gray & Christmas. Online commerce has a 4 per cent higher profit margin than traditional sales avenues, according to Forrester Research.

Fortunately for larger companies, brand-name recognition gives Web-sites a big boost. Ernst & Young's recent 'Internet Shopping' study found, for instance, that 69 per cent of online shoppers surveyed base their online buying decisions, in large part, on their familiarity with the company. Nearly three-quarters knew both the brand and the online store they were looking for when they made their last online purchase.

# Focus: How Two Industries are Conducting Business in Cyberspace

## The Music Industry

For a medium based on sight rather than sound, the Internet is having a tremendous impact on the worldwide music industry. It's become a base in which audiophiles exchange opinions, record labels push the artists on their rosters and music retailers hawk their wares.

Music-related content online includes information (tour dates, artist bios, new releases, reviews, etc.), message boards and chatrooms, live events, the sale of music and related merchandise, e-zines, contests, special promotions and fan clubs. Virtually every major record company has an online presence. Music-related newsgroups run the gamut from alt.music.techno to alt.rock-n-roll to alt.music.beethoven to alt.music. bootleg.

Music enthusiasts can 'attend' concerts and interviews online featuring the likes of Simple Minds, Smashing Pumpkins and flautist Eugenia Zuckerman, or they can choose to sample prerecorded audio selections courtesy of a variety of sites, many run by record companies. David Bowie took this concept one step further by releasing the song 'Telling Lies' exclusively on the Net (http://www.davidbowie.com). Despite a download time of seven hours (with a 28.8 modem), Netizens were undeterred: 100,000 downloads of the pitch-perfect recording were completed during the first month. Taking advantage of online marketing capabilities, Mercury Records made available for downloading a live, unreleased version of John Mellencamp's 'Key West Intermezzo (I Saw You First)' via AOL. A live cyberspace chat with Mellencamp followed.

A number of sites now use 'intelligent agent' software to generate a list of selections based on the visitor's musical preferences. Bignote (http://www.bignote.com), for example, surveys information submitted by its brigade of more than 1 million music fans to find artists the user is likely to enjoy, based on the user's ratings of other artists. The site, which is part of the Firefly network (http:/www.firefly.com), provides a free home page for each member, chatrooms, and links to reviews, audio samples and artist biographies.

**Converting Consumer Interest into Sales** CDs are among the top-selling items on the Net. Reasons for the success of electronic music mail-order houses include the buyer's ability to sample songs prior to purchase and to take advantage of modest discounts (typical price: US$9.95), and the seller's ability to reduce overheads and 'stock' a broader assortment of titles.

Internet Underground Music Archive (http://www.iuma.com/) got its start selling CDs of unsigned bands. Today, the Website carries titles from more than 1,000 bands, a number of which have been signed by major labels as a result of Net exposure. The site draws more than a quarter of a million hits per day and brings in nearly US$1 million a year. Relatively unknown artists are also getting a push from some major labels. For instance, the popular Sony Music Website (www.sony. com), which supports pages for all Sony labels and many of its artists, is credited with sparking booming record sales for the then largely unknown alternative band Korn (Epic/Immortal Records). Following this Net exposure, Korn's new CD, *Life Is Peachy*, broke onto *Billboard*'s album chart at number three, selling 152,000 albums in its first two weeks.

The Camelot Music site (http://www.camelotmusic.com) recommends music selections based on input from users, enables visitors to preview every track on a CD prior to purchase, and is supported by interactive computer-assisted ordering directly from the site. By early 1997, more than 1.2 million 30-second sound bytes were available from 80,000 CDs. The site attracts up to 120,000 hits a day.

Internet Music & Video Shop in the UK (http://www.musicshop. co.uk) sells discounted CDs online. With the UK already one of the cheapest places in Europe to buy CDs, the site receives approximately 60 per cent of its business from outside the country (14 per cent of which comes from the US). Approximately 5 per cent of those who visit the Internet Music & Video Shop make a purchase.

Despite all this activity, e-sales still represent a tiny portion of overall industry sales. According to Jupiter Communications, online music purchases were only about two-tenths of 1 per cent of the US industry's total in 1996. Look for that figure to grow rapidly in the next few years.

**Music Industry Next** Until recently, most companies shied away from distributing albums directly on the Net due to unanswered technical and legal questions. This has changed in the past year or so, as sites such as superSonic BOOM (http://www.supersonicboom.com) and Musicmaker (http://www.musicmaker.com) allow visitors to create and download custom CDs. Electronic delivery of music recordings could represent a US$2 billion market in coming years, according to the International Federation of Phonographic Industries. In anticipation of what's to come, there are now 'enhanced' CDs that combine sound and multimedia data and run on both audio CD players and properly equipped PCs. Enhanced CDs are identified in stores by a label that reads 'See What You Can Hear'. Internet music is also coming out of the box. Aristo International Corporation plans to put high-tech jukeboxes and video games linked to the Internet in bars, hotels and other public places. The company's MusicNet Plus plays high-quality digital music and enables customers to buy recordings and merchandise from bands, as well as tickets to events. (The machines are expected to sell for a price comparable to current coin-operated vending machines.)

## The Automotive Industry

The automotive industry is undergoing massive change already even outside the Internet, with car-makers revamping their distribution systems; large, national chains entering the market; and dealers experimenting with changes in service. On top of this, the Internet is beginning to change the way consumers research, buy and finance their new and used cars. This is particularly apparent in the States, where Internet usage is sufficiently common to make advertising and selling on the Net economical for dealers.

**The Educated Consumer** Increased access to information is putting car buyers in the driver's seat. Al the major manufacturers have sites online, featuring such information as product specifications, list prices, dealer locations and company histories. Most sites will also mail out additional information (in the form of a brochure, videotape or CD-ROM) on request. Microsoft's CarPoint (http://carpoint.msn.com) lets users search among more than 900 car models based on criteria the user selects. The search function includes 'Surround Video', an interactive feature that gives the user 360-degree interior views. Fighting Chance (http://www.fightingchance,com) features updated information on pricing and dealer rebates. IntelliChoice CarCenter (http://www.intelli-choice.com) provides product specifications, product reviews and advice for buyers. For US$4.95, the service will provide a downloadable report that includes information, invoice pricing for all options, current rebates and incentives and five-year cost-of-ownership evaluations.

The well-known *Edmund's Automobile Buyer's Guides* are online (http://www.edmunds.com), as is the *Kelley Blue Book* (http://www. kbb.com), which provides resale pricing on used cars. For used-car buyers, Vehicle History Report (http://www.vinguard.com) charges US$19.95 to take a vehicle identification number and search the vehicle's history for theft and accidents.

**Car Sales Online** In the past three years, car sales on the Net have become a viable business. Though online sales sites accounted for only about 1.5 per cent of all new-car sales in the US as of mid-1997, some analysts are predicting that as many as one out of five new-car buyers will make their purchases via the Net within the next two years. A study by J. D. Power & Associates has found that 70 per cent of new-car buyers in the US use or own a computer, and that 45 per cent of those people would consider using the Internet to shop for their next vehicle. In the past year, the number of people willing to buy an automobile over the Web jumped from 4 to 10 per cent, according to a study by the Dohring Company. And 38 per cent of consumers aged 35–49 said they would use the Internet to assist them in the car-buying process.

Some sites are even beginning to feature such services as online loan applications, credit approval and insurance sales, and a recent report from research and consulting firm Killen and Associates forecasts that within the next five years more auto loans will be processed via the Internet than through traditional channels.

Auto-By-Tel (http://www.autobytel.com) is one of the major sites that lets consumers order and buy new cars online. The company encourages consumers to access other online sites for vehicle information (the site provides links), then contact Auto-By-Tel for the actual purchase. Auto-By-Tel forwards the buyer's name and order to a local dealer (1,700 dealers were participating as of mid-1997), who calls the customer within forty-eight hours with a firm (no haggle) price, prepares all paperwork in advance, and may even drop off the car at the buyer's home. Auto-By-Tel charges dealers a sign-up fee of US$2,500–US$4,500, an annual fee of US$2,500, and an additional fee of US$500–US$1,500 a month per car brand. In return, dealers receive all customer inquiries within their exclusive territories.

In its first two years of operation, Auto-By-Tel reportedly turned 450,000 purchase requests over to dealers, approximately half of which resulted in sales. (As of spring 1998, the company reports that it is processing more than 100,000 purchase requests each month and generating US$500 million a month in auto sales.) Auto-By-Tel offers online financing through Chase Manhattan Bank and leasing through GE Capital. The company has also unveiled a used car cyberstore, which lists only vehicles that have been through a 135-point certification programme. They are backed by a seventy-two-hour, 100 per cent money-back return policy and a three-month/3,000-mile warranty.

A 1997 study by the National Automobile Dealers Association found that nearly 30 per cent of all US dealerships have Internet email addresses and report an average of forty-three leads from the Net each month. The average dealer sells an average of 2.5 more new vehicles and 1.6 more used vehicles per month because of their Net accessibility. Advantages to dealers who participate in online car shopping include decreased advertising costs, expanded sales areas, opportunities to establish an ongoing relationship with customers and decreased staffing needs. Advantages to buyers include increased leverage against dealers; no-haggle sales; savings in time and, in many cases, money.

Car dealers in the States are also using the Net to fight back against superstores such as CarMax and increase sales. In Atlanta, for example, a dozen new-car dealers and some private investors have formed the Used Car Network, featuring a toll-free hotline and Website. The site has photos and information on the used-car inventory of its thirty subscribing dealers. The Used Car Network hopes eventually to include a vehicle-inspection programme and used-vehicle warranty programme.

## What's Next?

**Web Hosts** Forrester Research estimates that building and operating a standard, in-house Website costs over US$300,000 per year; the cost of an interactive site with shopping capabilities can reach US$3.4 million. As an alternative, companies are using Web hosting services that install and operate sites for an average first-year bill of US$42,000. The Web hosting business is expected to generate US$5.3 billion in 2000.

**Performance-assessment Tools** InfoTEST International launched what it calls the first business performance assessment method for measuring how corporate Websites are meeting company goals in customer service, sales-lead generation and sales, brand equity and internal cost control. InfoTEST Benchmark features a standardized 1,000-point rating scale that combines quantitative and qualitative assessment techniques. The rating system and assessment guidelines can be downloaded free of charge at http://www.imation.com/infotest.

**Digital Signatures** Under drafted legislation, Germany is set to become the first country to set up a framework in which unforgeable digital 'signatures', backed by a personal ID code, will be legally acceptable.

**1:1 Marketing Online** According to the US Direct Marketing Association, 48 per cent of American direct marketers use online services for sales and marketing purposes. Web Screen Talk, a product of Sky Alland Marketing (http://www.skyalland.com), has effectively broadened the range of customer interaction that can be achieved by online vendors. A step beyond automated response forms and genetic 'contact@' options, Web Screen Talk supports real-time customer service in the form of a steamlined private chatroom (an Internet equivalent to 'operators are standing by'), as well as a 'Web Callback' feature that enables customers to schedule a convenient time to receive a follow-up call.

**Automated Customer Service** Interacting with consumers online can be both a blessing and curse. For example, Nike (http://www.nike.com) receives 2,000 emails daily. To ensure timely response without heavy manpower investment, high-tech companies such as Aeromail (http://www.aeromail.com) and General Interactive (http://www.interactive.com) offer technology that reads, analyses and mass customizes responses to email.

**Cyberscams** With the good comes the bad . . . In the US, federal and state regulators have announced that they are cracking down on marketers who tout business opportunity schemes over the Internet. As a first step, the Federal Trade Commission and North American Securities Administrators Association have issued warnings to 215 e-marketers, telling them that they must be able to back up all claims they make.

**Euro Cybergiants on the Horizon** Look out, Amazon.com and Barnes & Noble: German media conglomerate Bertelsmann AG has announced plans to open a global electronic bookstore. Tentatively called BooksOnline, the venture will offer titles in major languages from all publishers at significant discounts.

**Online Bargains** Aimed at filling some of the approximately 500,000 airline seats that fly empty every day, a new service called Priceline.com solicits bids from leisure travellers looking for bargain fares. At http://www.priceline.com, customers insert travel dates, destinations, and the price they're willing to pay; the service responds with a yea or nay within an hour. A dozen US and international airlines participate. Priceline.com initially will focus on airline tickets, but soon will expand to include cars, home mortgages, credit cards and computers.

# 16

# Faux Money

It is no accident that banks resemble temples, preferably Greek, and that the supplicants who come to perform the rites of deposit and withdrawal instinctively lower their voices into the registers of awe. Even the most junior tellers acquire within weeks of their employment the officiousness of hierophants tending an eternal flame. I don't know how they become so quickly inducted into the presiding mysteries, or who instructs them in the finely articulated inflections of contempt for the laity, but somehow they learn to think of themselves as suppliers of the monetarized DNA that is the breath of life.

Lewis H. Lapham, *Money and Class in America*

Love of money is the root of all evil, proclaims the New Testament. Not so, said English writer Samuel Butler, who asserted that it is the *want* of money that is the root of all evil. His fellow Englishman and author Somerset Maugham compared money to 'a sixth sense without which you cannot make a complete use of the other five'. And American economist John Kenneth Galbraith claimed that money 'ranks with love as man's greatest source of joy, and with death as his greatest source of anxiety'.

Why did we choose 'Faux Money' as the title for this chapter? Because, suddenly, money comes in so many forms – from plastic credit cards to certificates of deposit to e-cash – that it feels as though much of it doesn't *really* exist. We have no coins to jingle in our hand, no bills to pocket, no gems to admire under bright lights. Instead, we have pieces of paper telling us that we have money out there – somewhere. Much of our wealth these days doesn't look like money, doesn't feel like money – and we just have to hope it works like money when the time comes to spend it.

No matter where one lives, money is changing. And so are the institutions that safeguard and manage it. In fact, one could make a convincing argument that no industry is being reborn, mutated, reorganized and reconsidered at a greater rate than is the business of money. And this change all starts with our neighbourhood bank, the place where we keep our money, invest our money, borrow money and, perhaps most significant, manage our money, since we all crave control in a world that's in constant flux. This feeling of control will become even more important in the world of next, when the virtual bank will replace the branch, when smart computers will replace the oh-so-human beings who currently answer telephones, cash cheques, accept deposits and so on.

Financial institutions have a history of success in persuading consumers to adopt new technologies, particularly when they're accompanied by the carrot of convenience. (ATMs, after all, were many people's first experience with a computer.) However, technology's incredible pace of change in recent years has led to wide gaps in consumer confidence levels. At the same time that early adopters demand the very latest in technological innovation (smart cards, PC banking, online investing), traditionalists are uncertain that new applications have been sufficiently 'tested', and thus cling to the perceived security of face2face relationships.

Increasingly, financial institutions are expected to be all things to all consumers, while also distinguishing their efforts by providing unmatched personalized service.

This chapter details some of the primary trends that will shape the way we conduct financial transactions in life next.

## Next: The Invisible Pay Cheque

The best technological innovations are those that don't require our active participation. Direct deposit fits that bill precisely. It's no surprise, therefore, that direct deposit is becoming increasingly prevalent around the world. By depositing salaries into employees' bank accounts electronically, employers reduce processing and delivery costs. Employees like the system because it eliminates delays, loss or theft and trips to the bank. It's a service that plays perfectly into consumers' increasing demands for convenience and simplification.

Direct deposit is being championed by a variety of organizations. Even the US government (not known for simplifying anything) has gotten into the act. Since August 1996, all Social Security recipients applying for benefits must have their cheques automatically deposited to their bank accounts. By the end of this year, all federal payments, including salaries and other benefits, will be delivered electronically. The Treasury Department estimates that this conversion could save the government as much as US$500 million over the next five years and eliminate 100,000 cheque forgeries and thefts per year.

## Next: High Finance on the Net

Wired consumers aren't just purchasing books and airline tickets online – they've also discovered the value of Internet resources as an investment partner. In addition to researching potential investments, consumers can chat with fellow investors (both novices and veterans) and finance professionals in online forums, track stocks and bonds, and even conduct investment transactions online. SRI Consulting in California predicts that while only 8 per cent of US households will use Internet investment services by 2002, those 9 million households will represent 15 per cent of all households with investments.

According to a Retail OnLine Brokerage Study, released by Star Development Group last year, the convenience of electronic brokerage services has attracted thousands of new investors. At-home trading, account management and increased access to information also appeal to those investors with existing retail accounts. SRI Consulting estimates that of on-line-investing households last year, 3.8 million included heavy investors with low computer skills, 2.7 million contained active, serious investors with a high degree of familiarity with computers and online services and 2.6 million contained technophiles with moderate investment needs. All of the households tended to be affluent, ranging from a median net worth of US$236,000 for the technophile households to US$500,000 for the 3.8 million heavy-investor households.

At present, investors can trade online via a company's proprietary software, through commercial online services, or directly on the Internet. The American Association of Individual Investors reports that direct investment over the Net is the fastest growing segment of online trading, with 76 per cent of online traders offering Internet service today, up from just 42 per cent in 1995. Increased competition online has led to price wars, with some services offering trades for as little as US$9.

In general, personal-finance resources online are growing in both number and popularity. For instance, an estimated 250,000 households visit AOL's Motley Fool site each month (keyword: Fool), and the Silicon Investor Website (http://www.techstocks.com/) draws 30,000 daily visitors and 60,000 monthly postings. Interactive activities range from the practical (online trading) to the educational (financial-planning worksheets), and the entertaining (contests). In addition to posting prospectuses and other literature on its Website, Fidelity Investments (http://www.fidelity.com/) has incorporated interactive planning tools. For example: a program asks questions to determine a respondent's investment timeline and attitude towards risk, then suggests appropriate investments.

Quote.com (http://www.quote.com), which bills itself as the Internet's leading provider of financial market information for serious investors, reports that its 195,000 registered users are predominantly serious investors and traders who conduct an average of forty trades per year and have an average net worth of US$1.2 million. The typical user purportedly spends 3.5 hours per week on the Quote.com site.

Elsewhere on the Net, investors able to describe their 'perfect' fund can use software screening programs that search through a universe of funds for those that meet designated risk, return and management styles. Mutual Fund Expert (http://www.steelesystems.com), for example, lists 6,600 funds. The Market News Center on AOL (keyboard: Markets) features most of the major US and international indices (including the S&P 500, NASDAQ, Dow Jones Industrial Average and the Japanese, British and Hong Kong indices), breaking news reports, reports on upcoming earnings, a guide to mutual funds and a guide to conducting company research.

All of these Web capabilities don't come cheap: delivering Internet-based financial services can cost firms as much as US$23.1 million, according to 'Transaction Site Sticker Shock', a report from Forrester Research. 'Financial companies are shifting their Websites from promotions to transactions. Yet many of them are unaware of the rapidly escalating costs that lie ahead,' said Karen Epper, author of the report.

'As costs soar into the tens of millions, firms can no longer view the
Web as an inexpensive, under-the-radar-screen venture.'

## Next: The Faux Branch – Online Banking

Fifteen years ago, automated teller machines (ATMs) were just coming
into vogue. Today, ATMs are such an integral part of banking in North
America and elsewhere that at least one bank has begun charging a
small fee to customers who wish to deal with an actual bank teller.
Following on from the success of ATMs, a number of banks began to
encourage their customers to pay bills, transfer funds between accounts
and conduct other transactions via telephone. That was followed by
largely unsuccessful efforts to promote banking over one's PC using
proprietary software. Now, a growing number of banks are offering one
more option: banking via the Internet. Though we're only in the initial
stages of this trend, a study by Coopers and Lybrand estimates that
one-third of all American households will use computers for some form
of online investment or banking by 2004.

It's clear that many (if not all) banks consider the future of their
industry to lie online. A survey by Booz-Allen & Hamilton revealed
that major corporate banks plan to quadruple their Internet offerings
by the year 2000, and that 42 per cent of them plan to have advanced
sites that offer complete interactive corporate banking. Booz-Allen projects that nearly 40 per cent of corporate cash management customers
will use some form of Internet banking within the next three years.

Currently, a reported 519 financial institutions worldwide offer
online banking services to businesses; that compares with an estimated
1,200 retail sites. Jupiter Communications reports that the number of
home-banking users has already reached 4.5 million, and analysts predict that banks that wish to attract new customers in this growing
market will need to offer a breadth of services, including securities
trading and credit cards.

In the US, one big player in online banking is America Online; AOL's
Banking Center currently is partnered with more than twenty financial
institutions, including American Express, Bank of America, Chase Man-
hattan, Citibank, Mellon, PNC, Sanwa Bank California, Signet and
Wells Fargo. Each of these institutions has built a 'virtual branch' accessible via AOL. In the UK, Dot Matrix is developing the Digital Online
Terminal (DOT), a home-banking system that attaches to a television
and communicates with a participating bank via a standard telephone

line. Account holders will be able to view bank statements, pay bills online, make transfers between accounts and make purchases over the Internet. The system will use a smart-card slot that accepts any standard card, including Mondex.

Consumers who simply wish to pay bills online rather than enter into an online banking relationship can use a variety of services, from Atlanta, Georgia-based CheckFree, which currently handles online bill payment for 1.3 million consumers and 224 financial institutions, to CyberCash, a Virginia-based company, which enables consumers to pay bills directly on merchants' Websites.

## Focus: The British Banking Scene

British banks have already begun to experience what's next, after the deregulation of the 1980s, with building societies (savings and loans) offering banking services, and banks offering mortgages, insurance and any financial services their customer base might conceivably need. However, the biggest change from the consumer's point of view has probably been the widespread installation of ATMs and the arrival of telephone banking, pioneered by Midland Bank subsidiary First Direct. (Midland is owned by Hong Kong Bank.) Located in a business park in Leeds, and available 24/365, First Direct has picked up 650,000 customers since opening in 1989, and this number is increasing by 13,000 a month. The success of First Direct has prompted other banks to set up telephone banking services, reports the UK's *Daily Telegraph*. The eventual demise of brick-and-mortar branches seems assured.

## Next: Cash Goes High Tech

It is likely that the time will come when actual currency becomes obsolete. Electronic cash ('E-cash') is a totally anonymous, electronic debit card that uses an embedded computer chip; it's intended to replace currency (not credit cards or cheques). This innovation has huge potential, given that whereas an estimated 82 per cent of the value of daily US-dollar transactions occur in electronic form (e.g., credit card purchases, bank transfers), approximately 85 per cent of the actual financial transactions are in cash. Examples of e-cash at work include prepaid phone cards and metro and bus debit cards. Vending machines and other self-service devices are used as the introductory step.

Similar to e-cash, smart cards are embedded with a computer chip that tracks consumer spending and stores data about customers (e.g., product preferences, spending history). A smart card is considered more secure than e-cash, since it won't work without a personal identification number. Among other applications, the technology can be used for electronic supermarket coupons, paperless airplane tickets and electronic medical records.

Ironically, high-tech cash (including e-cash and smart cards) is something that's still next in computer-obsessed America – despite the fact that Europeans are already living a life of plastic smart money. The vast majority of consumers in Denmark, for instance, currently handle almost all bill payments and major transactions electronically; debit cards have largely replaced cheques. Some of the concerns hampering the adoption of smart cards in the States are the products' anonymity (which may benefit tax evaders, drug dealers, etc.); difficulty in taxing cyberspace transactions (where did the transaction take place?); questions surrounding who should issue e-cash (unlike currency, e-cash becomes worthless if the issuing entity goes bankrupt); and the potential for counterfeiting.

In all probability, smart cards will rise above these concerns and become standard practice throughout the world. The advantages for businesses and consumers are simply too strong to ignore.

A study by Killen & Associates, 'Non Banks' Smart Card Strategies: New Opportunities to Increase Sales and Profits', found that telephone companies are ideally positioned to apply smart cards to capture a significant share of the booming market for cash and Internet payments. Killen sees these markets growing from a worldwide total of 250 million transactions in 1996 to 25 billion in 2005. Because providers will aggressively introduce and market stored-value cards and smart cards, 30 per cent of these payments will be made by smart cards by 2005, the company reports.

Smart cards offer myriad applications. The principality of Monaco, for example, has created a smart-card loyalty system for visitors to the country's hotels and casinos. It's intended to encourage repeat visits to Monte Carlo. Users accumulate points every time they make a purchase at a participating store. Points can be exchanged for cash discounts on merchandise or applied towards a range of reward schemes, including discounted meals and airline tickets. Airlines are sure to be close behind in devising innovative frequent-flyer schemes facilitated by smart-card technology.

## Next: Increased Financial Interdependence –
## In Europe and Around the World

In chapter 2, we discussed some of the political and business implications of Europe's conversion to a single currency. There are also personal implications to consider – for, in just about any culture, money carries an emotional weight that extends far beyond its ability to procure goods and services. For Europeans, francs, marks, lira, guilders and other currencies are more than mere money – they're important symbols of each country's history, culture and sense of nationalism. In January 1996, more than 400 of Europe's brightest economic minds convened in Brussels to tackle a daunting mission: how to make Europeans love the euro. The three-day seminar kicked off a multimillion-dollar marketing campaign designed to convince Europeans that the EU's planned single currency will bring prosperity and order to the Continent. 'We have to help public opinion discover the euro and teach them to love it,' EU Finance Commissioner Yves-Thibault de Silguy told the French National Assembly.

Has the campaign worked? Not entirely. A recent newspaper poll among Germans, for instance, found that a clear majority oppose the launch of Europe's single currency in 1999. Fifty-eight per cent of respondents to the February 1998 *Handelsblatt* poll were opposed to the euro's adoption in 1999 versus 30 per cent who were in favour. While 27 per cent simply wanted the launch of the new currency to be delayed, 30 per cent were firmly against ever trading in their deutschmarks for euros. Only 24 per cent of respondents believed the euro would be as strong as the mark; 60 per cent feared it would be weaker.

As Europeans debate whether or not to participate in the EMU – and as a number of countries struggle to be eligible for that choice – there is a growing sense of financial connectedness among other countries around the world, as well. And this will only grow stronger. Already, investment banks from New York to London, Bonn to Tokyo have opened satellite offices in financial centres worldwide. News of financial shifts in one country can have a dramatic impact on markets thousands of miles away. But the interconnectedness of the global economy is seen on a micro scale as well. It is felt by the individual consumer who invests in an emerging market fund, makes a purchase over the Internet from a distant country, or subscribes to a newspaper in a country with which he or she has business dealings.

## What's Next?

**Consolidation Craze** Look for a growing number of bank consolidations, particularly outside the US. The *Economist* reports that as US banks have consolidated over the past decade, their costs have decreased from 67 per cent to 56 per cent of income, making them among the most efficient in the world. By contrast, the average expense ratio is 65 per cent among German banks and 70 per cent among French banks. Outside Britain, Europe is severely overbanked. Whereas the US has one branch for every 4,700 people, Italy has a branch for every 2,900 citizens, Germany has one for every 2,000 and Spain has one per 1,100. Since banks today must compete in the global arena, expect the rest of the world to join the consolidation craze.

**One-stop Shopping**  As in the telecommunications industry, 'one-stop shopping' is considered essential to reach finance customers who don't want multiple relationships with vendors and who want to facilitate the transfer of funds between current and savings accounts, mutual funds, certificates of deposit and other accounts. Miguel Velhinho of Y&R Portugal notes that in his country, hypermarkets have already blurred the distinction between shop and bank by providing such products and services as in-store bank branches and credit cards. The key to finance next will be convenience – whether that convenience comes via Internet access or switching funds between accounts while picking up the week's groceries.

**Internet-affiliated Charge Cards** Block Financial, a division of H&R Block and Visa International, have created WebCard Visa, a credit card for Internet users. Cardholders enjoy unrestricted access to account data and can download information directly into word processing, spreadsheet, database or personal finance software such as Quicken. Account numbers never appear online, and the card has a competitive interest rate and no annual fee.

**Online Machinations** To root out potential stock manipulations related to orchestrated hype or outright fraud, the US National Association of Securities Dealers (NASD has announced it will conduct routine searches of online sites for mention of stocks experiencing unusual trading activity.

**Investment Clubs** Across the US and in parts of Europe, people with limited disposable incomes are joining investment clubs. Participants typically contribute US$10–$50 a month and collectively invest the pooled funds. More than half of all such clubs have a better average annual return than Standard & Poor's 500-stock index each year.

**Bible-based Investing** In conjunction with a rise in spirituality, we're seeing an increase in bible-based investing. The practice is grounded in the Judaeo-Christian principle of 'stewardship', under which one is obligated to make the best use of resources entrusted to one's care. Under its tenets, bankruptcy is a sin, as is investing in so-called 'sin stocks'. Mutual funds that have been established to cater to the beliefs of specific Christian denominations include the Domini Social Equity Fund, which excludes companies involved in alcohol, tobacco, gaming, weapons-making and nuclear power. Organizations specializing in bible-based financial advising include the Timothy Plan's network of Christian Financial Consultants and the First Affirmative Financial Network. Among other investment guides available is one entitled *God Wants You to Be Rich*.

**Socially Responsible Investing** On a broader scale, consumers are insisting that the companies in which they invest maintain certain standards of conduct. The bottom line is no longer their sole concern. Shareholder requests have led Shell, for example, to release two new reports to investors: one about environmental preservation efforts and the other on human rights.

**Multiservice ATMs** Within a few years, multiservice automated teller machines (ATMs) are expected to dispense not only cash, but also such items as stamps, phone cards, travellers' cheques and theatre tickets. Sprint has even contracted with EDS to provide long-distance services through ATMs: users receive a receipt bearing Sprint's logo, an 800 number and an access code. NatWest's ATMs in London have begun to dispense advertisements along with the cash.

**Bartering** Bartering is back. Perhaps as an offshoot of our desire for simplification – in addition to being a cost-saving device – the barter industry is experiencing 15 per cent annual growth and has reached US$8 billion in annual trade. At the centre of the industry is the

National Association of Trade Exchanges, an association of business owners and professionals who have joined together to trade surplus goods and services. Members provide products and services to other members in exchange for trade dollars (which have the equivalent of cash dollars). Further growth of the industry is expected to be fuelled by the Internet, which has opened up global trading and communication possibilities that were once unthinkable. With expansion being the buzz in the barter industry, expect to see smaller, independent exchanges consolidate into larger, more sophisticated electronic clearing houses.

**Dying Broke** Coined 'dying broke' by *Worth* magazine, a growing American anti-inheritance movement is based on the decision to pro-actively use up one's financial resources while still alive. Rather than build a nest egg for heirs, so-called 'dying brokers' (DBs) use their savings for everything from paying off grandchildren's college loans to home improvements. The upshot: DBs see the benefits of their labour; recipients make earlier use of resources; and the government misses out on inheritance taxes.

**New Access to Investors** A couple of years ago, Destiny Pictures, a start-up film production company in Los Angeles, offered stock in a low-budget movie over the Internet for US$100 per share. Within a few months, more than 150 people from around the world had ordered US$15,000 worth of shares in the erotic thriller *Intimate Stranger*. (Not exactly a blockbuster, was it?) Look for other innovative investment opportunities online – and subsequent regulation.

**Eye-scanning** New Jersey-based Sensar Inc. will soon offer ATM manufacturers an alternative to passwords and PINs: when a customer inserts a bank card, a camera locates his or her eye and takes a digital image of the iris. In under two seconds, the resultant unique 'iris code' is compared with one initially provided by the customer. No match, no money.

**On-site Screening** Deluxe Corp., the largest cheque printer in the US, has joined with credit-scoring company Fair, Isaac & Co. and data warehouse Acxiom Corp. to create the 'debit bureau' credit-rating system. Deluxe will gather information from banks about bounced cheques and payment problems. Acxiom will combine that data with other financial information and pass it along to Fair, Isaac, which will use it to generate a credit rating. Retailers will soon use the system at point of purchase to help determine whether to accept an individual's cheque or debit card. The service will also be marketed to banks to help them decide whether to open an account for a particular person and, if so, under what terms.

# 17

# You are what Influences You

If what's happening in North America has any bearing on what will happen in the rest of the world – and with regard to cyberspace and media consumption, we feel sure it does – TV programmers had better be prepared for decreased viewing audiences once online services get into full swing. Seventy-eight per cent of respondents to a US study by Forrester Research said they make time for PC use by spending less time in front of the TV. For the most part, viewers are not giving up their favourite programmes but are cutting down on aimless channel-surfing. Though heavy PC users could watch a lot less television without dramatically impacting overall viewership, the attrition of these more affluent, better-educated viewers is likely to make the medium less attractive to some advertisers.

This chapter takes a look at some of the other major trends we're seeing in media today, with a focus on how various industries are responding to (and, in some cases, making use of) this upstart competitor: the Internet. We titled this chapter 'You are what Influences You' because as consumers gain access to more and more means of communication, the marketing communications future will be grounded in the idea of 'message layering'.

Paul Woolmington, president of media operations at Y&R Inc., shared the following insights with us: 'The new media order requires us to put consumers and customers at the centre of our media- and content-rich universe,' he says. 'From this vantage point we will be better equipped to select the most potent communication and media channels. These new rules of engagement require us to take a much broader view, use sharper media tools, break and remake the rules through better 'consumerized' strategies.

'Prime time, as we have traditionally known it, is being slowly but surely redefined. Redefined in the minds of ever-fragmenting audiences with regard to when, where, how, and in what format they want to receive and interact with their own, more personalized, media content.'

The core strategic challenge for tomorrow's marketers will be to ensure a consistent, uniform presentation of the brands in their care, recognizing the appropriate roles of each 'layer' of the communications plan in generating a coherent, effective whole. We watch with particular interest as marketing communications firms jockey for position as the 'custodian' of the layering strategy.

## Customized News

The proliferation of Internet-based media and other online sources of news and information means competition not only for newspapers and magazines, but for news services on TV (network, cable and satellite) and radio, as well. It seems inevitable that consumers will gain the ability to customize a media diet made up of niche-market publications, Usenet newsgroups, 'push' newsfeeds, cable news programming and other sources. The impact could be significant. It is possible, for instance, that nations will become increasingly fragmented in the absence of a handful of standard sources of news. There was a time when workers gathering at their place of employment could be relatively certain that they had all watched the same TV news the night before and read the same newspaper that morning. That assumption is no longer valid. With all the choices we have these days, the odds that one will choose the same media diet as one's neighbour or co-worker are slim.

Is the customization of news and information channels such a bad thing? Not necessarily. For many people, customized news is more convenient and useful than traditional sources. All of the authors of this book subscribe to at least one source of customized news, whether it be NewsHound, PointCast, or some other Internet-based venture. We receive a continuous flow of information on trends we're tracking and other topics of interest without having to spend time combing through dozens of publications in search of a few relevant articles.

Information can be specifically tailored to the needs of the individual. For example, a person with a food allergy can join the Food Allergy

Network's 'alerts' mailing list (http://www.foodallergy.org/index.html).
This provides immediate notification via email whenever the network
learns that a manufacturer has recalled or sent out a warning about a
product that contains an unlisted ingredient. (In most cases, the company in question covers the cost of sending the 'alerts'.) This ensures
that information unlikely to appear on national TV news and easily
overlooked when reading the local paper is transmitted as quickly as
possible.

That's the upside of customized news.

What will happen, though, if people begin to restrict themselves to
highly tailored news to the exclusion of general-interest news? The
same targeted resources that allow for the building of online communities among the elderly, gays and lesbians, stateside Europeans, environmental activists and the like can also provide a steady flow of narrowly
cast news and information to political extremists, conspiracy theorists
and so on. It's already difficult to tell fact from fiction on the Net, and
rumours are spread at blinding speeds. A year or so ago, we saw
respected US journalist Pierre Salinger go public with 'facts' purportedly
showing that TWA flight 800 was downed not by a mechanical mal-
function but by 'friendly fire' from a US Navy surface-to-air missile.
His source: newsgroups on the Internet.

The vast array of information channels available to consumers today
means each of us is responsible for selecting our own media diet. It's
up to the individual to determine whether his or her diet is rich in
news from top-notch journalists or made up of nothing but tabloid
reports, extremist e-zines and other forms of 'junk news'. Neighbours
living side by side who choose vastly different media diets may find
that their world views have little in common. There's also the possibility
that the market will cease to support the high-cost apparatus that is the
foundation of objective journalism, as audiences become increasingly
fragmented and subscription and advertising money is further divided.

## A Truly Global Medium

Cyberspace will be the first medium to become truly global; as such, it is
subject to debate over everything from freedom of the press to copyright
infringement, and to the risks and rewards of cultures becoming blurred
through common sources of news and entertainment. Although he has
visited China many times since, media mogul Rupert Murdoch, whose
News Corp. bought Star TV cable network three years ago, attracted

the most attention from Chinese officials back in 1993, when he made a speech in London saying that technological advances such as satellite television were 'an unambiguous threat to totalitarian regimes everywhere'. China's leadership promptly forbade individuals to buy satellite dishes, which had been selling fast. Since then, sales have quietly resumed, but the damage had been done. According to the *New York Times*, Murdoch's efforts to repair ties to Beijing – which included eliminating the BBC news service from Star TV's broadcast – have yet to win over government officials. Oddly, an unintended consequence of Murdoch's remarks was that Beijing started encouraging the growth of cable networks, until then very small, because leaders are convinced they can control the content of cable better than that of satellite broadcasts. Star TV is believed to be losing at least US$100 million a year, primarily because unknown viewership figures (it does not collect subscription fees) prevent the channel from selling sufficient advertising.

## Next: Globally Branded News

We've come a long way from the town crier, Gutenberg's printing press and Ben Franklin's almanac. Today, as with every other aspect of our lives, we want information delivery to be FAST. The terms 'instantaneous', 'real-time', and 'eyewitness' convey expectations that are far removed from those implied during the days of Walter Cronkite's weekly TV offering, *You Are There*, or Ed Murrow's *See It Now*. (Seven days later is anything but now.)

The press has risen to the occasion. CNN, for instance, has become an important worldwide source of information, whose influence is magnified during moments of 'breaking news'. CNN's coverage of the Persian Gulf War is considered to be the seminal moment in the network's coming of age as the preferred source for breaking coverage of world events – whenever and wherever they occur. In the States, the venerable news divisions of ABC, NBC, and CBS did not cede their hegemony as the 'source authority' in television news. Rather, CNN steadily chipped away at their domination through dedicated brand building. It brought to bear an unmatched combination of focus, reach and credibility (sometimes in the form of 'name' talent secured from traditional sources, but, more often, by rigid reporting standards and legitimate global credentials) – and harnessed the necessary technology to yield seamless and timely delivery. Today, CNN has new competition in the form of Britain's BBC World Service. Tomorrow, the rate at which information can span the globe means that competition can come from anywhere around the world.

## Next: Hyperlocal Offerings

We discussed earlier the degree to which consumers' media menus are growing more individualized as a result of the much broader selection of news and information sources available today. As we count down towards the millennium, we expect to see companies lay the groundwork for offering sponsor-supported customized Webpages to individual consumers who fall within specific demographic markers. Consumers will be able to fill out an online questionnaire specifying their areas of interest, rather than waste time surfing the Net for relevant sites. From those choices, cyberconsultants will design a personalized Webpage filled with links to an individually tailored assortment of ever-changing sites. Once a personal Webpage has been designed, it will be constantly updated and revised to reflect new and improved options available on the Web, customer feedback and the amount of time the customer spends at each linked site.

A few years down the road, we expect to see this customization concept extended to local television news reports. Viewers will be able to tailor their nightly news broadcast from a menu of options, specifying, for example, whether they wish to receive the total sports broadcast, just news on certain teams, or no sports news at all; whether they want just local news or national and/or international news, as well; and whether they are more interested in financial reports or 'human-interest' stories. It will even be possible for viewers to specify that they do not want to receive any news of a violent or sexual nature, or any 'bad' news. Hyperlocal news segments will also be available, as towns and communities provide footage of local events.

One of the most important implications of this trend will be that the increased segmentation of households and individual viewers will allow for hypertargeted advertising efforts. At the same time, national media organizations will struggle to stay relevant for a mass audience as resources shift to local news operations.

## Next: Facing Increased Competition from the Net, Traditional News and Information Sources Get Wired

Inge van Gaal, of the European Newspaper Association, Antwerp, Belgium, commented, 'Businesses and publishers in the newspaper market in Europe are looking with some worry to the future. New media – although they keep putting facts forward that this will not damage their business – is absolutely a source of worry. Quite a lot of money has been spent on being "with it". Consumers and advertisers on the one hand are trying out new media, but on the other hand are still sticking with newspapers as a reliable and traditional source of news and information.' As cyberspace becomes the 'next' mass medium around the world, it will spell even greater competition for newspapers, which will continue to see declines in readership and share of advertising revenue.

Newspaper publishers are taking steps already to stay competitive in a wired world. An April 1997 report from the Newspaper Association of America confirms a downward trend in advertising and circulation. In 1996, only 59 per cent of adults in the US read a daily paper, compared to 64 per cent one year earlier. In the same period, Sunday readership dropped from 72.6 to 68.5 per cent. This trend is particularly evident among young people, with only 45 per cent of 18- to 24-year-olds and 47 per cent of 25- to 34-year-olds reading a daily paper in 1996, down from 51 to 56 per cent in 1994. Given current trends, respected analyst John Morton has predicted that the entire newspaper industry in the US will essentially expire in the next thirty years or so as consumers increasingly turn to the Internet, TV and radio for their news.

Even newspaper journalists are bemoaning the demise of their medium. A survey by the American Society of Newspaper Editors found that journalists tend to be dissatisfied with the quality of their own newspapers and believe newspapers are losing importance in society. According to a report in *Editor & Publisher*, 64 per cent of the 1,000-plus journalists surveyed by the ASNJ said they only occasionally or rarely consider their papers a 'good read', and only 36 per cent find them 'usually very interesting'. A majority (55 per cent) think newspapers will play a less important part in life in ten years than they do now.

In a bid to keep pace with the rapidly changing world of information retrieval, more than 1,500 commercial newspapers have staked a site on the Internet thus far. Internet-based ad sales are expected to grow to more than US$5 billion by the year 2000, but for now, many publishers are building their sites with the expectation that they will be losing money in the short term. Time Warner's Pathfinder, for instance, is said to be losing between US$5 million and US$10 million a year. Parent companies are agreeing to take early losses with the expectation that growing reliance on the Internet will push a paying audience – and advertisers – their way in the months and years to come.

Of course, not everyone can afford to be in the red for so long. Companies whose pockets are not quite so deep are being displaced in what has come to be known as the 'great Web shakeout'; such significant news domains as Out and Politics Now, for example, have closed their sites in the face of serious financial losses. Nevertheless, the Newspaper Association of America reports that more than a third of online newspapers made money last year. An additional 24 per cent of online newspapers run by traditional media companies expect to be profitable within four years. The big money makers to date have been classifieds, display advertising and job listings. We expect competition among content providers to increase even more as a growing number of companies choose to build their brands via their own content-heavy Websites rather than simply place ads on other organizations' sites.

By most indications, there's a clear audience for online publications. Research firm NPD Group reports that 60 per cent of Web users surveyed indicate that they frequently read newspapers and/or magazines online. Nearly 40 per cent of the 1,527 respondents read an online daily newspaper. Among other findings: nine out of ten respondents who read print and online newspapers rated the two comparable in terms of accuracy and reliability; of magazines read online, computer titles are the most popular (read by half the sample), followed by entertainment (36 per cent), news (36 per cent), business (24 per cent), sports (15 per cent) and women's magazines (11 per cent). Approximately a quarter of the participants who currently read online publications said they would be willing to pay for a subscription to online computer magazines, newspapers, business magazines and/or sports magazines. Subscriptions to entertainment magazines, however, would only be purchased by 13 per cent of respondents.

## Next: The Convergence of TV and PC Content

Television executives are also taking the growth of the Internet seriously. In July 1996, Microsoft and the National Broadcasting Company in the US launched MSNBC (http://www.msnbc.com), a twenty-four-hour, online cable TV network. Core programming originally included three prime-time hours: a news talk show, a new-media and technology show and an hourly evening newscast with interview and discussion segments. The network has contributed some serious talent to help ensure the initiative's success: NBC News anchor Tom Brokaw, former *Today* host and current *Dateline NBC* anchor Jane Pauley, and Washington chief Tim Russert all have regular MSNBC slots, while Brian Williams is chief anchor.

The cablecast TV offering is closely linked to its companion Website at msnbc.com, which provides archived content (to provide depth on a given subject) and offers a host of interactive facilities, including viewer ratings of on-air content and opinion polls. MSNBC may well be what 'convergence' looks like.

Microsoft is appealing to a more narrow audience via its Web programming partnership with BET (Black Entertainment Television). And MSNBC has announced plans to launch ZDF.MSNBC, a German-language version of its online news site, in collaboration with ZDF, Germany's leading news network.

Hoping to compete with MSNBC in the category of computer-mediated news reporting is ABCNews.com (http://www.abcnews. com), an alliance of ABC News, Starwave, Netscape Communications Corp. and AOL. The online news service provides up-to-the-minute local, national and international news, as well as sports, entertainment, business and technology news. The venture currently has a reach of 16 million, including the 12 million visitors to AOL and 4 million visitors to Netscape, ABCNews.com will draw on the worldwide resources of ABC News, including ABC News Radio and ABC's affiliate newsrooms.

In a bid for a global audience, CNN Interactive (http://www.cnn.com) has launched a twenty-four-hour news and information service on the Web that includes regional products. The CNN site's once overloaded World News section has been broken into separate sites for Europe/Middle East, the Americas, Asia-Pacific and Africa. Last year, CNN Interactive averaged 10–12 million hits a day with two-thirds of all users based in the United States. A recent nonscientific survey found that most non-US users were drawn from Australia, Canada, Japan and the Netherlands. Clearly, we can expect to see more interaction between TV and the Internet in other parts of the world, as well. If the North American model is any guide, Websites increasingly will offer more in-depth analysis, interviews and background materials than would ever be practical in a TV broadcast forum.

## Next: Cyber-Radio

Radio also has entered the realm of cyberspace. Thanks to such technology as RealNetworks RealAudio (http://www.realaudio.com) and Xing Technology Corp.'s StreamWorks (http://www.xingtech.com), listeners are able to hear 'streaming' – or uninterrupted, live or prerecorded sound – without having first to download the full audio file. Bloomberg News Radio, the twenty-four-hour report from WBBR AM 1130 in New York City, is available at http://www.bloomberg,com/wbbr/index.html. The news broadcast is delivered in real time at most modem speeds via Streamworks. Minneapolis-based net.radio (http://www.netradio.net/) is the first live, twenty-four-hour-a-day, Internet-only radio station. The eclectic mix of vintage rock and cyberchat has attracted an audience from as far away as Australia, Germany, Israel and South Africa.

CNET radio (http://www.news.com/Radio/Index), a free daily audio news service exclusively for the Web, covers computers, the Internet and online services. The Monday–Friday segments run approximately eight to ten minutes each. To encourage interactivity, CNET has incorporated a 'your turn' forum, which allows listeners to speak out – literally – on the Web. Listener comments are recorded on dedicated phone lines and then translated to RealAudio segments that can be accessed by other online users. Launched on the Web in June 1995, CNET radio attracted more than 200,000 registered members within the first four months.

TST Audio-On-Demand (http://www.tstradio.com), a Tulsa, Oklahoma-based company, offers subscribers the chance to listen to radio shows from around the US via their computers. The service gives users the option of choosing the shows they want to hear twenty-four hours a day, when they want to hear them, as opposed to when they are broadcast. TST listeners can also choose the portions of the shows they want to hear by fast forwarding or rewinding (now there's an advantage over real-time transmission). Owner Ed Taylor says the mission of TST is not to compete with local radio but to appeal to small groups of people worldwide whose interests are ignored by their local stations – groups such as gays and lesbians, medical professionals, comic book collectors and UFO enthusiasts. TST On-Demand rates, which give users access to more than 6,000 hours of programming, range from US$6 for one hour (plus a one-hour bonus) to US$50 for 100 hours (plus a 100-hour bonus). TST also offers two 'streaming' channels: Liberated Women Channel and Your Personal Best: The Mind–Body Connection. Subscribers pay US$3 a month per channel or US$30 per channel annually.

## Next: Covering the News Online

The Internet and online services aren't merely a repository for publications; they've also become an important source of material for print and broadcast journalists. The third annual Media in Cyberspace survey (February 1997) confirms that journalists are growing increasingly reliant on the Internet as a business tool. Respondents to the study included more than 600 newspaper and magazine editors from across the US. More than a third of respondents reported that they or their staff go online every day. Two-thirds of journalists surveyed go online at least once a week, and 85 per cent go online at least once a month. Only 13 per cent of responding journalists do not have Internet access. Article research and reference, email and finding new sources are the primary ways in which journalists use the Internet. The bulk of interviews continue to be conducted in person or over the phone, however.

Most of the journalists surveyed prefer to get their facts from straight-text Websites rather than sites that contain audio and video features. Almost 60 per cent of respondents continue to get their story ideas via personal contacts; a mere 2 per cent indicated that their best source of story ideas is the World Wide Web. Forty-four per cent of respondents write copy that ends up online, but few publications are producing material specifically for online publication. More than 50 per cent of respondents work for organizations with Websites. Only 11 per cent report that their publication has no plans to go online. As in previous years, journalists are more likely to use free information services provided online by non-profit or public interest groups, rather than by corporations.

## Next: It's History . . .

In cyberspace, content is rarely permanent, as users reject yesterday's pages in favour of the latest and greatest. As a result, much of the information produced for the Web and other digital media is disappearing almost as fast as it's created. Among other reasons for the disappearance: site operators run out of money or time and disconnect their Websites or newsgroups from the Internet; and changing technical standards make older Websites unreadable. Denise Caruso, writing for the *New York Times* News Service, observed, 'Over the last two decades, an historic shift has occurred as an enormous amount of human endeavor – culture, commerce, communication – has moved from the physical world into the realm of electrons. Text printed on paper, the most persistent fossil of human thought, can still be read and appreciated centuries later. But a thought recorded only as electrons vanishes forever when the last machine that created it finally dies, or when a publisher purges all the files from what once was the Web server.' Just as much of recorded music history didn't make the transition from vinyl to CDs, a significant portion of current Web content is likely to fall by the wayside during the transition to the next generation of Web protocols. One possible way to prevent this is through the use of 'Web spiders', software programs that methodically index and archive the entire textual contents of the Web daily.

## What's Next

**Land of the Giants** Industry mergers are continuing to concentrate power in the hands of a few media giants. We can expect cross-marketing with these companies to be an essential component of marketing communications. Also increasingly common is newspaper 'clustering', as newspaper companies buy and sell properties to achieve greater concentration of ownership. In the US alone, more than 120 dailies changed hands in 1996, according to *American Journalism Review*. Advantages of clustering include lower operating costs, shared news coverage and feature sections, and increased advertising revenue (by offering a bigger circulation package, clustered papers can attract more advertising money than a single daily could hope to obtain).

**Nothing but Talk** Consumers' seemingly insatiable desire for news and information is forcing formatting changes in radio – just as consumer desire for entertainment is edging hard news out of TV broadcasts. Growing listener interest in news and talk radio in the US is illustrated by the popularity of such nationally syndicated personalities as Rush Limbaugh and Larry King – and by the willingness of Infinity

Broadcasting Corp. to keep 'shock jock' Howard Stern on its payroll despite having to hand over US$1.7 million to the Treasury Department in 1995 to settle indecency charges brought against Stern by the FCC between 1989 and 1994. Nearly 1,100 US stations specialized in talk and news in 1994, up 175 per cent from 1989, making it the fastest growing format. Other non-music formats being adopted by stations include all-sports and all-self-help.

**European Cable** In Europe, cable still seems new, maybe because its reach is just now achieving critical mass. Net revenues for western European cable operators are expected to grow to approximately Ecu 8.4 billion by 2005, according to CIT Research Ltd. The fastest growing markets include France and eastern and central Europe. Cable operators in Poland, for instance, are expected to triple their revenues by 2005.

**Educative Marketing** Remember when we used to pick up newspapers for news and information and expected nothing but account balances in our utility bills? No more. Nowadays, everyone wants to inform us – print advertisements contain recipes and 'fast facts', while inserts placed in the envelope alongside our bills contain information on keeping our home at a moderate temperature, protecting our children from bug bites and keeping the dog's coat shiny. Who needs schools when we have marketers?

**Electronic Slush Piles?** Budding novelists now have a new outlet for their work: Enchanted E-Books (http://www.e-books.com). For US$99, an editor will read an uploaded manuscript; if he/she likes it, the manuscript will be published for sale on the site at around US$2–3 per copy. The books are downloaded to the buyer's hard drive – no paper is involved. Of the first fifty submissions, the site published forty.

**Hypertargeted Press** As newspapers grow more successful in decoding user demographics, readers can expect targeted zoned editions and tailored ads. 'We started out geographically, with ZIP codes, which made inserting ads easier,' Eric Wolferson, VP for technology at the Newspaper Association of America, told the *San Francisco Examiner*. 'Now advertisers want even narrower niches, so we're [using] database technology that allows us to have household-specific designations.'

Eventually, says Wolferson, 'you and your neighbour will get different newspapers,' with most differences being in the ads. A house hunter's newspaper, for example, would feature a majority of real-estate ads for as long as the reader is in that market.

**Increased Personalization** Digital printing – which weds computer-generated content with high-speed copiers – eliminates the economies of scale associated with offset printing, making it easier to turn a profit when publishing books in small quantities. Print times are reduced to a few minutes, enabling 'on demand' printing, a cost-effective alternative to warehousing and stock overruns. Using Xerox DocuTech printers, Simon & Schuster (http://www.sscp.com) produces more than 125,000 customized books per month. Possible implications: an end to 'out-of-print' books; ongoing 'updates' from authors; books printed at the bookstore, while you wait; and greater access for unknown writers and those in marginal categories.

**Audience Feedback** To improve news-stand sales, *Men's Health* is inviting readers to vote for preferred cover text and graphics at http://www.menshealth.com/. Instantaneous feedback means broadcasters and publishers can more accurately tailor their content to meet the changing needs of their audiences.

**Media Filters** To stave off information overload, consumers will depend on a variety of trusted sources (think Oprah Winfrey's book club) to help differentiate between worthy and unworthy.

# 18

# 360 Degree Branding

It's the mission of advertising agencies and marketing communications firms to connect people to brands. As put by Jeanne Binstock van Rij, managing director of the Honeycomb Institute, at the 1996 Strategic Leadership Forum: 'Brand image is no longer a marginal dimension of business, but the very core of business identity and strategy. With a world culture evolving, customers everywhere respond to images, myths and metaphors that help them define their personal and national identities and relationships within a global context of world culture and product benefits . . . Powerful brand identities and corporate branding will be the main engines of continuing international growth.'

We agree with this assessment. We also note that to build one's brands successfully, marketing strategies today must be holistic. It is our job as marketers to publicize, position, promote, advertise, sell, reinforce brand image and loyalty, resell and more. As marketing partners, ad agencies have a meaningful role to play in each and every step of the marketing-selling-promoting-loyalty-building cycle. To our detriment, the 'brain drain' that the worldwide ad agency business is suffering has led clients to have lesser expectations of their agency partners, causing them to turn instead to other consultants with whom to collaborate.

Current thinking speaks to the fact that an ad either registers with a target consumer or doesn't, and that constant repetition of the message doesn't make much difference. What does make a difference is a holistic approach that integrates the campaign launch with a proactive 'educational' campaign to ensure that the consumer is told what to expect and then hears what he/she was expecting, thereby 'getting it' more often than not. When Marty Cooke gave birth to the Chiat/Day advertising agency's Idea Factory in New York, the basis of his theory was simple: everything communicates. One's brand message must be conveyed not only on TV, in magazines, or in other traditional forms of media advertising, but also on the product's packaging, on delivery trucks, at point of sale, on souvenir giveaways at trade shows, and on and on. Today's consumer is increasingly likely to wear multiple hats and to be reachable in multiple ways. He or she may be a shareholder in the company, a consumer of the actual product, a third-party validator (either as an influential or a journalist), or even an employee of a company in some way connected to the brand. Reaching this consumer with consistent and positive message layering is the key to connecting him or her to the brand in question.

Ira, who was president of Chiat/Day while Marty Cooke was creative director, notes that when Chiat/Day launched Fruitopia for Coke earlier this decade, the agency practised what Cooke was preaching and used message layering and a media mix that incorporated everything from packaging and point-of-purchase displays to in-theatre videos and a roving New Age bus, brought to consumers courtesy of Fruitopia. Advertisements were painted on the sides of buildings in New York, San Francisco and other key markets. The product may not have been an ideal fit for the Coke distribution system, but smart, integrated marketing that effectively targeted the new consumer ensured that the Fruitopia message of New Age inspiration reached its target – again and again – educating, entertaining and inventing desire, as all good marketing communication does.

## Building Brands in Cyberspace

In our view, every business today must compete in two worlds: the physical market*place* and the online market*space*, a virtual world of information, entertainment and interaction. Activities that take place in the marketspace mirror those that traditionally have taken place in the marketplace, but that does not mean that the process of creating value is the same in both worlds. New consumers who log on to the Internet are looking for instant solutions and for direct and efficient interaction with the brands amongst which they must choose. In the face of information and sensory overload, these consumers will turn to

a trusted face in the crowd – choosing the brand with flawless credentials, a continuous history and the drive and ability to anticipate the
consumer's needs.

What some analysts have failed to notice is that the power of the
Internet goes far beyond shopping, entertainment and research. Of even
greater impact will be the Internet's role as a vehicle of persuasion. The
world was stunned by the mass suicide of members of the Heaven's
Gate cult in California and the group's ties to the Internet immediately
became fodder for an oftentimes-uninformed discussion of the 'dark
side' of the Net. People who had probably never even logged on to the
Web immediately began to decry its base nature, warning of its sinister
power to brainwash the weak-minded. Calls rang out for governments
to monitor and regulate content on the Net, but thus far free-speech
advocates have ruled the day.

### 10 Realities of the Next Millennium

1 If you know the marketplace, you can own the marketspace.
2 Any company that establishes a site on the Internet automatically
  becomes a multinational company.
3 New-product announcements on the Net will generate immediate
  demand, making it more difficult to conduct slow test-as-you-go
  rollouts.
4 Greekspeak is the newest international language – and has a
  better chance of surviving than does Esperanto.
5 Thanks to Usenet and other online forums, the distinction
  between news and gossip is becoming increasingly blurred.
6 Everyone – no matter what age or income level – has the
  potential to be influential in cyberspace. Conversely, those who
  wield great power in the 'real world' find themselves on a far
  more level playing field when they come online.
7 Privacy is an increasingly rare – and treasured – commodity, and
  consumers will pay a premium to ensure that personal
  information remains just that. Companies that can't be trusted
  with one's personal data are less likely to be trusted in any other
  category.
8 New technologies are giving small and midsize companies far
  greater access to consumers than they have ever before enjoyed.
  Established corporations would do well to watch their flanks.
9 The homogeneity of traditional media images and messages will

break down as ethnic and other minority groups gain a greater
share of voice via the Internet.

10 The Internet is turning the population into creators of content as
opposed to mere consumers of it.

At present small companies are utilizing the enormous power of the
Internet in three ways: as a conduit of information to and from consumers; as a vehicle for consumer and market research: and as a platform for cyberpersuasion. We'll look at each of these in turn.

## Information Pipeline

A corporate Website can be nothing more than an electronic version
of a product brochure. It can tell the consumer what a product is, how
much it costs and where to buy it. But the potential of a Website as a
conduit of information is far, far greater. An effective site will offer
an opportunity for interaction with the consumer. It will provide a
mechanism for customer service, whether in the form of email, a bulletin board, or ichat,[1] and it will take advantage of opportunities to
garner personal information from consumers visiting the site. Some
Websites do this by requiring basic demographic information prior to
allowing the user to access the site's full content, whereas other sites
gather user data by means of entertaining surveys and message boards.
In addition to being useful for general marketing purposes, this captured
data can be used very effectively to target individual site visitors with
product information.

One of the great advantages of advertising online is the ability to
tailor ads to individual consumers. With the ClickWise ad management
program from ClickOver Inc. (http://www.clickover.com), for example,
site managers can increase the odds of effecting a click-through by
delivering advertisements based on known information about the site
visitor. A visitor who had indicated upon registering that she is a tennis
player who travels extensively and plans to buy a new computer within
the next twelve months can be targeted with ads from such sponsors
as Adidas, Samsonite and Gateway 2000 when she logs on to the site.
A visitor from London or Helsinki or Boston can be targeted by companies doing business in those locales. Some sites tailor ads to each
visitor's computer platform (Macintosh, Windows or DOS, to ensure
that they are selling only those products that are technologically compatible.

To appreciate fully the implications of this targeted advertising, imagine if TV commercials and magazine ads were different from household to household, consumer to consumer. An amateur athlete watching local TV news might be targeted with an ad for Nike athletic shoes, while a gardening enthusiast down the street could receive instead an ad for Ortho lawn-care products. Of course, this has long been the quest of marketers. Procter & Gamble began producing soap operas nearly half a century ago to target homemakers. And the increasingly targeted magazines available today are attempting to reach everyone from gourmets to golf enthusiasts to Nintendo addicts. Still, the Internet has an edge in that it is able to verify interest in a product or category, and can produce and disseminate a much greater variety of ads than would be practical in other media.

Recognizing the potential of cybermarketing, more than 90 per cent of top advertisers in the US have established one or more Websites. And a study conducted among the 125 member companies of the Association of National Advertisers Inc. found that more than half already sell or plan to sell products and/or services via the Internet, and approximately one-third advertise on other companies' Websites, with advertising expenditures averaging US$250,000.

## Keys to a Successful Website
- Attention-grabbing door
- Engaging, interactive content – beyond high-tech bells and whistles
- Visually stimulating but without the overload of time-consuming graphics
- Content unavailable anywhere else
- Emphasis on consumer needs vs company 'chest thumping'
- Numerous links and plenty of opportunities to return to the home page; ease of navigation
- Regular updates
- Registered with search engines/catalogue listings
- Email link to company (must encourage consumer interaction/ comments)
- Attitude (quirky/offbeat humour, willingness to push envelope, exudes e-confidence and credibility if subject is more serious)
- Organizational and/or institutional support – in terms of both budget and personnel

- Integrated with/supported by other media channels (e.g., print media, TV, radio)
- Capable of gathering information about users for:
  - –Tailoring site to accommodate users' needs/requests
  - –Consumer research
- Graphics/design in sync with corporate image

## Creating an Online Dialogue with the New Consumer

In our work, we continue to rely on cyber-research, regularly conducting online focus groups and one-on-one interviews, and sending out e-polls on behalf of a variety of clients. For example, while still with TBWA, the four of us conducted an intensive research project in the US on behalf of Denmark's Lego. Participants, who were recruited online, filled out a number of e-polls and detailed questionnaires. They even visited a specially constructed Website to view a product in development. The entire project was conducted electronically, which meant we were able to use participants in all areas of the country without incurring a single travel cost or even the expense of renting research facilities. And because these children and their parents were able to participate in the study from the comfort of their homes and on their own schedule, we were able to recruit the busy, relatively affluent families who are the product's target.

This convenient and relatively inexpensive forum is the most time- and cost-effective way to access consumers of all ages, in a variety of occupations, in many parts of the world. In addition, citizens of cyberspace (particularly outside North America and Scandinavia) are widely regarded as change leaders. As a result, although online research may not always be scientifically representative, it is predictive of trends and attitudes that are making their way toward the mainstream.

Research conducted in cyberspace can be qualitative and/or quantitative (though given current penetration rates, 'quantitative' data will almost certainly involve a skew). Online focus groups are like their face2face counterparts in that a moderator leads a session based on a formal discussion guide; they are unlike face2face groups in that participants enjoy a certain amount of anonymity, often alleviating embarrassment and facilitating honesty. Transcripts are available immediately following the group, and clients can be invited to 'sit in' on the sessions.

E-polls are a cost-effective, timely means of obtaining answers from a broad consumer sample to a well-defined set of questions. Although there are limitations with respect to length (for obvious reasons, shorter polls yield a greater participation rate), respondents can be recontacted easily for participation in a follow-up poll or interview addressing more in-depth questions. Given an average poll-completion time of no more than fifteen minutes, our experience dictates that a sample size of 300 can typically be secured within five days of aggressive distribution.

## The Art of Cyberpersuasion

As mentioned earlier, a third critical way in which marketers can reach the new consumer online is via cyberpersuasion. By this we mean more than simply building an engaging Website that attracts consumers and keeps them coming back for more. (Although the potential benefits of building such a community online should not be underestimated.) What we are referring to instead are the ways in which one can establish a corporate presence throughout the Internet. Whether using news-groups, chatrooms, online forums or email, marketers have valuable opportunities to connect with their customers and build their brands in cyberspace.

In our work with clients, we often talk about 'whisper campaigns', a means by which one can spread one's message to an online audience without becoming intrusive – and, thus, unwelcome. The best whisper campaigns are conducted by people who genuinely have their fellow cybernauts' best interests at heart. By way of example, when we were conducting some background research for a client in the animal healthcare field, we visited a forum on AOL for pet lovers. One of the message boards was devoted to the topic of coat and skin problems common to household pets. A new flea-control product had recently been introduced, and many of the visitors to the board were searching for information regarding the product's safety and effectiveness. Some participants were also relating rumours they had heard about various negative side effects associated with the product. What caught our attention was the presence in this forum of a former veterinarian who now works for the company that makes the product in question.

He did absolutely everything right.

Whenever someone posted a question or rumour about this product, the company representative responded within twenty-four hours. He stated his affiliation with the company, as well as his former position as a private-practice veterinarian. He then proceeded to answer the question or squelch the rumour, providing spccific data from research projects that had disproved whatever the rumour happened to be. This company rep was so effective because he was a *member* of this online community. He didn't just answer questions pertaining to his company's products, he also provided advice on all sorts of ailments and conditions in his capacity as a trained veterinarian. So instead of being regarded as a corporate shill, he was valued as a trusted and well-regarded member of the community. His company benefited from his presence there – and so did the pet owners and animal-care professionals who frequented the site.

One of the first companies to feel the potential backlash of the Internet was Intel. As you may recall, the company had a problem with its Pentium computer chip a few years ago. It attempted to respond to email complaints by issuing a notice online that the 'bug' in its Pentium chip was 'rare' and would affect only a minute percentage of users. IBM responded by posting a notice on its Website that contradicted Intel's claims (and later refused to ship any computers that contained the defective chip). The result: Intel issued a recall and replaced the chip.

Since that time, a number of companies have made use of the persuasive powers of the Net or been the victim of them – sometimes both. In 1997, for instance, a rumour circulated on the Internet that American fashion designer Tommy Hilfiger had made some racist comments on the *Oprah* talk show in the US. The resultant call for a boycott of Hilfiger's products (which was heard both on and off the Net) spurred the company to fight back – using the same means as its rumour-mongering detractors. It created a memo contradicting the rumours (see opposite) and circulated it throughout a number of popular Internet newsgroups. This incident serves as a reminder that smart companies don't only work to spread their message in cyberspace, they also monitor Internet content and take whatever actions are necessary to protect their brand.

*Subject: An Official Response From Tommy Hilfiger Co*
*From: hilfigerco@aol.com (HilfigerCo)*
*Date: 20 Mar 1997 04:42:33 GMT*

TO: TOMMY HILFIGER CONSUMERS AND FRIENDS
FROM: TOMMY HILFIGER CORPORATION
SUBJECT: MALICIOUS RUMORS

We are disturbed to learn that an ugly rumor has been circulating about our company.

Since we understand that you have been the recipient of false information we wanted to set the record straight. The facts are simple and incontrovertible. Tommy Hilfiger did not make the alleged inappropriate racial comments. He has never appeared on the Ophrah Winfrey show, although the rumor specifically asserts that he made negative remarks in that forum and that Ms. Winfrey asked him to leave. The show's producer has confirmed the fact that Tommy has never been a guest.

Similar rumors have circulated about comments supposedly made on other television shows. All of them are completely false. Tommy Hilfiger has never appeared on Larry King Live or on CNN's 'Style with Elsa Klensch' despite persistent misinformation to the contrary.

Whether these rumors are part of a misunderstanding or a deliberate act of malice, they have absolutely no basis in fact. Tommy Hilfiger wants his clothing to be enjoyed by people of all backgrounds and his collections are put together with the broadest cross section of individuals in mind. To reinforce this, he features models of all ethnic backgrounds in his fashion shows and advertisements. Tommy Hilfiger and the entire company are extremely pleased that the brand has been received so enthusiastically by individuals of all ethnic backgrounds around the world. We hope you, too, are a satisfied customer!!

If you have additional questions or concerns, please contact Tommy Hilfiger Corporate Communications at 25 West 39th St., New York, NY 10018.

The remainder of this chapter takes a look at some of the important (or just plain interesting) trends we're seeing in marketing efforts aimed at the new consumer. Most have in common the attributes of personalization, multiple channels of communication and innovative techniques

designed to break through the clutter and chaos surrounding consumers.

## Next: Increased Emphasis on 1:1 Marketing

Mass marketing is obsolete. Changing demographics, new distribution
channels, intensified competition, additional media channels, new technologies and declining advertising effectiveness have combined to make
personal marketing a must.

Around the world, we're seeing innovative marketers customizing
their offerings to extend the impact of their messages on targeted consumers. In the UK, American Express personalizes offers to cardholders
based on their purchase history and demographic data. Sports enthusiasts, for instance, might receive a special discount offer from a local
sporting goods store along with their monthly invoice. These personalized inserts have achieved an extremely impressive 'take' rate of
just under 40 per cent.

In the Netherlands, Moore Corporation (http://www.moore.com)
and KPN have teamed up to offer consumers customized catalogues.
Customers can phone, fax or email a request for a catalogue of products
with specific features, within a specified price range. According to
*Marketing Tools*, an initial market test of more than 100,000 households
resulted in 15 to 35 per cent of customers placing an order. Further
tests are planned in Canada, the UK and the US. Moore has also set
up a voice-response phone system Dutch consumers can call to get
information on products ranging from appliances to personal electronics. Printed responses to queries are mailed within two days.

In the increasingly competitive airline industry, American Airlines
representatives now call their most valuable frequent flyers before their
flights both to thank them for choosing American Airlines and to see
whether there's anything they can do to make the trip more comfortable. British Airways is installing new software that will allow them to
'remember' the preferences of their frequent flyers (favourite magazines, beverages, special meals, etc.) so they can greet these customers
with the items upon boarding.

## Next: Global Branding

Satellite television, Hollywood movies and cross-border marketing
efforts have created a world culture with implications for brand strategy,
market intelligence and management techniques in every business that

hopes to be international. In a world in which national borders present little obstacle to culture, advertising and media, marketers are now called upon to make sure their brands are marketed in a way that is most relevant – and least offensive – to every nation in which they are sold. One of the world's best-known brands, Levi's, has tackled this mission by building a Website (http://www.levi.com) that delivers one overriding message: unity crosses borders. Visitors to the site can view Levi's advertisements from all over the world, while absorbing such messsages as 'Many voices, many cultures, many venues, one message: Levi's jeans, true originals for true originals' and 'Around the world, down the street, across points of view, Levi's jeans are there.'

Launched in 1983, the Swatch watch company has grown into the most successful maker of wristwatches of all time. The watches are now available in seventy-two markets worldwide. In addition to a global print advertising campaign, the company spreads its message through innovative marketing promotions. In one example, Swatch ran a promotion in conjunction with the Museum of Byzantine Civilization in Thessaloniki, Greece. Anyone wearing Swatch's commemorative watch to the exhibit of the treasures of Holy Mount Athos was granted free admission.

*Swoosh*. Not just the sound of a tram careening by you on a street corner in Amsterdam, but also the symbol that runs the length of the cars. US-based Nike has managed to make its geometric logo one of the most recognized symbols across the globe. By plastering its logo on billboards, phone booths, all forms of mass transportation and on the shoes and clothing of top athletes worldwide in just about all sports, Nike has become synonymous with athletic excellence – and marketing savvy. (Interestingly, as the authors were completing this book, Nike had begun to drop the swoosh in some of its advertising, replacing it with NIKE. It would appear to be an attempt to shake up its advertising in the face of increasingly gloomy financial news.)

## Next: Creating the Ad Biz in a Parallel Universe

'Internet spending is real. It does reach an upscale demographic. The Internet is eroding TV use. It is measurable,' says Rich LeFurgy, chairman, Internet Advertising Bureau Board (IABB), and senior vice president of advertising, ABC News/ESPN Internet Ventures. Net-based advertising revenues continue to grow: IAB reports that revenue topped US$906.5 million for 1997, with last-quarter revenues of some

US$330.5 million marking the eighth record-setting quarter in a row. '1997 was definitely a breakthrough year for Internet advertising,' said LeFurgy. 'When we compare advertising revenue for the television industry in equivalent dollars for its third year, the Internet is slightly ahead, at US$907 million compared to television's US$834 million.'

For now, US companies dominate the market. Jupiter predicts that non-US online revenues will reach US$704 million in 2000. By comparison, the American market is expected to reach US$5 billion-plus in that time. Dresdner Kleinwort Benson expects the value of UK advertising on the Internet to reach US$450 million by 2001. Internet advertising in Japan reached US$32 million in 1997, an increase of more than 250 per cent from the previous year, according to Dentsu, Inc.

According to a study by Coopers & Lybrand, 90 per cent of all Internet ad spending is generated by five categories: computing products, 30 per cent; telecommunications, 22 per cent; consumer-related businesses, 17 per cent; financial services, 11 per cent; and new-media businesses, 10 per cent. For now, banner ads continue to be the standard, but new advertising business models and formats continue to evolve. Among recent developments: 'in-lines' or 'one liners' (visitors performing a search are presented with a simple sentence, such as 'Buy a new car at a great price – click here'; the line appears as just another entry on a list of search results); ad-supported email; and ad-supported chatrooms.

Though the medium is developing rapidly, we still have a long way to go before optimum use is achieved. A 1997 study by *Ad Age* and Mediamark Research Inc. found that marketers still use two-way technology to deliver primarily one-way messages. Nearly three-quarters of respondents use interactive technology to provide information about their company, 48.2 per cent use it for promotion and 45.8 per cent use it as a public relations tool. In contrast, only 37.2 per cent use interactive media as a basis for one-to-one marketing – and even fewer conduct electronic commerce.

A number of organizations are taking steps to facilitate and encourage online advertising. Among them Audits & Surveys (http://www.surveys.com) and CyberGold (http://www.cybergold.com) have formed an alliance to help online advertisers gauge response to their ads and develop responder and non-responder profiles. The new service combines Audits & Survey's polling and sampling programmes with Cyber-Gold's incentive arrangements, which reward consumers for responding to ads and surveys. The combined effort is intended to elicit demographic and lifestyle data and to probe consumers with regard to how online advertisements influence or fail to influence purchase.

## Next: Brand Building in Cyberspace Via Content
Though less obvious than banners and other forms of advertising online, branded content provides a valuable opportunity for companies to build their brands in cyberspace. By luring consumers with information on everything from parenting to classic cars to the fight against breast cancer, companies are able to associate themselves with a positive message or cause, while also gaining access to a steady stream of potential customers.

OshKosh B'Gosh, which has focused recently on clothing for kids, has created the OshKosh B'Gosh Genuine Parents Club at its Website (http://www.oshkoshbgosh.com/cgi-bin/de/gpcintro). Among other features (including store locators and a 'gift gallery'), the site posts a newsletter containing parenting tips, gift ideas and kids' fashion trends. Parents who join the free club are given a complimentary gift subscription to *Parents* or *Child* magazine.

Procter & Gamble is also attempting to align itself with parents online. P&G has entered into a multi-year advertising deal with ParentTime, a joint venture of Time Warner Cable Programming and Procter & Gamble Productions. The site (http://www.parenttime.com) is designed to 'inform and entertain parents and expectant parents'. Contributors include sex guru Dr Ruth Westheimer and authors William and Martha Sears (*The Birth Book* and *The Discipline Book*); Dale Burg, Carol Boswell and Ron Barrett (*How to Mom*); and Adele Faber and Elaine Mazlish (*Liberated Parents and Liberated Children*).

The Adidas webZine (http://www.adidas.de) features sports news, profiles of and interviews with Adidas-sponsored athletes and information about Adidas-sponsored events. The webZine is offered for six markets: Germany, Spain, Sweden, Switzerland, the US and the UK, with each edition focusing on local sports heroes and issues.

Johnson & Johnson's Website (http://www.jnj.com) is devoted to 'caring'. Information is provided on such topics as infant care, issues related to motherhood and breakthroughs in healthcare products. There is also a link to the Library of Healthcare Information, a list of organizations that provide support for new parents.

## Next: Innovative Branding and Image-Building Techniques

**In-school Marketing** Despite the controversies surrounding it, in-school marketing is becoming increasingly common as cash-strapped schools welcome equipment, materials, programming and products from companies eager to reach the youth market. In the US Channel One continues to beam satellite news programming and sponsors' advertisements into secondary-school classrooms in exchange for providing the schools with free satellite and video equipment. Other companies enter schools more subtly, with lesson plans and materials on such topics as nutrition, recycling and the like. The inclusion of product logos, marketing messages and – some charge – biased information continues to infuriate many parents and educators.

**Shape Shifters** These days, organizations of all stripes are working to get their message across without letting us know they're behind it. A few examples:

- With US$100,000 in federal grants from the National Science Foundation and the Department of Energy, a group of US scientists recently tried to reshape their profession's geeky image by commissioning the writing of a prime-time TV show that, they hoped, would do for scientists what *ER* is doing for doctors. So far, there have been no takers for the series.
- Among some organizations an increasingly common practice is 'greenscamming', giving environmentally friendly names to groups on the other side of the battle. Two examples: Friends of Eagle Mountain, organized by a mining company that wants to create the world's largest landfill; and Northwesterners for More Fish (since dissolved, we're happy to report), created by companies accused of depleting the fish population.
- Whereas root beer provides a taste of nostalgia for many boomers, it's being pitched to younger male consumers as 'The foam that goes straight to your brain.' The slogan, for PepsiCo's Mug brand, accompanies ads that appear primarily on MTV.
- To give start-ups a fighting chance in a market that favours unique, personalized products, mass-market giants are opting to distance themselves from certain of their lines: Miller Brewing Co.'s Red Dog beer was launched as a microbrew of Plank Road Brewery. R. J. Reynold's Moonlight Tobacco Co. markets cigarettes

under the brand names Politix, City and Northstar in selected markets, with scant mention of their parent company. Detroit heavyweight General Motors distanced itself from Saturn by setting up shop in rural Tennessee and packaging its offspring as a small-town enterprise.

## Next: Music As a Marketing Tool

Eager to tap into the lucrative hip-hop market, manufacturers are increasingly forming alliances with big names in rap. Most successful thus far has been fashion designer Tommy Hilfiger, who lured rappers into the fold with free wardrobes. Last year, Hilfiger used hardcore rappers Method Man and Treach (of Naughty by Nature) as runway models. Designer Louis Vuitton has also jumped on to the hip-hop bandwagon, with print ads featuring pioneer deejay Grandmaster Flash.

The use of CDs as premiums and promotional products is also on the rise, with recent releases of music compilations from such companies as Godiva, Ralph Lauren, Pottery Barn and Fila. Intended to build customer loyalty by bringing the stores 'into customers' homes', these compilations also allow retailers to develop a brand image based on a signature sound. Philip Morris has raised the ire of tobacco foes by creating a record company – Woman Thing Music – to promote its Virginia Slims brand. In addition to giving away CDs with cigarette purchases, the company is sponsoring a series of concerts. CDs produced by The Body Shop raise money for causes the company supports; compilations have included *Protect Respect: Artists Who Care About AIDS* and *Voices Against Violence* (female artists).

Tying together three areas of keen interest to teens – music, fashion and beer – Anheuser-Busch produced a Budweiser-branded tour in the UK that coincided with the company's launch of a line of branded clothing. In an example of the new emphasis on integrated marketing, Kahlúa teamed up with the UK band M People, first sponsoring a global tour and then branching out to include on-bottle CD offers and radio promotions, including Kahlúa Groove, a branded radio programme.

## Next: Mega Movie Marketing

From action figures, prepaid phone cards and breakfast cereal to toothbrushes, pyjamas and toys, merchandise tied into blockbuster movies has become a huge business in the past decade. Universal Studios reports that licences from *Jurassic Park* alone generated US$1 billion in sales.

Ira Mayer, publisher of the *Licensing Letter* in New York, told the *Los Angeles Times*, 'Up until 1991 or so, licensing was an ancillary revenue stream, a bonus that went straight to the bottom line. Now, some films wouldn't even get made unless they get this licensing agreement out front.' By the time the remake of *101 Dalmatians* was released, Disney had licensed a grand total of 17,000 product tie-ins. A Cruella de Vil tennis visor, anyone?

## Next: CEOs as Celebrity Spokespeople

Corporate executives equipped with the personality and credibility to serve as spokespersons would do well to try their hand. With 500 commercials to his credit, Dave Thomas, founder of Wendy's Old Fashioned Hamburgers, has emerged as one of America's most recognizable corporate spokespersons – second only to basketball star Michael Jordan.

At the same time, however, companies are increasingly alert to the potential downside of real-life spokespersons (Dave Thomas's recent heart attack, for instance, wasn't the best advertising for the company's product). Tying one's brand to the fate of any celebrity appears risky in this era of such 'fallen' stars as O. J. Simpson and boxer Mike Tyson.

Consumers are also rejecting celebrity endorsements in cases in which there is not a 'logical fit'. In conducting a series of online focus groups for a parenting product, we were told time and time again by the parent participants that they would not accept a celebrity spokesperson for the product because most celebrities are too busy (or uncaring) to be good parents. To be effective, an endorser must somehow be linked in consumers' minds to the product category. Rock star Tina Turner, for instance, has been a big hit in ads for Hanes hosiery because she is well known for her great legs and active lifestyle. She would be far less effective endorsing, for example, a credit card or automotive company.

## What's Next?

**Thoughtful Convergence**  Convergence isn't just about digitivity; it's also about connecting people to brands in ways that leverage insights into consumer patterns – all without being mistaken for Big Brother. 'Brand convergence' is about brands bonding because their combined power is greater than the sum of their parts. A case in point is Citibank's

Driver's Edge card, which enables Ford Citibank members to earn points towards the purchase or lease of a new Ford vehicle.

In the coming months and years, we can expect a growing number of alliances among investment banks, management consulting firms, public accountancies and even ad agencies and public relations firms. All are selling knowledge – and in this age of brand zeal, knowledge is the only bankable power.

**Anti-advertising Backlash** With all the branded babble thrust at modern consumers on a daily basis, who can blame them for being a bit jaded? In the online arena, techies are even devising ways to get around banner ads. Cybersitter software has launched WWW Advertising, a filter that prevents browsers from loading banner ads on numerous Websites. The company says the feature helps its 1.2 million users save bandwidth and avoid intrusive pitches.

Warning to marketers: this backlash will get worse before it gets better. A survival tactic for smart marketers: talk smart to smart people about smart brands.

**Discreet Branding** Discretion is the better part of branding. Intel inside is far more honourable than Microsoft everywhere. Discretion doesn't mean an absence of branding; what it means is steady branding without being intrusive or overpowering. Today's mantra should be that more is not always most memorable and quantity isn't a substitute for quality. While others were peppering the world with multiple thirty-second commercials, Ford sponsored the US network television debut of award-winning film *Schindler's List* in 1997. No commercials aired – not even during the intermission. Sometimes, the best way to call attention to a brand is by being very, very quiet.

**Brand Action Marketing** Peter Storck, director of Jupiter Online Advertising Group, warns: 'Brands are choosing an either/or strategy in which they focus on brand building or direct marketing initiatives. This ignores what makes online different from other media – interactivity.' According to Jupiter Communications (http://www.jup.com), successful brand action marketing consists of six component tactics: media, retail enhancement, customization, promotions, sales service and support, and distribution and transactions.

**Digital Coupons** Chicago-based CoolSavings (http://www3.cool savings.com/) offers personalized coupons via the Net. Just over a year old, the company has 400,000 members, each of whom has completed a personal-preferences profile. Advertisers target customers geographically, demographically or by stated preferences.

**Microbrands** Narrowcasting will enable microbrands to create, and then own, niche categories (e.g., climate-customized furnishings or DIY materials).

**Heritage Trail** Watch for brand spokespeople who focus on the legacy of the brand – and expect these individuals to be members of the brands' employed ranks rather than celebrity endorsers. It should have come as no surprise that Anheuser-Busch's spot featuring family members made its way on to 1997 best-of lists.

# Conclusion

## [19]

## America by Americans

A main premise of this book is the interconnectivity of the global village. As we come to the end of our global travelogue into the future, this brief conclusion affords us an opportunity to narrow our focus in terms of content and context.

The authors are American by birth and currently live in the United States, although, between us, we've logged two dozen trips to Europe in the last seven months and have spent more than six weeks of the last two years in Africa and Asia. Marian and Ira both were raised in and around New York City, are relatively knowledgeable about US history and immersed in its popular culture, and as, with most heavy business travellers, we watch more than our fair share of CNN. So why is forecasting what's next for the US a more difficult challenge than forecasting global and regional nexts, as we've done in completing more than half a dozen editions of this book? In some ways, we're disadvantaged when it comes to analysing life next in the place where it'll impact us most: what we're seeing as next for America isn't all good news, and maybe this somehow causes us to freeze.

Because we have lived 'life next' in many respects, and because we subscribe to a strong belief that the future is now, we're often confounded by the disinclination of many of our fellow countrymen and women to embrace anything new – that is, beyond trendy disposable, wear-outable products and popular fashions. Beta (trial) launches seem to have taken a toll on the American psyche, exhausting our capacity to become thrilled about newness. Instead, we are content to put our excitement on hold until presented with a personal opportunity to 'see and believe'. While the media's tendency to hype invites (some say demands) a standoffish reaction, the undercurrent of hesitation and pessimism betrays our history as the nation that courageously took 'one giant step for mankind' back in the sixties.

## A Joseph Heller Plot – For Life

Until it ended its run, the most successful TV show in America for the past several years had been *Seinfeld*, a comedy in which 'nothing happens'. The empty plotline mirrors much of daily life in America. Perhaps the appeal of nothingness is a response to information overload: nitty-gritty details of current affairs routinely evolve into big stories and blend into little stories, all against a backdrop of analytical commentary that, naturally, is further balanced by so-called 'hard news'. Perhaps Americans have shut down because life beyond the TV screen is changing too fast. Then again, perhaps we're simply a nation that's become complacent in its success, both as an economic and a cultural force.

Americans' general passivity and detachment with regard to the future will probably spell a series of nexts that are both interesting and unfortunate – including an underinvolved outlook towards globalization, a fact that we understand all too well. Why was a team of American authors able to attract publishers in the Netherlands, Germany, France, Australia, Brazil, the UK and Italy before lining up an American counterpart? One explanation we received: 'You have far too global a perspective. Americans want to hear about what's next in America, preferably in their own state, not around the world.' Go figure. It just depressed the hell outta us . . .

We note that only 23 per cent of Americans have ever had a passport. Why do Paris if we can do Paris Island instead? The French may take a lot of heat for being jingoistic, but the truth is that we Americans are much worse – at least the French are more apt to speak a second language. (In 1998, half of all Europeans aged fifteen to twenty-four can converse in English, according to the European Union – this is up from one in three in 1987.) Each of the authors knows financially well-off Americans who have never been abroad, and countless others who consider Paris truly exotic and the thought of a trip to the Acropolis or the Partheonon completely over the top.

## What's It Got to Do With Us?

Another striking example of Americans' 'head-in-the-sand mentality' is our reaction (or lack thereof) to the Asian economic crisis, which just a couple of months ago threw our financial markets into turmoil. 'Who's wringing their hands over the fallout from Asia and other potential economic problems?' queried *Business Week*. 'Not the average American ... Personally, Americans believe that they are doing very well [despite analysts' predictions of an economic slowdown].'

So, will America Next be marked by blind faith? Or will our façade of optimism crack apart when some act of fate, or a series of them, reminds us that we're not as isolated from economic problems in other parts of the world as the huge expanses of water separating us from other continents would lead us to believe?

Given that change in America is often motivated by financial self-interest, we predict that, as the world shrinks and as the United states of Europe pulls together to provide the kind of economic challenge to US hegemony heretofore unseen, Americans will be forced to abandon the modern-day cultural 'isolationism' that would have made Woodrow Wilson proud. Today's kids and teens (who, thanks to the Internet, are growing up with an electronic 'window on the world') may prove to be the first generation that will fully embrace the opportunities of the global stage.

An American friend of Marian's recently asked whether she resents having to spend so much time in countries in which few people speak English fluently. In their time spent around the world, the only thing Ira and Marian have resented is their own limitations as linguists. In the face of changing global realities, it is our fervent hope that more US schools will grasp the importance of introducing students to other languages and cultures at an age when students can most readily absorb those lessons. As futurists, we recognize that a more globally oriented America is an eventual Next; as Americans, we sincerely hope the US wakes up to that reality sooner rather than later.

## USA 2005

Just this afternoon, Marian was ending a friendly chat with Philippe Krakowsky, a colleague. 'You're going to Copenhagen on Monday?' he asked. 'After I read the English translation of the first edition of your book, and saw your 'next' about planes falling from the sky due to budget cuts and inadequate maintenance, I have to ask you, 'How do you get onto airplanes? Are you actually comfortable flying?' Good question. Marian's answer, by her own report, was weak: 'I believe in fate.'

In contrast, trendtracking is about believing in intuition, which is based neither on fate nor faith. It's about testing hunches, about tossing balls into the air and about watching the patterns as they fall. In closing, we've outlined a series of trends – macro and micro – that will help to define life in the US in the near future. (And, for the record, Marian still believes we'll be seeing a rise in airline casualties in the years to come.)

## Next: Rebirth of Big Cities

Our nation's cities are our centres of commerce, art, politics, even religion. They draw in newcomers with the lure of job prospects and cultural attractions, and they house the decision-makers and bureaucrats who plan infrastructures and oversee policymaking and implementation on a national scale. In recent decades, our cities have also been decried as centres of crime and indifference, as sprawling 'asphalt jungles' teeming with people yet somehow devoid of any sense of community. Some cities have all but driven out the middle class, who work there by day but flee to the suburbs at night.

A number of trends are converging to change the very nature of cities in the US. First, there's the impact of dual-career couples. Whereas women once had the time to run the household and complete errands while their husbands worked, today most working couples must scramble to fit in such mundanities as dropping off the dry-cleaning, getting the car serviced, picking up something for dinner and getting the kids to and from daycare or school. In response to these changing needs, business districts are gradually making space for everything from drugstores and dry cleaners to hair salons and video-rental outlets. Daycare centres and preschools are also opening up in business districts.

Eager to recapture the revenues that have been taken away by sprawling suburban shopping centres, many cities have redoubled their efforts to revitalize downtown areas. Providing tax and other incentives to one-stop entertainment destinations (e.g. GameWorks) is one of the high-profile ways in which city leaders are demonstrating their commitment to draw suburbanites back into the city after dark.

At the same time, our cities are changing – and will continue to change in the years ahead – because the nature of work is changing.

With more people working at home (whether telecommuting or running home-based businesses), more temporary and part-time workers and a growing population of retirees, residential neighbourhoods are no longer the sole province of stay-at-home mothers and preschoolers during the day. This has an impact on everything from the sorts of businesses these areas require (copy shops and computer supply stores among them) to the hours during which restaurants and other businesses must operate.

The implications of this trend include opportunities for 'personal-services centres' to succeed in downtown locations, development of home-office hubs (offering everything from meeting space to on-site computer repair) and global banks that offer specialized products and services for SOHO clients.

## Ageing Workforce

More than 75 million baby boomers were born in the US between 1946 and 1964, a number that has increased through immigration to approximately 83 million boomers in the country today. According to a recent report from the US Department of Labor, 'The Aging Baby Boom: Implications for Employment and Training Programs', the continued presence of boomers in the labour market will contribute to a steady increase in the median age of workers, from thirty-eight in 1994 to forty-one by 2005. According to the Employee Benefit Research Institute's 1998 Retirement Confidence Survey, 72 per cent of boomers interviewed expect to continue working past sixty-five. In keeping with boomer mentality, many of these people will work longer by choice rather than necessity.

In consequence, we can expect retirement to change dramatically in the twenty-first century, with a rise in part-time consulting and a drop in the volunteer force being just two of the trends we'll see. Implications for employers include greater emphasis on healthcare plans and retirement packages and increased necessity of providing job-skills training to mid-career employees.

## Next: Sound-bite Nation

Media consumption by sound bite is a reality of contemporary America. While MTV is regarded as the pioneer of this form, the love affair with sound bites has been reflected in all media forms: CNN 'Headline News' gives us the world in a half hour (every half hour, twenty-four hours a day), and, in print, we have *USA Today* – news from around the nation in colourful, condensed form.

Today, we're already hearing analysts decry Americans' short attention spans – particularly when it comes to the topics of politics and economics. Tomorrow, we can expect to see an even greater chasm develop between the majority of the population and those few who continue to dine on hearty media diets that come complete with global perspectives and analysis. Tragically, trusted sources of such perspective and analysis will become far fewer, as economic realities continue to force 'news' organizations to emphasize entertainment over education. With a growing number of students being taught the fundamentals by such means as puppet shows, computer games and videos, what are the odds that upcoming generations will generate demand for 'hard news' and in-depth coverage?

## Next: Workplace Stresses

According to the '1997 National Study of the Changing Workforce', a report from the Families and Work Institute (http:/www.familiesand-workinst.org), one in three US employees brings work home at least once a week, an increase of 10 per cent over the last twenty years. Not surprisingly, the number of employees who would like to work fewer hours rose 17 percentage points over this time period.

Employee stress is a big topic right now, as companies being to grasp its enormous impact on worker morale, retention and productivity. According to the above-referenced study, nearly a quarter of today's employees often or very often felt nervous or stressed; 13 per cent often or very often had difficulty coping with the demands of everyday life; 26 per cent often or very often felt emotionally drained by their work; 28 per cent often or very often have not had the energy to do things with their families or others; and 36 per cent often or very often felt used up at the end of the workday.

Rather than help to alleviate these stresses, new technologies have contributed to them. As unbelievable as it sounds, a survey of 1,035 US workers found that, on average, each receives 190 messages a day. In an eight-hour workday, that's nearly twenty-four interruptions every hour!

| Source | No. of Daily Messages |
|---|---|
| Telephone | 52 |
| Email | 30 |
| Voicemail | 22 |
| Interoffice Mail | 18 |
| Postal Service Mail | 18 |
| Fax | 15 |
| Post-It Notes | 11 |
| Phone Message Slips | 10 |
| Pager | 4 |
| Overnight Courier | 4 |
| Cellular Phone | 3 |
| Postal Express Mail | 3 |

'We're drowning,' said Meredith Fischer, a VP at Pitney Bowes Inc., the office products company that funded the study. 'We're working in an interruption-driven workplace . . . You can't finish the project, finish the thought.'

Implications for the American workforce will range from on-site mental health counsellors to new limits on electronic communication to mandated communication 'blackouts' for employees on vacation (or simply on break).

## Next: Fear, Fear Everywhere
**Big Brother on Steroids** There are some Americans who practically consider Bill Gates the anti-Christ. No, not because of Microsoft's allegedly unfair business practices, but because Gates embodies all that we fear about technology. In the opening chapter of this book, we talked about global technofears – concerns that new technologies increasingly will invade our private lives and our businesses. In the US, some of these fears may well become realities ahead of much of the rest of the world. The degree to which we welcome technological innovations into our lives and homes makes us vulnerable to those who would choose to monitor our interests, our purchases – even our thoughts (via Internet postings).

Legislative action may work to restrict some prying 'digital eyes', but the reality is that we've already lost much of the privacy we once took for granted. With satellites overhead and databases filled with our financial, medical and other personal details, true anonymity is no longer a possibility.

**Lock the Gates, Load the Guns** Already shaken by the World Trade Center explosion two years earlier, Americans were jolted awake by the 1995 bombing of the Alfred P. Murrah Federal Building in Oklahoma City. The fact that this terrorist act was committed by Americans, took place in what the media love to call 'America's Heartland', and involved the deaths of small children combined to make this event an almost unimaginable horror. Subsequent news stories about America's militias further fuelled our fears and feelings of insecurity.

There was a time when Americans feared acts of terrorism only while travelling abroad. That was before the World Trade Center bombing, before Oklahoma City, before the deadly explosion at the Atlanta Olympic Games. Fears of foreign (typically Islamic) terrorists are real, but many of us now feel even more acutely the threat posed by America's paramilitary groups, armed with high-tech weapons and heightened paranoia. After all, they're already in the country, they're already armed, and, for the most part, they look just like the rest of us.

Not surprisingly, the result of increased violence (terrorist, random and other) is that Americans no longer feel safe at home or on the street. We watch news reports about drive-by shootings and in-school massacres; we see kids die of drug overdoses and drunk-driving accidents; we follow trial coverage of Ted Kaczynski and Timothy McVeigh on TV and via the Net. Many of us react to this bombardment of violent images by clinging to the feelings of security afforded by familiar faces, places and products. Others of us engage in extreme sports or other high-risk behaviours, getting a rush out of facing our mortality head on. Still others take steps to help ensure our own safety, perhaps by enrolling in a martial arts class, advocating gun control or moving into a gated community.

In the years to come, expect efforts to bolster our security to become even stronger, particularly among the wealthy. 'In the next millennium the chasm between rich and poor is bound to grow even wider,' forecast an article in *Maclean's*. 'At the moment, the world's 358 billionaires, according to the United Nations, control more wealth than 45 per cent of the Earth's population. As this imbalance becomes even greater, social unrest will increase. In response, the upper crust could share its wealth – but more likely its members will retreat behind guarded and gated fortress enclaves, where they will live in safety – and perpetual fear.'

Personal security will be a growth industry to watch, featuring every-thing from stylish bulletproof vests to trained attack dogs and sophisti-cated aerial surveillance. *Maclean's* reports that the newest gadgets will include satellite images and helicopters with infrared cameras that can detect the heat from a burning cigarette. 'The proving ground for such equipment is the Los Angeles Police Department,' the magazine says, 'which already operates four Aerospatiale helicopters with 30-million candle-power spotlights to turn night into day, and a separate fleet of Bell Jet Ranger whirlybirds that can ferry SWAT teams into action at a moment's notice. It is only a matter of time, in the corporate world of tomorrow, before such services are privatized and offered to the highest bidders.'

**American? Who Me?** The *Wall Street Journal* reports that record numbers of Americans are claiming binationality in order to obtain a foreign passport. Among the nations allowing binationality: France, the UK, Mexico, Colombia, Ecuador, Brazil and the Dominican Republic. Though some travellers are motivated by a need or desire to work abroad, others are obtaining second passports to protect themselves from anti-American terrorists.

For those unable to claim dual nationality, there's still hope. As reported in the *Financial Times*, when an American on a hijacked aircraft was shot ten years ago on the basis of his nationality, Texan Donna Walker came up with the idea of camouflage passports. For US$215, International Documents Service provides a fake passport (and support-ing materials), which, while not meant for legal matters, just might come in handy should one be caught in a war zone or on a hijacked ship or plane.

The passports sport a burgundy, EU-style cover, along with the usual personal information. The key difference is that IDS issues them under such defunct names as Ceylon and Rhodesia. The idea, says Walker, is to look like 'a not very interesting man from a not very interesting country'. IDS clients are primarily businessmen from the US and Germany.

'Our finest hour', Walker told the *Financial Times*, 'came when Iraq invaded Kuwait, and Americans and Europeans went into hiding. A group of six oil company guys had my passports and used them to get through Iraqi checkpoints to escape to Jordan.'

## Next: Serial 'Life' Partners

US baby boomers are only just beginning to admit that the institution of marriage doesn't work for most people their age in the late 1990s, whereas this is an accepted fact in the UK. When one 'pushes' a boomer – male or female – who has been married for more than a couple of years, one quickly learns of lustful yearnings (acted upon or not) outside the marital bedroom. Being denied these extramarital dalliances – or made to feel guilty for participating in them – makes boomers feel fenced in. This is, after all, the generation that wants it all. An array of public events has brought the issue out into the open, most notably the scandals erupting around President Clinton.

In an era in which people entering the workforce are likely to have five or six careers over a span of five or more decades, we'd be naïve to assume that one's shifting needs will be met by a single life partner. Given the unprecedented rate of change in our world, people now live multiple 'life spans'. And the recently announced breakthrough in cellular research suggests that one's 'productive' years may soon extend far beyond those of the average person today. Will second, third and even fourth families become increasingly common? Will movement from one 'life' to the next be planned for and celebrated? How will long-term financial planning be affected by the knowledge that one's life – and 'life' partners – will undergo radical shifts every decade or so? the social, economic and commercial ramifications are extraordinary.

# What's Next?

**New Cultural Influences** Studies by the US Census Bureau have pinpointed 2009 as the year in which the number of Hispanic-Americans nationwide will exceed the number of African-Americans, making Hispanics the largest national minority. The proportion of Asian-Americans also continues to grow.

The influence of these diverse cultures on American life may be somewhat more dramatic than in years past as a result of a shift towards multiculturalism rather than assimilation. One obvious area of influence will be in the foods we eat. In an *American Demographics* article entitled, 'Some Like It Hot', marketing writer Brad Edmondson reported, 'Ethnic foods have gone mainstream in the last decade, and so have the spices behind them. Imports of ginger root for consumption – in Asian-influenced stir-fried dishes, for example – increased 83 per cent between 1984 and 1993, then another 80 per cent just between 1993 and 1994. Imports of cumin, a mainstay of Mexican food, increased 55 per cent between 1984 and 1994. Poppy seed imports leapt 29 per cent, and imports of anise seeds rose 50 per cent, as bagels and other East European baked goods migrated from New York City to the heartland.' Expect 'fusion foods' to drive food consumption in the future.

**Parenting Platform** As parents are increasingly blamed for the sins of their children, we'll see more organizations devoted to providing parenting assistance and to serving as parent advocates. In an early example, economist Sylvia Ann Hewlett and Harvard philosophy and religion professor Cornel West, co-authors of *The War Against Parents*, recently founded the New York City-based National Parenting Association (NPA) in an attempt to reorganize and mobilize the country's 62 million parents of children under age eighteen. As reported in *Business Week*, Hewlett, a mother of four, asserts that parents 'face stressful lives with little cultural or social support from business and government'. By uniting parents across political and racial lines, the NPA hopes to become the parents' equivalent of the American Association of Retired Persons.

**De Facto Polygamy** Look for more people to take on new 'life' partners without bothering to shed previous ones; arrangements will be made for multiple partners to live under one roof, ensuring greater financial security and more hands to cope with household responsibilities.

**Privacy Contracts** Prior to engaging in sexual relations, parties will insist on signed confidentiality agreements detailing penalties if information is leaked to the press – or to a spouse.

**Patriot Prep** Parents unhappy with the trend towards multiculturalism in American schools will form private schools based not on religion but on the supremacy of Western thought and patriotic ideals.

**Car, Sweet Car** The American fascination with automobiles grows ever stronger. Today, we do a whole lot more than run errands and commute to work in our cars, we practically live in them. In our fast-food society, as many as one in ten restaurant meals is now eaten in a car. Automakers are facilitating mobile dining by introducing such features as shallower pleats in seat stitching to reduce collection of crumbs; redesigned cupholders that accommodate diverse sizes and shapes, including kids' juice boxes; and dashboards with as many as three power plug points for use with portable stoves or refrigerators. Manufacturers are also facilitating the trend of car as office, outfitting new models with such things as power outlets and laptop computer-size platforms between the driver and front passenger seats. The prototype Mercedes E420 goes one step further: It's 'Internet ready'. Potential applications include Internet access, email capability, customized traffic alerts, remote roadside assistance, navigational aids and links to one's office. Engineers at Daimler-Benz predict that such applications will be available commercially within the next few three or four years.

**Catching up with the Jetsons** The daily commute may never be the same. NASA, the FAA and seventy aviation-related companies in the US have created a consortium to start building personal aircraft that would cost no more than a luxury car – and be nearly as simple to use, reports *Newsweek*. When the pilot touches the words 'Boston' and 'New York' on a computer display in the cockpit, for example, a flight plan between those cities would automatically be calculated. 'Computerization of complicated flight procedures and airbags in the cockpit can make this type of flying very, very safe,' contends Bruce J. Holmes, NASA's general-aviation manager.

**Redefining Community** More than 40 million Americans live in condominium, co-operative and homeowner associations today, according to new estimates from the Community Associations Institute. The number of community associations has skyrocketed from 10,000 in 1970 to an estimated 205,000 today.

To maintain physical assets and enhance property values, community associations collect US$24.6 billion in assessments annually and hold US$18 billion in reserve funds to cover future capital expenditures. Look for such associations to become far more exclusive and to play a much larger role in social affairs as Americans grow increasingly wary of people who aren't just like them.

**Isolation begets Isolation** A society of singles is growing nationwide, especially in America's cities. *New York* magazine recently reported that, among surveyed singles living in the Big Apple, 29 per cent of women in their thirties say they don't want to get married. While increased job opportunities may be a big factor in this choice, it's important to understand just how far-reaching this trend may be. We live in a nation that, like just about every other nation, was constructed with 'families' as its essential building blocks. Our laws, our moral precepts, our social mores – everything is predicated on the notion of the family unit. Should an increasing percentage of Americans choose to remain single for life, this trend will impact on everything from how cities are built to how products are packaged.

**Nostalgia Tourism** Just as some people currently enjoy re-enactments of Civil War battles, tourists next will pay to 'participate' in such high-energy experiences as the race riots of the sixties and the gang wars of the nineties.

# Notes

## Chapter 1
1. *American Demographics*, December 1997

## Chapter 2
1. *Electronic Telegraph*, 11 May 1997
2. *Electronic Telegraph*, 3 May 1996
3. BBC, 3 February 1998
4. 'Suharto's End Game', Simon Long, *Economist*, 26 July 1997
5. *1998 Information Please Almanac*

## Chapter 5
1. Nua Internet Surveys
2. *Wired News*, 23 March 1998
3. 'Bulk Buys and Tax Breaks Boost PCs', *European*, 23 March 1998

## Chapter 6
1. *Los Angeles Times*, 9 October 1997
2. *Business Daily*, 24 October 1997
3. Gannett News Service

## Chapter 7
1. *Independent*
2. Reuters
3. *The Atlanta Journal and Constitution; Forbes ASAP*

## Chapter 8

1. Louis Harris and Associates, Families and Work Institute, Whirlpool Foundation, *Research Alert*
2. American Animal Hospital Association

## Chapter 13

1. *International Business Strategies* defines SOHO businesses as all sites that are not part of a larger enterprise or company and where fewer than twenty employees work regularly. Home offices are usually not organized legal entities (businesses) but are located in a household where a person regularly works at least one day per week.

## Chapter 15

1. As quoted in *Management Stats Daily, Innovation Line*, 30 June 1997

## Chapter 18

1. A recent study by Jupiter Communications suggests that servicing customers via online chat could cost as little as 25 cents a transaction, compared with US$1.25 per phone transaction.

# Index

# Acknowledgements

*Next: A Vision of Lives in the Future* is the work of four individuals, spun through the voices of two who trekked the planet, and was made possible only through the support of the multinational advertising agency Young & Rubicam. In November 1997, just three weeks before the Dutch edition of this book was unveiled, Marian, Ann and Christy joined Y&R as its Brand Futures Group. Later that week, before she had even settled into her new workspace, Marian left for Helsinki, where she was scheduled to address the marketing community. Two weeks later, she and Ira were back in Amsterdam to celebrate publication of *Trends Voor De Toekomst*, the original title of this book. As publishers around the world began signing on for updated versions of *Trends* (now called *Next*) in a variety of languages, Ira and Marian went to work revising the manuscript, which they then handed over to Ann and Christy for their input.

Though *Next* still has its origins in our original Dutch edition, it now benefits from a more global perspective, thanks in large part to extensive analyses offered by Marian's (and Ann's and Christy's) new colleagues at Y&R offices around the globe. For this, we have to thank then Y&R vice chairman Tim Pollak, who was the first to understand the importance of facilitating this input and who turned to all his country managers in the Pan-Pacific region for help. From his base in Sydney, Australia, we also received generous assistance from Richard McGowan, who oversees corporate communications in the Pan-Pacific region –

where Young & Rubicam is partnered with the largest advertising agency in the world, Japan's Dentsu, under the name DY&R.

Philippe Krakowsky, senior vice president and director of corporate communications for Y&R, was responsible for getting word about the book and its importance out to all the Y&R offices; and his intelligence and wit have eased Marian's transition to Y&R. By arranging for Marian to join him in briefing Y&R Inc. chairman and CEO Peter Georgescu, as Peter prepared comments for the World Economic Forum in Davos, Switzerland a few months ago, Philippe ensured that Marian, and this book, would be embraced by the man who is leading Y&R's transformation from now to next. Mark Stroock, who has been with Y&R for thirty years in senior communications roles, also lent insights and context for opening up editorial dialogues with offices near and far.

Ed Vick, COO of Y&R Inc., and Stewart Owen, vice chairman and chief strategic officer, are the pair who attracted Marian (and her team) to join the company, and who continue to support the efforts of Brand Futures Group as we take our rule-breaking thoughts to offices near and far.

Stan Stefanski, Mike Zeigler, Stephanie Abramson and Jim Pharo have helped sort through the tedium of agreements, contracts and agency commitments to make the book a vibrant archive of insights about now and next. Leonard Orkin of Kaye, Collyer was a godsend in sorting through our past, present and future agreements regarding the publication of *Next* and its planned companion, *The Generation and the Gaps.*

Barbara Jack, then CEO of Wunderman Cato Johnson and now executive director, Y&R Inc., turned to her personnel worldwide for their perspective on what's next. This book also benefits, as a result, from the influence of those who are involved in 1:1 marketing next. It benefits, too, from the generous contributions we received from colleagues at reputation managers Burson-Marsteller, publicists Cohn & Wolfe and brand identity specialists Landor Associates.

Finally, at Peter Georgescu's request, Fernan Montero, chairman & CEO Y&R Europe, and Joe De Deo, chairman Y&R Latin America & Canada, helped interest their offices in this book. Jim Williams, director of strategy & research, Y&R Europe, mobilized colleagues throughout Europe to find time to contribute. Special thanks to the following individuals, all employees of Y&R companies, for providing us with insights into what's next in their local and national markets. (Some of these individuals asked that their comments not be attributed to them, but simply to their office, so this may be the only place that their contribution is noted – and lauded.)

Europe: Edward Appleton (Y&R GmbH Frankfurt), Adrian Day (Landor London), Lola Gonzalez (Y&R Madrid), Arianna Grigoriadis (WCJ Rome), Sonja Huerlimann (AY&R Zurich), Zoya Ivanova (Y&R Europe Moscow), Marco Lombardi (Y&R Italia Milan), Dominique Missoffe (Y&R Paris), Sus Røedgaard (Y&R Copenhagen), Katarina Varenius (Hall & Cederquist/Y&R Stockholm), Miguel Velhinho (Y&R Portugal) and Jim Williams (Y&R Europe London)

International Task Force members within 285 Madison Avenue (Y&R headquarters): Barbara Bruinsma, Nikki Karani, Tammy Lechter, Mary Peng and Kamila Tischler

North America: Daisy Exposito (The Bravo Group NY), Leslie Gaines-Ross (Burson-Marsteller US NY). Louisa Holland (Sudler & Hennessey NY, Meridith Jamin (Y&R NY), Scott Marticke (Y&R Atlanta), Lia Nikopoulou (Landor NY), and Todd Ochsner (Y&R Vancouver)

Pan-Pacific: Yoshitaka Abe (DY&R Tokyo), Anne Ainsley (WCJ Sydney), Maria Evangeli (Cohn & Wolfe Sydney), Jonathan Holburt (DY&R Vietnam), Lara Hussein (DY&R Malaysia), Daniel Ko (DY&R Beijing), Sharon Lee (DY&R Shanghai), Steven Lyons (Burson-Marsteller, North Asia Hong Kong), Mila M. Marquez (DY&R Guangzhou), Melissa Miller (Y&R Sydney), Karen Ng (DY&R Hong Kong), Angela Pih (DY&R Hong Kong), Lucinda Sherborne (Y&R Auckland), Sachin Talwar (Burson-Marsteller Roger Pereira Communications Pvt. Ltd, Mumbai, India), Han van Dijk (DY&R Asia Singapore), and 'the groups' at DY&R Korea, DY&R India and DY&R Taiwan

Latin America: Adolfo Garro (Y&R Mexico), Claudia Gonzalez (Y&R Colombia) and Jennifer Moore (Y&R Colombia Medellin)

And, in the moral-support category, special thanks to Y&R's Jennifer Alexander, Maggie Brennan, June Blocklin, Daryl Elliott, Lisa Epstein, Sophie Glovier, Jemma Gould, Liz McKee, Cristina Merrill (now of *Adweek*), Kate Milano, John Partilla, Julie Rothhouse, Mike Samet, Jaime LeVine and Paul Woolmington, each of whom provided some laughs, extraordinary assistance at various crisis points, and witty insights, as Marian pulled her hair out – and drove our research analysts, Merritt Walters and Amy Woessner, to do the same. Merritt and Amy deserve thanks not only for helping Marian contain the chaos that is apt to be generated by such a book project, but also for their invaluable assistance with administrative details and fact-checking.

Also invaluable were the assistance and insights we received from Stuart Harris, a frequent freelance contributor to the thinking archives of Y&R's Brand Futures Group. For the past two years, he has been living in Kuala Lumpur, Malaysia, where he has been employed primarily as a market research director. A native of Britain, Harris has also worked and lived in Italy and the Netherlands, and his insights into Europe and Asia contributed greatly to this project.

## Next and Past
The authors also are grateful to a number of people with whom we worked while in Europe, especially Robbert Ammerlan and Martine Litjems of Anthos Publishing, and Fleur Dusee, Willemijn ter Weele and Friso Westenberg, our Dutch staff at the Department of the Future, who made our international adventure so deeply personal, as well as professionally expansive.

## Born at Chiat/Day
This book took root because Chiat/Day, our former employer, believed in the future. By challenging his employees and himself to reinvent marketing communications and the process of obtaining and making use of consumer insights. Jay Chiat created a face-to-face and virtual environment in which the curious thrived. Jay gave both of us the most important professional legacy any pair could dream of: confidence to evolve in revolutionary ways; quirky, unconventional working styles to ensure that good enough is never enough, and, especially, our tradition of forcing change into and up organizations.

This book is a team effort. In preparing the Dutch edition, Ann O'Reilly and Christy Lane Plummer energized Fleur, Friso, Will, and Ira's eldest son, David, to stay with us, round the clock when necessary, so that a great book was possible in a matter of weeks. Ann and Christy are very much co-authors of the book, and their brilliance is reflected throughout.

Finally, we want to acknowledge the opportunities and support we enjoyed during our two-year international odyssey with the Department of the Future. Laurie Coots, COO of TBWA Chiat/Day; Colette Chestnut, CFO; and Velda Ruddock, director of intelligence, were strong supporters. Alasdair Ritchie, then president, TBWA Europe and now senior vice president, operations, TBWA International; Perry Valkenburg, chairman and CEO of TBWA's presence in the Netherlands (known as the Company Group and including the award-winning Campaign Company advertising agency); and Jonathan Hill, managing director, TBWA Europe (now based in Capetown), made our success possible. Reg Lascaris and John Hunt, founders of TBWA's second jewel, Hunt Lascaris (Chiat/Day being the first, in our biased opinion), brought Marian to Africa and, in about two weeks, expanded her world view dramatically.

Keith Smith, regional director, TBWA Asia Pacific, opened the eyes of both of us to the beauty and potential of that part of world next. Gavin Heron, TBWA's Greater China planning director, was and is a dear pal, and a great sounding board, as is Robin Lauffer, who had been planning director with us in New York and who moved to Brussels around the time Marian and Ira departed for Amsterdam and Milan, respectively. She is now managing partner, director of strategic planning at TBWA.

Ira Matathia
Marian Salzman